Exchanges Between Us:
More Intergenerational Connections

Edited by:

Ellen Bouchard Ryan
Gail M. Elliot
Ann P. Anas

The McMaster Centre for Gerontological Studies
McMaster University
Hamilton, Ontario
CANADA

BOOK TITLE: **Exchanges Between Us: More Intergenerational Connections**

EDITORS: Ellen Bouchard Ryan, Gail M. Elliot, and Ann P. Anas

Cover Design: Eugene Martinello

First Printing: November 2000

Canadian Cataloguing in Publication Data

Exchanges Between Us: More Intergenerational Connections

ISBN: 1-894088-22-0
1. Aged, Writings of the, Canadian (English).* 2. Children's writings Canadian (English).* 3. Canadian literature (English) – 20th Century.* 4. Grandparent and child- Literary collections. I. Ryan, Ellen Bouchard. II. Elliot, Gail M., 1957- .   III. Anas, Ann P., 1945 - . IV. McMaster University. Centre for Gerontological Studies.

PS8235.S45E92 2000   C810.8'0920432   C00-931953-0

For further information contact:
The McMaster Centre for Gerontological Studies
KTH - 226
McMaster University
Hamilton, ON   L8S 4M4

(905) 525-9140 Extension: 24449
Printed at: McMaster University,
Hamilton, Ontario, Canada

ACKNOWLEDGEMENTS

The McMaster Centre for Gerontological Studies expresses its sincere appreciation to the Franchisees of Jumbo Video across Canada for their generous financial contribution in support of the production of this book.

Sincere gratitude is also extended to The Writer's Cramp Group of Dundas for their encouragement with this project as well as for their charitable donation.

Proceeds from this publication will be used to support the McMaster Centre for Gerontological Studies, McMaster University.

Table of Contents

CHAPTER 3 – Connections From Two Generations

CHAPTER 4 – Connections From Children

CHAPTER 5 – Connections From Young Adults

FOREWORD

*"I have two living grandparents...They are 78 and
85, and I'm only 20. Being on the same wave length
as them would be almost miraculous"*
                                        -- An undergraduate

In one of our courses on aging, students - mostly young adults - hear many stories. They read from an anthology of poems, essays, and short fiction with themes relating to the aging experience. They hear also from older volunteers who help to facilitate small discussion groups on these readings. Then the students write about the stories they've read and discussed, incorporating their own personal experiences and thoughts about the meaning of growing older. What may begin as an academic exercise in a required course often becomes an intergenerational journey as these young adults call upon their grandparents for advice and guidance. Frequently, the near miracle mentioned above does happen, as communication is facilitated and relationships strengthened through shared stories.

Our research also underscores the importance of stories in the lives of older adults and their families. We have found that adults of all ages recognize a "good" story, one that is coherent and interesting. For the individual older person, telling such a story to others can be a kind of mental exercise that promotes healthy and successful aging. It sharpens perceptions of the event and enhances understanding of it. A better understanding, in turn, promotes a strong sense of the self and helps in the process of life review - putting together the stories of one's life in a positive and integrated fashion. Stories can also serve as an expression of the investment in the care of the young that older generations feel. Erik Erikson termed this "generative" investment in the nurturing and guidance of the young a kind of intergenerational gift that benefits both tellers and recipients. In our research, stories with such generative themes are especially enjoyed and preferred by younger listeners.

For families, story-telling cements intergenerational bonds. Older people, in general, have a positive view of their families and a strong commitment to their successful future. This commitment is called "intergenerational stake" by gerontologists. Helping young members understand their family's history can help facilitate caring and respectful communication. As Ellen Ryan says, when we know little about someone of another age, we may be tempted to rely on stereotypes in our interactions: for example, all teenagers are moody; all seniors grumpy. When we know more, our interactions take into account the complexity of individual lives. For each generation, the stories of another provide a glimpse at that complexity.

From our point of view as social scientists, this is an important book. We know very little about how younger and older members of a family use stories as a way to build their relationships. The stories in this volume provide some insights into this process. They demonstrate bridges of understanding, which can be shared by other families whose story-telling abilities might not be as well honed. We hope that it will encourage all families to take time for one another and create new generations of oral historians.

Joan E. Norris, Ph.D.
Department of Family Relations
& Applied Nutrition
University of Guelph

Michael W. Pratt, Ed.D.
Department of Psychology
Wilfrid Laurier University

INTRODUCTION

Exchanges Between Us:

More Intergenerational

Connections

Exchanges Between Us:

More Intergenerational Connections

Intergenerational exchanges contribute to lasting memories for all involved. Whether these exchanges take place in person, over the phone, via email or on paper, the outcomes can prove to be rewarding. The exchanges recorded in this book have been written by people of all ages and the themes are incredibly diverse. The authors have written about family, historical events, identity, love, learning, trials, challenges, tribulations, aspirations, success, healing, hope, and humour. These stories, poems and letters reinforce the message that meaningful connections continue to be made across the life span. As the pages unfold you will find that young ones often find it surprising to hear that grandparents got into mischief, made mistakes, have dreams and goals for the future and look at life differently today than they did many years ago. Moreover, young people benefit from hearing about the sacrifices, large or small, that were made in the name of honour and pride, such as the story about chocolate ration tickets that is so eloquently told in the Connections From Older Adults chapter of this book.

Within the framework of a life course perspective, individuals age within a social, economic, and political environment that may otherwise be referred to as history, or historical events. Many of these historical and life circumstances may be recorded to varying degrees in history books, but the relationships that evolved, the trials that were faced, the hardships that were overcome and the joys that were shared may be lost if they are not captured during meaningful exchanges between family and friends. Perhaps even more importantly, this dialogue may take on new meaning when shared with loved ones of another generation.

It is interesting to read through these contributions and reflect on the many different life perspectives that have been developed by those retelling their stories and looking forward to the future with a sense of fulfillment, anticipation and integrity. Some of the pieces clearly illustrate how the

3

passage of time can bring the past and the present together and, most interestingly, contribute to shaping the future. For some, when the past comes together with the present, feelings of contentment, peace and gratification unfold, as in the story written by the Australian grandmother for her grandchildren.

These contributions remind us that our world is filled with people who have had interesting lives, yet have never achieved fame or fortune. They are stories about the families, friends and relationships of normal, everyday people. Many have experienced hard times, but they have also developed creative solutions to difficult problems. These accounts also convince us of the diversity of living that takes place over time. Some individuals have led their lives with a great deal of continuity, while others have experienced an over-abundance of transitions and a life of innumerable changes.

The children's contributions relay loving messages of warm memories about meaningful exchanges with their grandparent(s) or other older adults. Through these tributes the children express their appreciation of and respect for their older loved ones. In some cases, they speak openly about the regard they have for a grandparent they have never met or who has recently passed away. They eloquently share their sentiments and express how they will hold onto their memories for years to come.

Many of the young adults expand on these messages of love, gratitude and appreciation and speak about the role that older adults have played in their lives. Older loved ones are often seen as role models with excellent words of advice that the young adult can use to guide them through life's journey.

Our first volume, *From Me To You: Intergenerational Connections Through Storytelling*, was inspired by the International Year of the Older Person, and by our desire to promote intergenerational communication. Encouraged by the enthusiastic response to that collection, we decided to follow up with this second publication. Like our first volume, this book contains chapters from older adults, young adults and elementary school students. In this publication, we have added two additional chapters; one is entitled

"Connections From the Middle Generation" and the other is entitled "Connections From Two Generations".

As you read through this collection, you will see how the variety and breadth of these offerings reflect the rich individuality of the authors, young and old and in between. We hope these exchanges will reap many benefits in the months and years to come and that the family conversations they generate will continue long after this book goes to press.

Acknowledgments

A book such as this is the culmination of the work of many people. First of all we would like to express our sincere thanks to all those who shared their stories with us. We received a tremendous response to our request for intergenerational contributions. The entries presented in the pages that follow were selected based on the ratings of a panel of reviewers. The reviewers were given coded stories, letters and poems and asked to use standardized criteria when rating each submission. The ratings were averaged and the top scores were selected for inclusion in this publication. We thank all who took time to prepare something for our consideration.

Thanks also to all those who reviewed and rated the many submissions we received. A special thanks is also extended to the following people, whose enthusiasm and hard work helped to make this book possible: Dr. Alan Bishop, Professor, Department of English; Dr. James (Jim) Johnson, Professor Emeritus, Department of Economics; Miranda Beamer and Kristine Pearce, Gerontology Program graduates; and Amrita Raghunathan and Colleen Lowe, Gerontology Program students, and Office Assistants, in the Centre for Gerontological Studies. Thanks also to Kim Lizotte and Joanna Shepherd for their assistance. Dennis Ryan is also acknowledged and thanked for sharing his excellent editing skills and we thank all those who allowed us to present pictures of their loved ones on the cover of this book.

Finally, we would also like to acknowledge the students and teachers of Sheridan Public School in Oakville. Their interest in this project was sincerely appreciated and the stories were truly amazing.

Ellen Bouchard Ryan
Gail M. Elliot
Ann P. Anas

CHAPTER 1

CONNECTIONS FROM OLDER ADULTS

POOH STICKS

Dr. David Inman
Dundas, Ontario

Old Ben's inability to read or write had been neither here nor there to his grandson. Being illiterate seems perfectly normal before you are five years old. Their friendship had been based on trust and understanding – and, of course, love; but let's not get sloppy about it. They had treated each other with tolerance and dignity and had never had any reason to lie to one another.

Then a day came when each of them realized he was keeping something important from the other. As it happens, each of them already knew the other's secret but felt that to speak about it would be indelicate. Both of these lies of omission were prompted by the one really acceptable excuse for lying, the fear of hurting a friend; but they were not treating either of their consciences gently.

Little Ben had been not much more than one-year-old when his grandfather had introduced him to the absorbing ritual of Pooh Sticks. At the bottom of his parents' garden there was a slow-moving stream spanned by an elderly wooden bridge. The bridge's reason for existing was no longer obvious. If you wanted to cross the stream, there was a much safer, uglier bridge a short distance away. Almost no one ever used the Pooh Sticks bridge except the two Bens. It was their favourite place. If you have something overdue to say to a friend, an ideal time to get it off your chest is when the two of you are leaning dangerously over opposite sides of a bridge looking at each other beneath its arch. You are both the same way up but the rest of the world is upside down, suspended beneath your bottoms; and time is suspended with it. It is reassuringly intimate, and the best of all times for broaching matters of great delicacy.

It was little Ben's turn to drop the stick in the water and count – a fairly recently acquired skill – while his grandfather waited for it to appear on his side of the bridge. He dropped it carefully to make sure it got lodged behind a rock.

After reaching twenty, he stopped counting and said, "Looks like it's stuck."

"Maybe," said Old Ben, "but it may unstuck if we wait a bit longer."

This was Little Ben's moment. With that exaggerated air of nonchalance, which five-year-old boys assume when risking everything by revealing a secret, he said, "I've been learning to read a bit."

"That's good," said Old Ben. "Very good. Wish I'd got around to it myself. Never seemed to have the time, somehow. Too busy making money. Got a lot of money in the bank now. Don't have much use for it. No books on the shelf though. Wish I had some use for them. Glad to hear you aren't going to make the same mistake."

Little Ben knew he was the only person in the world privileged to share his friend's pain. Prodding vaguely, he dredged up another white lie.

"It's not important. Just something they sort of expect me to do now that I'm going to proper school. Thought I might as well tell you, though."

Old Ben marveled at his friend's tact. He could only guess how excited the boy must really be about entering a magic world, which was forever beyond his own reach.

"Sure, sure; but you keep at it, Ben. Never know when it might come in handy. Maybe you'll be able to read stuff for me sometimes. They teaching you to write as well?"

"Well, only just. I mean, we've only just started. I can write my name. So I suppose I could write your name too, since it's the same as mine. If you wanted me to, that is."

The Pooh Stick was firmly jammed; they both knew it was not going to get free on its own. It was Old Ben's turn.

"Supposing I had to move out for some reason. I mean, not live here any more. If that happened we could still play together. Here at the river, I mean. Couldn't we?"

"Sure," said Little Ben. Then, after a delicate pause, "When do you think you might have to go?"

"Well, pretty soon, I guess. Your Mom and Dad are too busy to have me on their hands all the time. Especially now that . . . hey, is that stick never going to free itself? Anyway, it's high time I spent some of that money on something. Might as well pay someone else to look after me for a change."

Old Ben prodded ineffectually at a rock, carefully avoiding the Pooh Stick, before adding, "You could come and see me a lot, of course. If you wanted to, that is."

"That would be great," said Little Ben.

The two-way confessional was over. Absolution had been sought and given. It had been unnecessary to reveal either the ecstasy of discovering literacy in preparation for adulthood, or the agony of losing functional control on the way to second childhood.

As they returned to the house, forgetting the Pooh Stick, which had served its purpose, the old man said, "I won't be able to take all my stuff with me, of course. Just as well; lot of old junk, most of it. Come to think of it, there's one thing you might like to take off my hands. Since you're learning to read and write, that is."

He dragged an exquisite little writing desk out of his closet.

"There you are", he said, "this belonged to *my* grandpa. Supposed to be hundreds of years old. It's called an excreta, or something. Never been much use to me. It can be yours now, if you want it."

Little Ben's height doubled. It was the first beautiful, grown-up thing he had ever owned. He ran his finger lovingly over the elaborately carved, Elizabethan oak and something even more wonderful happened. A section of the carving swung open to reveal a sheaf of yellow pages.

"It's a secret hiding place! Did you know about it?"

"No, it never did that for me. It must like you."

Old Ben pulled the pages out and said, "Here's your big chance, then. See if you can read what's written on them." No sooner had he said it than he wished he hadn't.

Little Ben looked proudly at the faded writing. It did not look like anything he had ever seen before.

"I can't read *any* of it," he said miserably, fighting back tears of frustration.

Old Ben understood his grandson's feeling of inadequacy. He had been there many times. "Never mind. It's probably in some foreign language. No use to anyone anymore. Probably never was."

Then, seeing that his friend still felt that he had failed his first big test, he added, "They would make great boats though, wouldn't they?"

An hour later they were on the bridge again, launching a parchment armada. The little boats sailed bravely; but not for long. The first to sink was the title page. As it went down the centuries old ink dissolved. Only the old man and the boy had been privy to the brief disclosure of its message; but its secret had remained safe from them. Now it was lost forever.

What it had been trying to say for four centuries, in a script which had defeated both of them, was this . . .

Loues Labour Vvonne
A Comedie by Vvm. Shakfpar.

BURIED ALIVE

Robert W. Allan
Port Dover, Ontario

Forty hands, twenty shovels and a large bucket crane dug the way to a dramatic victory on August 24, 1949, in mid afternoon in the rescue of a fifteen-year-old boy. He had been buried forty minutes under tons of sand piled forty feet high on a dockside at the foot of Victoria Avenue beside Mixed Concrete Supply Ltd.

This could very well have been my own obituary, almost fifty years ago, but the Great Man above decided to give me one of my nine lives to tell this story.

My brother Don and I were together a lot when I went out to run for track training. Don would ride on the crossbar of my bike when I went off to a couple of my favourite training runs. One was out past Dundurn Castle and down Valley Inn Road, the other was through the H.M.C.S. Star and along the revetment wall on the bayfront. Don would usually sit and play by himself while I ran for over an hour.

On this day Don was playing in the sand pile behind Canadian Vegetable Oil and in front of the Mixed Concrete plant while I ran on the docks. Every twenty minutes I would join Don for a breather and we ran up this big sand pile. We had probably done this routine dozens of times without anyone ever coming around to chase us away.

Unknown to us, under this sand pile a screw conveyor fed sand to a hopper over a hundred feet away in the cement plant to be mixed into various grades of concrete. In running up the south face of this sand pile, I broke through an air pocket directly over the feeder hopper and dropped down to my waist. I was trapped and could feel myself slowly sinking deeper as Don was clambering over to help me. I kept yelling at him to stay away but he kept on coming until he was right in front of me and tried to reach for me. I could see a train parked on the tracks behind the soya bean plant and told Don to go there for help but he just stood there as I was

14

sliding deeper into the sand. I reached out, slapped Don across the face and screamed at him to "get the hell out of here and get some help at the train."

As Don tumbled back down the slope, and was running the hundred-yard dash of his life for help, I disappeared below the sand. I had enough sense to put one hand over my nose and the other straight up over my head. The pressure kept building against my chest as I continued to slide further into this tomb of sand.

I remember my feet hitting something solid, then I blacked out as several thoughts and images whirled through my mind and coloured lights flashed, even though my eyes were closed tight. It would be an hour later before I regained any memory of the surrounding events.

Meanwhile the train engineer and his fireman, Jim Noble and Owen Bray, saw Don coming, knew something was wrong, grabbed their shovels and went to meet him.

Inside the cement plant, an operator named Marvin McLenaghan went up the conveyor tunnel to see why the screw had stopped feeding sand and began poking into the small opening at the bottom of the hopper. When my two feet suddenly dropped down he cut off all power and ran up to the plant telling people to call the fire department, police and ambulance as someone was trapped in the conveyor hopper. Fellow workers grabbed shovels, sheets of steel, boards and anything useful for digging, while the gathering crowd of twenty policemen and firemen used their bare hands to start moving twenty-five tons of sand. A huge clam shell power shovel was brought over to move the first fifteen feet off the pile but the last eight or ten feet was dug away manually for fear of the heavy clam shell grabbing me.

After forty minutes of digging someone yelled, "Here he is, I've got his arm." It was Detective George Caton who held on and directed the rescuers to abandon their shovels and dig only with their bare hands. My head was uncovered and Lieutenant George Newcombe of the Victoria Street fire station clapped an inhalator mask over my face, which was blue, and I began to respond almost immediately.

"I didn't expect him to come around," Lieutenant Newcombe said afterwards. "Then I was afraid there would be another cave in before they could get him out of here. That would have finished him for sure. But as soon as we put the inhalator on him, he gulped. I guess the oxygen perked him up a bit as he started to fight it." Being careful not to hurt me further, as I was still unconscious, they started using their shovels again and to shore up the walls to free me while the inhalator was held on my face, which was still blue.

A few minutes later when my body was free, six workers lifted my inert form and carried me to a blanket. Firemen and policemen immediately began applying artificial respiration.

My final removal from the sand had been effected through the efforts of Constable John Fraser who had entered the hopper tunnel under the ground and pushed upward on my feet as detective George Caton who was still holding my arm, pulled me free.

Within moments after being placed on the blanket, I coughed, then was sick and finally tried to roll over and sit up. Nobody cheered, but apparently there were grins on nearly every face, except Don's. He had been crying for an hour but when a photographer who wanted his picture said, "Your brother's going to be all right," a big slightly buck toothed but very grateful grin crossed his wet face and he said "Yeh."

A big husky fireman stood up and, mopping his brow with his shirtsleeve, asked, "Anybody's got a cigarette?" One of the waiting newsmen handed him a pack and said, "How do you feel now?" The fireman smiled, "I feel good now. When I first got here I didn't think the kid had a chance – boy, what a scrapper eh?"

I was carried to the waiting ambulance accompanied by Lieutenant Newcombe, a trained specialist in inhalators, and Drs. J.W. Faris and T.M. Black who were staff members at the General Hospital where they were taking me. A Detective Bill Stamp who was George Caton's partner took Don home as trucks and cars pulled away and we headed up Victoria Avenue to the hospital.

About the time the ambulance got blocked by a train across Victoria Avenue, I started to regain consciousness and felt sick. I tried to sit up but was being held down by a couple of guys in white coats who were holding a terrible smelly rubber mask over my face. A siren was wailing and people outside the ambulance were hollering at the train crew to split the cars apart to let us pass, and I knew I was going to be sick. I was able to jerk my head to one side as I threw up all over one of the white coats holding me down. Now I started to feel better and realized where I was.

While all this was going on, my mother was informed by a busybody know it all from down the street, that I had been hit by a train at the peanut factory. Of course mother was now getting opposing scraps of information from the press and police as the rescue was still in progress. A neighbour, Isabell Rollo's husband, said he would find out what was going on. He jumped over the veranda railing and ran down the street to the General Hospital.

Meanwhile the police had gone to my dad's office at Donald Rope & Wire to tell him he should go to the hospital as I had been buried alive, was unconscious and on my way to the General Hospital. They took him down in a cruiser to the emergency department before I showed up.

Back on Victoria Avenue they finally split the train apart so we could continue up the street. I don't know why they didn't just drive the whole damn train down the track.

A whole medical team was waiting when we arrived at the General. While they were taking x-rays, doctors and nurses were busy cleaning sand from every orifice of my body and also from some places I didn't even know I had. The only marks on me were a scrape on a forearm where a shovel hit me. The doctors couldn't understand why or how I survived. The only possible explanation was the moisture left in the sand from the previous day's rain held enough oxygen. I could suck it through my fingers covering my face and not inhale the sand, which sure would have suffocated me in a short time after going under.

By now I was feeling fine so they wheeled me to an examination room where dad and two neighbours were waiting. I sat up and said, "Hi - lets go home," while everyone stood around looking at each other in amazement. Bill Woods and Jack Dynes said they would run back home to tell mom that I was just fine. Meanwhile, dad and I had to check out by the cashier's office to sign out and collect a bill for two dollars for the use of the emergency room.

We walked up Barton Street to Wellington, stopped in a corner store for ice cream cones and continued to walk home talking about this

17

adventure as though it was just another one of our Sunday afternoon runs together. I don't remember dad showing any great emotion, but I'm sure I probably scarred his heart forever.

Mother was typical when we arrived home just after six o'clock. She said, "Your supper is cold now, heat it up yourself or go without." Dad, Don, Maureen, Veronica and me sat around the kitchen table eating and talking while mom sat in the living room pretending to read the paper, as she probably had her cry by herself. The only thing she ever said to me was, "You are going to get fined yet for riding Don around on your bike."

The reporters and photographers started phoning and knocking on the door by seven that night looking for additional pictures of family and any information they could write about. The following day we allowed a Mr. Horrigan from the Toronto Star to come for a follow-up story and pictures. When Don, dad and I went up to the Star's office to view the pictures a couple of days later, he charged us twenty-five cents for each copy we wanted.

But the story doesn't end happily ever after at this time in August 1949 as I thought it did.

Olive was working at St. Joseph's Hospital in the spring of 1971 covering all floors and departments as a member of the nurse's pool. One evening she was called to a room where a patient asked if he might get a cup of tea. Olive obliged as she had some time, so she delivered it to this old gentleman who was extremely grateful and asked her to sit with him for a minute. In the course of conversation he said that he was a retired cop and he spotted her nametag as they talked about his career exploits. Olive knew his name and asked him if he was at a boy's rescue from a sand pile twenty-two years earlier. He said he sure was and remembered the lucky lad's name was Allan. Then he realized Olive's nametag read O. Allan, R.N. He asked her if she knew the boy or was a relative and when she said, "I am Bob Allan's wife" he grabbed her arm as he had grabbed mine many years before. The policeman was Detective George Caton who had directed my rescue.

Stranger yet was that George Caton's wife was down the hall in another room dying of cancer with her family around her.

Needless to say the Catons received Olive's attention completely for the balance of the week. When she came home and told me whom she was nursing, it seemed as though fate had stepped in to return a great favour to someone who was instrumental in helping to save my life. I know Olive couldn't save Mrs. Caton's life but she certainly made the end more comfortable for the whole family, particularly Mrs. Caton.

I went to visit George and his wife before she died and met their son who sat with his dad and me as we related the story of my rescue and George Caton's leading role in the operation.

George's son never knew his dad had been a hero until that night and was so proud of his dad that we both wished we had a medal to give him. George Caton was grateful to Olive who was with his wife when she died. And he was so pleased to visit with me on a couple of occasions before he went home to God two years later.

I am even more thankful for having met this man almost fifty years ago. Unfortunately it took me twenty-two years to meet him face to face and say thank you, and another twenty-seven years to write this story so people will know of this fine gentleman who is partially responsible for my existence today, which has been a happy forever after story.

God bless George Caton.

On October 29, 1949, Eaton's GOOD Deed Club awarded Don a watch and the Gold Star Pin with a certificate stating that this is their highest honour to be obtained for the best good deed of the week. I have the letter advising Don of this award and also the Gold Pin displayed with the certificate and one of the newspaper photos of the two of us at home.

God bless you brother!!!!!!!!!!!!!!!!!!!!!!!

JUSTICE FOR JIMMIE

Glenna N. King
Hamilton, Ontario

Dear Kaitlyn,

I was so happy when you decided to come to the reunion with us last summer. I realize that it was a long tiresome trip for you but didn't we have fun! The whole weekend would not have been so fine without you, and a tear was in my eye when I saw you light the candle for your great-grandfather. I wish that you had known him, Kaitlyn, but even your mother has no real memory of him. She was not yet two years old when he died.

Memories are important, Kaitlyn, and that was what that reunion was about; remembering a couple named James and Elizabeth and their sons and daughters. My father and your great-grandfather was the second son of James and Elizabeth. The family was a large one consisting of six boys, two girls and two dead in infancy. It was not a notable family as some families are. None of the offspring achieved great things or became famous. They were simply honourable, upright people well respected in their community.

I had hoped that at the reunion I could have gathered some family stories but I wasn't able to. Perhaps the people I approached really thought that they did not have any to tell but I suspect that we all have stories; we just have to dig a little for them. My father was a storyteller as anyone with a little Irish blood in them should be, and I am so glad that he was, for now we can know James and Elizabeth as something more than names etched on a tombstone or church window. I am sending you a story I have written which is based on a true story concerning James. It is rather sad, but it has a nice Irish twist to it, which pleases me.

James or Jimmie as he was commonly known died at the age of fifty-nine. While he lived, he farmed a few acres and worked for a man who behaved very much like the O'Brien of my story. I think it was not uncommon in those long ago days to find situations such as I describe. I won't go into detail about what took place when Jimmie's sons went to get a coffin in which to bury their father. I'll let my story speak for itself.

Love You,
Nanny

*　　*　　*　　*

Jimmie Cullen died on August tenth at exactly two a.m. His death was not unexpected for he had taken to his bed early in April and as spring gave way to summer, it became obvious that he would not get better. It was tuberculosis. The Cullens seemed a special target of that dread disease, and although Jimmie had fought this last battle with great courage, he could not win. Perhaps if he had been able to stop sooner; but a man just can't give in too quickly, especially when there are young ones in the house. Yet Lizzie was luckier than some. Their two oldest children were boys, and were big enough to work when there was something for them to do. Fortunately O'Brien had given the eldest boy, Jordy, work at the mill soon after his father had taken sick and what he earned kept bread on the table. Jordy, at sixteen, was now the sole support of the family.

Lizzie Cullen did not call the boys when Jimmie passed away at two o'clock. She and her neighbours had stayed with him when they saw that the end was near and they did what was necessary. When the boys came down to breakfast their father was already laid out in his best suit waiting to be put into his coffin.

"You'll ask O'Brien to get a coffin sent up from town, Jordy," Lizzie said.

"Yeah Ma, I'll tend to it."

Lizzie hated O'Brien, as did everyone else in the village. They hated him because they were dependent upon him for the food they ate and the clothes they wore and the coffins in which they buried their dead. They hated him because he controlled everything and they controlled nothing. They hated him because he held all the weapons and did not hesitate to use

21

them. The lumber camp belonged to him and the sawmill and because this was all there was, their very lives belonged to him also.

O'Brien did not believe in regular paydays. Of what use was it to hand out good money to these simple people who would most likely waste it on drink or fancy clothes. Much better to keep them supplied with food and necessary clothing, and when necessary, hand out a twenty dollar bill so that taxes might be paid and nickels and dimes supplied for the offering plate on Sunday. Few were in a position ever to question his way of doing business and no explanations were given.

Jimmie Cullen had worked for O'Brien for twenty years. Now he was dead and there would be enough money to bury him. Lizzie had seen to that. As soon as Jimmie had been forced to leave work, she had drawn no more of his "time." She had not discussed it with her husband but they had both understood. What he had earned the last month at the mill would not be touched so there would be plenty on hand to look after things and to pay for a decent funeral.

Jordy put on his Sunday suit when he went to the mill. He would not work on the day his father died, nor would O'Brien expect him to. Neither did Jordy expect to be told that there was not enough money in back wages for a coffin.

"But Ma said there was still time owin.'"

"Your Ma has made a mistake, Jordy. After all I ain't been payin' you the wages I paid your father. A boy ain't able to do a man's job, but the groceries is still goin' outta here and there ain't been none of ya hungry. Then there's been the medicine for your Pa. Medicine is dear. No Jordy, his time was used up weeks ago. There ain't any left for a coffin."

"All right then, give it to us on tick and take it out'a my time." Jordy was desperate.

"Now Jordy, what way is that to do business?" O'Brien pulled a red and white handkerchief out of his pocket and blew his nose.

"With the way things is goin', I maybe won't be able to give you work much longer." O'Brien blew again. "Times is hard right now. No, Jordy, it can't be done. Tell your Ma I'll be glad to pick up a real nice coffin in town but it will cost her thirty dollars in cash. It's the best I can do."

"Thirty dollars!" Jordy turned away quickly so O'Brien wouldn't see the tears in his eyes.

"Bastard," he thought, "He knows damn well I give him a better day's work than Pa was able to give him for more than a year. How can he say there ain't no time owin' us?"

Lizzie turned pale when Jordy told her what O'Brien had said. "He's a dishonest man Jordy," she said. "Yer Pa killed hisself workin' fer him and now he denies him a decent burial. Thirty dollars, thirty pieces of silver, the traitors is all the same. Greed, crooked greed, that's what it is." She covered her head with her apron.

Jordy could not bear it. He left the house but there was no place to go. He felt strange and uncomfortable in his good suit and remembered that he should have changed but he couldn't go back in again, at least, not now. A man had to do something. He had to think.

Jordy went to the barn, and there, he began to build a box. It was a rough box built of rough board and badly put together for he was no carpenter, but it was strong and big enough to hold Jimmie Cullen. When it was finished with three leather handgrips attached to each side, he called his brother to help him carry it into the house. There in the front parlour, supported on two kitchen chairs and lined with Lizzie's best patchwork quilt, it became a coffin for Jimmie.

Jordy sat in the parlour looking out of the window, his back turned to the relatives and neighbours as they came to pay their last respects to the dead and to sit around and talk in whispers with each other. When they spoke to him, he seemed not to hear and they agreed that he was taking it hard.

At last O'Brien came. Jordy knew he would. He always came when there was death. He was proud of the fact that he did the right thing by his people. He never failed to shake hands with a certain number of them at church. He visited with them if there was serious sickness in the family, at which time he stayed a comfortable distance from them so as not to catch their germs. He congratulated them when there was a new baby and looked sorrowfully at them when they died and sent a wreath for the funeral. Jordy turned away from the window when O'Brien came into the room.

The big man took off his sweat brimmed hat and held it in his hand. He seemed not to notice the box.

"So young to die," he said. "So young to die. They don't come better than Jimmie Cullen." It was a fine tribute. He reached into his pocket for the red and white handkerchief.

Jordy came and stood facing him on the opposite side of the box.

"You'll be a pallbearer at the funeral to-morrow, won't you, Mr. O'Brien?" he asked.

O'Brien seemed flustered.

"Now Jordy, I'm mighty honoured to be asked, but won't you be wantin' yer relatives and close friends?" He fumbled with one of the leather grips on the rough box.

"No, Mr. O'Brien," said Jordy softly. "We want you."

"Well now Jordy, I'm a busy man."

"Ya won't be busy to-morrow, Mr. O'Brien. The mill will be down to let the men off for the funeral."

Others had now gathered around to hear the conversation. They knew what had happened. It was the talk of the village. Jimmie Cullen laid out in a rough wooden box made by the hands of his own son because O'Brien had refused to pay Lizzie his back wages. It wasn't the first time something like this had happened, but it seemed that this time he might have to pay. This boy of Jimmie Cullen's was keen and they were with him all the way. They recognized a wonderful kind of justice in forcing him to carry Jimmie to his last resting place in the rough box to which he had damned him. They would give him the place of honour right at the head of the box.

O'Brien looked at the faces around him and saw clearly what was in the eyes of each. He looked at Jordy and saw that he had met his match.

"We'll see what we can do boy," he said. "We'll see what we can do." He left the room hurriedly.

Jordy turned back to the window. He was still there at dusk when O'Brien's old wagon drove up to the house with a fine pine coffin lined with purple silk for his father.

PRECIOUS PIRATES

Alex Graham
Delhi, Ontario

A sly devilish pirate
Has invaded my heart,
And, in search of my treasures,
Has torn it apart;

You would never suspect
Her sweet innocent air,
Eyes as deep as a coal mine
And as dark as her hair;

There is perfume and powder
Scattered round in her haste,
And my peace and decorum
Are forever laid waste;

I confess, as a Grandpa,
This has happened before,
And in truth we enjoy it
So we don't bar the door;

They hold us to ransom
As all pirates would,
And we yield up our love
As Grandparents should;

The sacks in the strongroom,
With affection are full,
And there's always a drawstring
For a pirate to pull;

We hope that their booty
Will last them for years,
They can hoard all the smiles
And trade off the tears;

And someday looking back,
They may yet realize,
They may have been pirates
But we captured the prize.

BIRTHDAY CAKES

Ruth Murdoch
Burlington, Ontario

On my older brother Lawrence's seventeenth or eighteenth birthday he was bringing his new girlfriend, Betty, to dinner for the first time.

When I got home from school that third day of January, Mother asked me to ice the cake, which she had already made. In our family birthday cakes were usually a white layer cake with jam, lemon, or icing filling and white icing with coconut on it. This time we were to have a little change. Lawrence did not like coconut but would I please make his favourite, maple cream. Jam was the chosen filling that day.

I set to work, measuring the brown sugar and milk into a saucepan and put it on to boil. A full rolling boil for three minutes, exactly, the recipe specified. Add butter and vanilla later and beat well with a spoon. This I did and, when ready, poured it on to the awaiting cake.

Oh! Oh! Something was not quite right. The icing only covered about half the cake and down part of the side. It was suddenly too stiff to budge. Not to worry. Another batch would set matters to rights. Lawrence's favourite icing was maple cream so lots of it he would have.

Same procedure. This time I aimed for the other side of the cake with approximately the same results. The sides were sparsely covered and the top was about an inch thick. Lawrence would love it. At least it looked nice and shiny where no knife had touched it to spread it thinner.

Lawrence arrived with Betty and dinner proceeded. I cannot recall the menu but at the end of the main course, Mother and I went into the kitchen to put the candles in the cake. Soon giggles were heard coming from the kitchen and then outright laughter, although we tried to stifle it.

At that time we had candleholders for birthday cakes, which resembled pink flowers with wire pieces by which they were stuck into the cake. No way would or could these holders penetrate that thick icing of concrete consistency. They just bent. Finally there was only one answer that I could see. That icing was hit a couple of hard smacks with a hammer. The candles were lined up along the ensuing cracks wherever we could fit them in. A few had to go through thin spots near the top of the sides.

We triumphantly carried that odd-looking birthday cake in, complete with candles sprouting in all directions. There was certainly no discernable pattern to their placement.

At first Lawrence was mortified at the behaviour of his Mother and sister but very soon saw the funny side of it as the whole table of people exploded in laughter.

After the candles were removed we eventually turned the cake upside down, cut it into slices and broke a piece of icing off to go with each piece. It tasted fine.

Do you know, I never made that icing again until my own children were nearly grown. Then it was done very, very, carefully – not overcooked or over beaten. I like the taste of it but it's not my favourite because of the memories.

Oh yes, later on March 20, 1944, Betty and Lawrence were married so it did not have disastrous effects on their relationship.

THE SECOND BIG BANG

Ruth Murdoch
Burlington, Ontario

It was July 18, 1945. Halifax was recovering from the devastation of the VE Day riots. Dad was up in Toronto on a few days' leave preparing for his impending discharge from the Royal Canadian Navy. My younger brother, Jim, was in port for a short time while his ship was preparing to sail around to take part in the Pacific activities. Mom and I, together with our cocker spaniel puppy Skipper, were holding the fort at 348 Gottingen Street in Halifax.

That evening, Mom, Jim and I decided to see a movie. Just as we were walking over to the streetcar stop about 6:30 p.m. there was a horrific explosion in the direction of Bedford Basin, immediately followed by a mushroom shaped cloud. At the same time, the glass window of the shop we had just passed blew out, missing us by inches.

We looked at one another wondering just what we should do. Finally we decided that there was nothing we could do about it and it was over, at least for now. We took the next streetcar downtown and proceeded to the movie. I'll never forget it. The show was called *Journey for Margaret* about a little evacuee in England, I believe, starring Margaret O'Brien. One or two things puzzled us. While there was a nice pastoral scene on the screen, we could hear sounds of explosions. As the movie was about the war and there were bombings going on, we kidded ourselves that it was all part of the show, albeit unexplained. When, however, people started walking up and down the aisles asking all Air Raid Wardens to report to their stations immediately, we decided it was definitely time to leave.

As it turned out, we were able to get the last streetcar allowed back up to Gottingen Street. When we neared home, we heard loud speakers on patrol cars telling everyone to evacuate that area immediately and to leave all doors and windows open so the force of any blast would dissipate without damage. At least, that was the theory and hope.

Apparently some depth charges being handled on the loading dock at the Naval magazine had fallen into the water. That was the initial bang. There was great danger of the whole main Munitions Dump going up. If this happened it could destroy the whole north end of Halifax. That's where we lived. Remember, they had the memory of the first Halifax Explosion in 1916, I believe, when hundreds of people were killed.

We grabbed a couple of blankets and Skipper and we hurried down to Citadel Hill. From time to time the sky would light up with the glow from an explosion. I never did understand what all the minor explosions were about but they were definitely there throughout the night. I had just finished reading Hugh Maclennan's *"Barometer Rising,"* the story of the first explosion. In it they said either one side or the other of Citadel Hill was far more dangerous than the other because either the force of the explosion would hit that side of the hill or debris from the explosion would go over the hill and, losing force, would drop on the other side. I couldn't remember which.

From time to time patrol cars would drive around asking people to move to the other side of the hill. I guess they couldn't decide which side was safer either, as through the night we moved several times. All around us people were stretched out on blankets on the ground in the darkness, some talking in subdued voices. Whenever we had to move, Jim looked after Mother and I looked after Skipper. Many a time we would be standing when an explosion would occur. That is when we were told to crouch on the ground. Later we kidded Mom and called her our "Dive Mommer." She would get her head down all right but her rear end was usually sticking up in the air. At one time Jim ran into his commanding officer. He was supposed to be back aboard the ship that evening but was told to stick with us until things settled down, hopefully the next day. All other naval personnel were occupied with their ships or the explosion. I believe they moved as many ships as possible if they were considered in a danger zone.

The next day Halifax made up for all the bad feelings leading up to the riots. We were told to go to the Commons, a large park area. There all babies were taken from the mothers, fed, changed and cleaned up before being returned. Sandwiches and coffee or milk were handed out to everyone. When I put my hand out, I was thoroughly ashamed of just how filthy it was. Johns were set up with long line-ups, of course, but they did their best and nobody complained. Blankets had been handed out through the night by the Red Cross.

That afternoon we were allowed to go home again. We had no damage done to our belongings but many others had different stories to tell. The force of the explosions broke dishes in one home and nothing next door. There seemed no rhyme or reason as to why it took that pattern. My uncle, who was also in the Navy for the second time, was a pretty stubborn fellow. He wasn't going to leave. After one explosion the trap door leading to the attic came down on top of him. He left.

For the next few days the radio kept broadcasting requests for people to return to the Red Cross the blankets they had been loaned. We could see several with the distinctive red stripe on grey blanket hanging on the lines at the back of the homes on the next street, airing. I guess that is human nature and it was a rather poor neighbourhood.

Miraculously, there was only one casualty. That was the rating who had phoned in the alarm when the depth charge went in. It was thought that the force of the explosion had killed him when he was in such a confined space as a telephone booth but he had no other injuries.

Dad, in Toronto, was wondering what was happening to his family in Halifax. We reassured him by phone that all was well. Some time after that Jim's ship sailed for the Pacific but by the time they reached it, that war was over as well. He was discharged in Victoria, B.C. and returned to Toronto without most of his gear, as he wanted no part of it anymore.

The night we spent on Citadel Hill, Mom and I were very glad to have that fine sailor looking after us.

POEMS

Alex Graham
Delhi, Ontario

GRANDMA'S LOVE

There are chambers of love
in a Grandmother's heart,
And each Grandchild is given
the key to their part;
It gets topped up with memories
of each year as they grow,
and we daily share pride,
That only Grandmothers know;
Graduation today is a step on the
way
To the lifetime of dreams
That we wish for and pray;
You may visit your chamber
Any time you feel free,
To pick up some love,
And leave memories for me.

GRAMPA'S HEART

They often show you pictures
of hearts upon TV,
All rounded smooth and throbbing,
alive and plain to see
But they never show a
Grampa's heart
with the tiny strings that tug
When little arms wrap
around the neck
to give a loving hug
I don't know if they just trim them
or they're much too fine to show
But though they are invisible
the strings are there I know.
There's one for every Grandson
and each Granddaughter too
I know there must be
strings to spare
prepared for someone new.
I don't care if you believe me,
think me just a silly mug,
All Grampas know the
strings are real
because they've felt the tug.

31

A LETTER TO MY GRANDCHILD

Florence Leet
Hamilton, Ontario

Dear Grandchild:

We are approaching the year 2000 or the second millennium. I have had the pleasure of living during the last 60 years and have noticed many changes in the way we think and feel, and seen more opportunities than were previously available. There were also some cruel wars.

Those who used their dreams and opportunities have made great strides in the field of medicine, transportation, communication, toys and many other inventions.

World War I (1914-1918)

Your great-grandpa Leet was an American citizen. He fought in the Engineering Division. Armed with a bayonet, gun and a folding shovel, he dug trenches in France and captured prisoners.

World War II (1939-1945)

It started when the Japanese bombed Pearl Harbour. The cruelest man in the entire history of the world was a leader and dictator of the Germans. He ordered the slaughter of millions of people. His name was Adolph Hitler.

During World War II your great aunt Lois and I were not permitted to read the newspaper or listen to the news as your great-great-grandparents considered it too horrific.

One day I asked my mom why so many families didn't have daddies. She replied that the daddies were away fighting and that they were very brave. We would pray that they would return safely.

When we saw a neighbour running to our neighbour, Bob Seymour's home, we would let mother know, because the Seymours had the "community phone." A family could be getting news.

It became evident that war must be stopped. The war ended when the U.S. dropped three atomic bombs on Japan. The use of atomic power is now channeled for peaceful means.

The League of Nations and later the United Nations was formed to maintain world peace.

During the 1950's there was the Korean War. Later there was the Vietnam War and the Killing Fields of Cambodia.

As the century draws to a close the Bosnians, Serbs and Croations are at war. Some people who were fortunate enough to escape from the war zones have reported cases of "ethnic cleansing." The United Nations sent peacekeeping forces.

Human Relationships

The role of women has changed dramatically during the 1900's. Early in the century women were considered to be chattels of their husbands. They were to cook, clean, sew and have babies. As there was no effective means of birth control, it was not unusual for there to be ten children in a family. It was considered proper for a man to beat his wife. Divorce brought shame upon the family, as did living together without benefit of marriage. In 1999, living common-law is normal and divorces are frequent.

In 1900 women didn't attend school. The only jobs considered suitable for ladies by the 1950's were in nursing, libraries, teaching and other so called feminine kinds of work. Women so employed were considered to be "Old Maids" (unmarried ladies). Today's women run companies and literally do every job that men do. (Although they only earn 80¢ for every $1.00 men earn for similar work.)

Today it is considered important that women receive as much education as they possibly can. However, in the 1950's it was a well-known fact that a woman's reason for attending university was to receive an MRS degree (find a husband). In the early 1900's a married women who worked was considered inferior as "she could not make ends meet on her husband's income." Today's family needs two well-educated parents working at an above middle class wage to support a family.

In the early part of the century children were reprimanded by the use of a birch switch or a board or belt across the backside for such naughty acts as swearing, not showing respect to elders, or not helping neighbours or other family members.

The breakdown of the family unit is said to be caused by lack of discipline, mothers working, violent TV programs, availability of drugs, guns and gangs. Now some parents are fearful of their children and the problems they could bring upon themselves.

My dear grandchild, you and your parents are so fortunate to love and share life with each other. There is no problem you cannot ask about for their advice. Pick your friends very carefully. Good friends last a lifetime.

Choose your future with great care. Thoughtfulness, caring, loving and loyalty are some of the best attributes you should consider. Your best friends are your family.

Inventions

Can you imagine a life without radios, TV, VCR, CD's, tapes, automobiles, airplanes, telephones, computers, and space travel? Your great-grandpa Leet saw the first motorcar in Chicago. It was a Model A Ford. When your mother was a baby she watched the first man in space.

I believe your great-grandpa and great-grandma Leet had a wireless radio when I was born. Great-grandpa Leet had a car, which was sold before I was born (1939) as it was too expensive. Today most families have more than one car.

Every winter morning was cold, and while your great-aunt Lois and grandma Leet huddled under the covers, your great-grandpa Leet stoked the coal furnace until he purchased an automatic oil furnace. He used to turn on the water heater and wait for hot water to have our once weekly bath. When we got an automatic hot water heater, we could bathe daily, have an automatic clothes washer, and automatic dishwasher. Previous to the automatic clothes washer was a large tin washtub and a scrubbing board. The washtub doubled for bathing. The wringer (hand and electric operated) was dangerous as my mother got her hands caught in the wringer.

It is impossible for me to write all of the changes. Many men worked on plans for a computer. Bill Gates completed the task thus becoming very important. Your uncle Jeff works with computers.

Medicine

Our family has benefited most from the dedication of physicians.

On April 5, 1949, my mother and father were crossing the street when a car hit my mom. She had serious head and leg injuries. Dr. Cooper put in the first metal plate in our city by reading and following the Medical Journal instructions while he operated. Although splinters of bone would come out of her leg from time to time, she walked for almost 30 years.

My cousin Eleanor was just a child when she became ill with Poliomyelitis, also known as Infantile Paralysis. She was rushed from Owen Sound, Ontario to Sick Children's Hospital in Toronto, Ontario. Many children died during the outbreak. Some were maintained for a while in an Iron Lung. We were lucky, Eleanor's problems were in her legs and she worked faithfully at her therapy and regained her ability to walk. She now has Post Polio Syndrome and will need a wheelchair soon.

Many dedicated medical scientists worked tirelessly on treatments and medications. In the 1950's the radio bulletins were announcing hourly for people to listen to a special news bulletin at 8:00 p.m. We gathered around the radio and heard that Dr. James Salk had invented the Salk Vaccine, which prevented Polio. The last case of Polio was in the 1970's in Africa and the world is now free of a crippling and killing disease.

When I was a child, my mother noticed I was stiff and that my joints were pinkish, hot and swollen. My mother, a nurse, took me to the doctor as she thought I had arthritis. The doctor told her that children couldn't get it. It was also thought that arthritis was only one disease. Mother treated me from her limited medical knowledge. It is believed, now, that I was born with five of the more than 100 kinds of arthritis. I have been treated by many skillful, dedicated, and knowledgeable rheumatologists and neurosurgeons including Dr. Watson Buchanan, Dr. Walter Kean, Dr. Reddy to name only a few, as well as the Arthritis Society. (I know I can do my exercises in my sleep.)

Two weeks ago it was announced that an abnormal gene is responsible for rheumatoid arthritis and that one patient had been "cured." However, rheumatoid arthritis can go into spontaneous remission and it will take many patients to be rheumatoid free with no return until they can announce a cure.

YOU and your family, my wonderful grandchild, are the newest medical miracle in our family. Your mother and father wanted YOU so much that YOU are a very special person, an in vitro baby. (Had the same situation existed between your grandfather and me, when your mother, aunt and uncle were born, it would have been impossible that any children were born.)

It is now December 26, 1999. You have been growing inside your mother's womb for the past 7 ½ months. Your family and extended family are excited and looking forward to loving YOU and the joy that YOU alone can bring.

Dear grandchild, I have only one more thing to add. When you pick your life's vocation decide on something you enjoy doing. Learn as much as you can about your chosen vocation. You may have to take a related career but don't give up.

May you have many happy, healthy years in this wonderful world!

Love,
Grandma Florence Leet
St. Peter's Hospital
Hamilton, Ontario

P.S. - Kathryn and Loran, you decide when my grandchild is old enough for my letter.

WEDDINGS

David G. Dawson
Burlington, Ontario

To my grandchildren from Papa

  We had a wedding in our family in May 1998 when our daughter Jean married Steve. They had become engaged the previous year and had several months to make all the arrangements. As was normal, Jean along with her sister Sue, her friends and her mother planned, discussed, altered, and planned some more. Steve did not have much to do, other than attend a few parties and be there at the right time.

  In contrast, when Lorraine and I were married in 1955, most of the arrangements were in my hands. I had left Alberta in October 1954 for two years of work and study in a Rugby England factory (BTH), and there was no "understanding" between us. Lorraine remained in Edmonton to finish her nursing course, which would run until the end of September 1955.

  Our romance continued by lots of letters, mostly using the blue air mail forms, with an extra blue sheet inside to beat the post office on the postage rate. After a long winter I proposed by selecting a ring from the current Birks catalogue (sent by my family) and my folks bought the ring for me (in a blue box) and gave it to Lorraine. She didn't send it back, so we were engaged. To return to Canada for a wedding would require going by sea (to save money) and would take over two week's travelling time. So we decided to get married in Britain. As we both came from small towns, a wedding at home with extended families nearby would have had to be a very large affair. The date was set for Saturday, December 3, and then it was over to me.

  First step was to contact the minister, Reverend Dr. A. Murray-Smith of the Presbyterian Church where I had been attending. He agreed to perform the ceremony in his church. He also was Canadian, and had spent some time with Frontier College before settling in England after the war.

Then I went to the library to borrow many books on weddings, and to learn what needed to be done to do it right. One particular book became my guide, as it had simple guidelines to follow.

Some parts were easy. The Best Man was to be John Godfrey from Winnipeg (also at BTH), who was my roommate in the "digs" where I was living. Over the winter I met the Hughes family in Rugby, John, his sister Pat and their mother. John agreed to give the bride away and became "Papa John" for the occasion, with Pat and their mother acting as consultants. For the reception, I made a booking with Pattison's Tea Room, located in High Street next to Over's bookstore.

There were lots of other details, ordering engraved invitations, flowers, the photographer, the hired car for the wedding day (a black Daimler), and formal clothes for the men. For the only time in my life, I wore "Morning Dress" - striped gray trousers, black jacket with tails, gray vest, and spotted gray tie (all rented from Moss Bros. for the day). Lorraine had bought "the dress" and her mother made the wedding cake, which was shipped over, and we had it iced (marzipan) by the folks at the Tea Room.

One problem was finding a place to live, as rental space was then in short supply. I heard about a flat, which was coming vacant, from Pierre Gauvreau who was living there on the ground floor rear. It was available sooner than we needed but I took it early just to be sure of having it. There were three furnished flats at 9 Murray Road. We had a sitting room with coal fireplace, kitchen with gas stove (gas from coal at the local gas works), a bathroom with a hot water geyser, and then a bedroom one floor up, under the sloping roof, also with a coal fireplace. When I moved in, Mrs. Hughes helped me buy pots and pans, blankets and towels at the Rugby Co-op. (We still use one of the pots today.)

Francine, wife of Pierre (they were from Montreal and he worked in the factory too), agreed to be Matron of Honour, so I felt all the major things had been solved, and I only had to worry about a few (many) more details. The guest list was prepared, consisting of Canadians in Britain who were there on the fellowship program and people I had met in Rugby and London. One guest was Dave Birenbaum, a classmate of mine from Edmonton, who Lorraine knew. The honeymoon would be in London, staying at the Ruebens Hotel, near Buckingham Palace, and having lunch at the Boulogne (all of these on John Hughes' recommendation). Travel would be by train and we would splurge on First Class fares.

Lorraine would fly over, on a North Star from Calgary to Montreal, then Super Constellation from Montreal, to Shannon and London. She would stay for the week prior to December 3 with the Hughes. Robbie Rhodes would lend us his car Ruby (a pre-war Austin 7) for all the running around prior to wedding day.

It was too good to be true. The first complication was the church. The Presbyterian building had only been consecrated for three years, and any wedding held there would not be legal. So I was able to get the Congregational Church, which included 75-year-old Mr. Aust, who would hear the necessary legal words uttered during the ceremony. He would sign the official register, documenting that we were legally married. Because Lorraine would only have been seven days in the country a special (more expensive) wedding license was required.

Then Francine discovered that her priest was uncomfortable with her taking part in a non-Catholic ceremony, so she had to refuse. Jean Turnbull, the recent bride of one of my work friends Andrew (both from Scotland and now in Australia), agreed to be the bridal attendant, and we were OK again.

Lorraine's plane arrived on time, the wedding took place, the reception was a success, and my "friends" managed to scatter confetti outside our first class compartment on the train before it left Rugby.

We just passed our forty-third anniversary, so we did it right.

TO MY DEAR GRANDCHILDREN

Margaret Lewington
Orillia, Ontario

August 1999

To My Dear Grandchildren,

There are many things I could write about your Grandma's and Grandad's families, but I will start by telling you about your great-great-Grandparents (my Grandparents). My Grandmother and Grandfather were engaged in England and shortly thereafter learned that my Grandfather was being transferred to South Africa. My Grandmother made the difficult decision of going with him and leaving her family behind. Grandad was a buyer for a big company and often travelled to other countries, such as India. Grandma decided to meet him in South Africa, where they were married after her long trip by boat; they didn't have airplanes in those days. They had a large family of 10 children and loved living in such a beautiful country. They especially enjoyed the climate. My Grandmother always said it was a great country for raising such a large family.

Grandad was transferred back to England when the oldest children were in their teens, but the damp climate did not agree with him as he was asthmatic. They then decided to move to Canada – the land of opportunity – with all the family. Grandad came first with his eldest son to look for a place to live. They found a farm in Stayner, Ontario, where they thought they would enjoy farming. The rest of the family followed soon after by boat. They were all in for quite a shock when their first Canadian winter arrived.   They had not realized how much snow the Stayner and Collingwood areas would receive in the winter. This type of weather was extremely difficult for them after being used to the mild South African winters. They stayed a few years in Stayner and while there, my Mother, your Great-Grandmother, taught piano lessons.

After the rough winters in Stayner the family decided to sell and move. They bought a General Store in Brooklyn, Ontario where the younger family members finished their schooling. They attended St. Thomas' Anglican Church where my Mother played the church organ. My Mother was later married to my Father in Brooklyn, but they decided to settle in Toronto.

Your Great-Grandparents

As previously mentioned, your Great-Grandmother was born in South Africa and came to live in Canada with her family. Your Great-Grandfather's mother unfortunately died when he was just a boy of nine years. He lived with a married sister for several years. After working for a while he and a chum decided they wanted to travel and see the world. By the time they arrived in Toronto, they ran out of money so had to find work and settle for a short period of time. (Your Grandfather found work in a wholesale chinaware and gift office writing the descriptions for their sales catalogue, where he ended up staying for many years.) He found a boarding home and stayed with a lovely Christian family who treated him as another son. The family already had two boys of their own. He considered them his Canadian family, as they were so kind to him.

After this new family of his learned that he was from South Africa they told him they knew a South African family who lived close by. A meeting was set up with the family, but everyone knew that your Great-Grandmother's brothers had their eyes set on my Dad, and had every intention of introducing the couple to each other. It seemed that this meeting was meant to be since Mom and Dad were married after a short courtship. They were married on December 26, 1929 and the next year, on December 19, 1930, they welcomed triplets into the world – three babies born after only just a year of marriage. What a surprise for them! All three of us were incubator babies, and in those days there was no such thing as Social

Assistance or financial help with medical expenses. I recall Mom saying that they were being charged more per day for hospitalization and incubators than Dad was earning in a week. That was indeed a big setback for them in the early days of the Great Depression. However, they survived and were always loving and caring parents.

Dad joined the army while the three of us were very young. He was stationed in many places across Canada prior to being sent overseas. I recall going with Mom and my brothers to the Union Station to see Dad off and I remember how hard it was not knowing each time whether we'd see him again. They were anxious days.

As you know, my one brother was, and is, legally blind. He ended up having to attend the School for the Blind in Brantford. Making the decision to send her son away to school was one of the most difficult things my Mother said she ever had to do. Uncle Don learned how to be independent and later secured a job at the Canadian National Institute for the Blind in Toronto, where he stayed until he retired. We were all proud of him and were thankful that he became so independent and self-sufficient in spite of his handicap. He met his wife, Aunt Marianne, at the CNIB while they were both working there.

Remember as you go through life to think about the good things that happen and focus on these. For example, my Dad did go overseas and thankfully returned. While overseas the army would hold concerts to entertain the troops. The officers would ask my Dad to prepare a play or recite poetry. He was so very good at making people laugh and thinking of something witty or meaningful in a poetic way. He also wrote a play for the Belgian people, and that went over very well. He told us that the audience really applauded. Unfortunately I don't have copies of some of those special pieces he wrote. However, I do have a copy of my favourite poem and I will submit it to you now

The Soldier's Wife

R.Q.M.S. Thomas S. Thompson
Ghent Belgium, Dec. 20, 1944

Who faces war with courage,
Yet facing it has fear,
The fear of losing him,
That life holds so dear?

Who bears the burden bravely,
And cheers him on to fight,
With pleasant news of home,
That is not always right?

Who tells him of his children,
Keeps a smile upon his face,
When things are all against him,
And smiling is out of place?

Who trusts him without question,
Yet remains loyal beyond doubt
And casts aside temptations
From the wicked world without?

Who dreads to get a cable,
And opens it with fear,
And when the news is pleasant,
Softly wipes away a tear?

Who thinks of him in every
prayer,
And prays that God will spare,
The man now serving far from
home,
Whose burden she doth share?

Who is the bravest in this war?
Who suffers most in life?
Who loves and cares about him?
His best friend - his wife.

While overseas, Dad was presented with a special award. I recall it was an acorn, for meritous service overseas. We were all very proud of him. So the message is, even though those were difficult years for us all, that we also carry some fond memories I can now share with my grandchildren.

Dad should have been a writer or gone into Journalism. However, in those days he didn't have the opportunity. I know that you, my grandchildren, are excellent writers. I encourage you to pursue your goals and to take every opportunity to achieve them.
Lots of love to each of you, your Loving Grandma (and Grandpa sends his love too) . . .

GRANDMOTHERS

Ann Elson
Picton, Ontario

Both my parents came from large families, but when I was growing up as an only child, we did not live in geographic proximity to any of my aunts and uncles. Consequently, I heard very few of the family stories or myths, and all I have are disjointed snippets of information. This story is a gift to my four grandchildren to share what little I do know and to give them a sense of the people who went before them.

One Friday afternoon when I was about 8 we were waiting to be dismissed from school, and the teacher told us all to find out how old we would be in the year 2000. (This was very clever on her part because it involved addition and subtraction, but none of us seemed to realize this.) I came up with the answer 70, and I did not think I would ever survive to that incredible age. Now, of course, I don't think it is very old at all. At the same time, my grandfather was 88, and my grandmother was 81, but I don't think I knew that. Besides they were not old, they were ancient. Then I began to wonder if you think I am ancient – which would make your great-grandmother prehistoric – or if you think of our age at all. And I wondered how I learned to be a grandmother, since I only knew one of mine, and she was dead by the time I was eleven.

Helen, my paternal Grandmother, was born in 1858. She was short and square, like me, only she was quite stooped over so that the back of her skirt was always shorter than the front, and she wore her hair scraped back in a knob. In fact, most old ladies had "knobs." She, as did most of the women her age, wore black cotton stockings and black laced-up shoes called oxfords, which I thought looked dreadful though they would be an improvement on the orthopedic shoes I have to wear today. A few really old ladies who were not expected to do any more work wore a low-heeled kind of black slipper. My grandmother always wore a black dress, usually with a little white design. Her housedresses that she wore in the mornings to do her work were probably white, but I would guess that they had a black design on them and, of course, her sweater coats were black. What I remember most clearly was that the skin on her face was so very soft and was covered with lots of fine wrinkles. She knit me a pair of red mitts every Christmas and let me play with her quilt blocks when she was piecing them together, but she was not the kind of grandmother who read to me or told me stories, or played games with me. Every time we visited her, she always gave me a dime, but my grandfather gave me a quarter!

I was the eleventh of twelve grandchildren, and we lived over 60 miles away, so I did not know my grandparents very well. My father tried to visit them once a month in good weather to check on their health, and they did live with us the winters I was 8 and 9. They lived in the red brick tenant house on my uncle's farm – or my uncle and his family lived in the main house on my grandparents' farm - I don't know which. I do not think they had electricity in the house because they had no radio. When she visited us, my grandmother loved listening to the soap operas between three and four in the afternoon, and I had to keep quiet until they were finished. My grandparents did not have an indoor bathroom, and I really hated having to walk down the path to the outhouse where they had pages out of Eaton's catalogue instead of toilet paper. (It was not shiny coloured paper like they have now in catalogues.) The only water was from a pump at the kitchen sink. However, they did have a phone on a party line. I can remember my grandmother once saying that she and her good friends Mrs. Bouie and Mrs. Bell all got on the line together and just went ahead and planned the next Institute meeting.

My grandmother, Helen, did not have an easy life. She was born on a farm south of Barrie, Ontario. Her mother was very anxious that her children be educated. The best she could manage for Mary, the oldest girl, was painting lessons, and my grandmother, the second, had piano lessons, and the two of them rode horses to Barrie every week for instruction. The next two girls were primary school teachers, and the last two she managed to send to university. One was a medical doctor in China and the other was the first national secretary for the YWCA in Canada. (The older boy attended medical school; the other was a business man.)

My grandfather was Helen's first cousin. He was a barn farmer, and he left home in Sandford near Uxbridge and went north to Wasaga Beach where land was available to open farms. On the way he stopped to visit his uncle, met my grandmother and they were married. He went on ahead to build the house, and she, by then expecting her first child, joined him later. She took the train to Elmvale, but for some reason my grandfather did not meet her, so she set off to walk 7 miles in the rain with her long heavy skirts dragging in the mud. She came to a cousin's farm first, and they took her in and dried her out, and drove her the rest of the way.

Any history book about early Ontario will tell you how difficult farming life was in the old days. When Bill, my oldest paternal cousin, was visiting our grandparents as a small child, only their youngest son, who later took over the farm, was living with his parents. By then my grandmother had a couple of Jersey cows and chickens of her own, and every Saturday she drove to Elmvale to sell butter and cream and eggs, and Bill went with her. Bill told me she was a great talker and loved to visit her customers, so it was often dark when they returned to the farm. My grandfather would not see to it that her cows were brought it for milking, so she and Bill would set off into the bush, she with her ball of wool tucked under her arm and knitting all the way. She must have made some money with her cream route because when I was a child there was an old touring car sitting out behind my uncle's barn and my cousins told me that it had been Grandma's car. Bill also told me that she was "mighty light on her feet" but I don't know when he saw her dancing. I am quite sure my grandfather did not dance.

My grandfather was a very strict Presbyterian who did not believe that any work should be done on Sunday by people or animals, but he did hitch up my grandmother's horse so she could get to church on time to play the organ, and he walked. Bill told me that Grandma was always late so that she jumped in the buggy with her boots unlaced and gave the horse his head while she did them up.

During the First World War, Helen's only daughter was in France as a nursing sister. Two of her sons were overseas also, my father as a stretcher-bearer and his brother as infantryman. Harvey was killed when he was caught in a British artillery barrage.

My grandfather was struck and killed by a car when he was 90, and my grandmother lived a little over a year longer. She did not want to continue living without her Willy.

Maggie, my maternal grandmother, was born in 1867, the same year as Canada. She died before my parents were married, so I have only a picture of her. She too had her hair in a knob, but I think her hair must have been curly because she had waves around her face. In another picture she is dressed in a long dark dress, wearing an enormous hat covered with frou frou. She lived all her life in Hamilton. Her husband died in a train crash when she was only 36 years old, and left her with eight children, the youngest being born five months after his death. Those were the days of no pensions and no insurance, and I cannot imagine how she managed to hold the family together. She sold most of her jewellery (her father was the first jeweller to settle in Hamilton) and at various times had boarders and took in laundry. The four oldest children had to work. My mother left school at fourteen to help support the family and send her oldest brother to theological school. No sacrifice was too great for any Scotch Presbyterian family to make to have a son become a minister.

My mother, Nettie, was born in 1892. One of her greatest trials was being called "Nettie." She hated the name, but she was no fonder of her second name, "Agnes." She claimed the only other creature she ever heard called "Nettie" was a dirty old white horse.

My mother met my father when she was twenty years old. He was a fellow theological student with my uncle who took him to Hamilton to visit one weekend. My parents met about 1912 but they did not marry until 1925. First my father was in France during the war, and then he had to finish his medical education, and my mother, Nettie, had to look after my grandmother until she died in 1923, make a home for her two younger sisters and send her youngest brother to university. Fortunately, according to the Business and Professional Women's Club of the day, she was the highest paid woman in Hamilton at that time. Somehow she also managed to find time and money to train as a professional singer. In a different way, she had as hard a life as my two grandmothers.

My mother never wore black, though she did wear brown frequently, which I thought was just as bad, but she always wore high heeled shoes, and had her hair bobbed. She was quite sophisticated compared to the village women with whom she spent most of her life. I can't imagine what it was like for her to leave the high-powered and cultured life she had in Hamilton to live in a village of 600 where she was relegated to being "wife of." She acted as my father's secretary, receptionist and bookkeeper, looked after a large flower garden, preserved everything there was to preserve in the way of fruit and vegetables, sat on the library board and was secretary of the Women's Missionary Society of the United Church. The only time she ever began to use all her skills and energy was during World War II when she was president of the township Red Cross Society.

The war was agony for my mother. She had lost a younger brother during World War I and her oldest brother had been so badly wounded he had been sent back to Canada in 1917. This time her youngest and favourite brother was overseas (he was in Bari, Italy, when the harbour blew up) and for six months during the worst of the U-boat war on the Atlantic, my father served as a medical officer for troops being sent overseas – convoy duty. My mother never really recovered from the strains of the war, and two years later had breast cancer when the only tools to fight it were deep X-ray and radium. Though she lived for another fifteen years, she never believed she was free of the disease. By the time Margie was born, my mother was 64, and she lived for only five more years and died before Janet was born. She adored her grandchildren, and always elected to look after the youngest one in the summers when your grandfather and I spent a week in Stratford at the plays. The older one or two stayed with Granny.

Dorothy (Granny), my mother-in-law, was born in 1902. Her father was a paperhanger, and he was very much the head of the family, and what he said was law. Granny also had to leave school early so that her brothers could be supported. She was a telegraphist, and made very good money for a woman in the twenties. She took her pay packet home every week, as did her sisters, and they gave them to their father. He gave them back car fare and some spending money and kept the rest. He told the family that he was going to stop working when he was 60 and that they could support him. He did, and the sisters did. I am not sure if the brothers contributed to his upkeep, or if they had to turn over their pay packets when they lived at home. Granny never has had her hair cut, and still wears her braids wound around her head, just like she did when she began to work in 1916.

Until the day he died, Granny never knew what her husband's salary or pension was. He managed all the money and gave her an allowance to run the house. He was kind and generous, but it meant that, when he died, she did not know if she had enough money to live on, or how to manage her income. This was strange to me, since both my mother and I managed the family finances. Even my grandmother Helen had her own income and Maggie had certainly had to look after whatever money she had when she was widowed.

Granny did not begin to wear very bright clothes until she was in her 90's. Maybe it was to compensate for the fact that she had to stop swimming when she moved into the retirement home at 91, or maybe it was because she was going blind and I began to buy her clothes for her. She was ten years younger than my mother, and had the energy to play games with her grandchildren, and to teach Margie and Pat how to skip, and Donald how to braid hair, and to tell innumerable stories about when she was a little girl as well as exciting adventures from the Bible.

I was born in 1929, after women were finally recognized as persons in their own right. Before that women were somebody's wife, mother, sister, daughter or grandmother. And what kind of a grandmother am I?

I certainly do not wear my hair in a knob, nor do any of my friends. I wear all of the colours of the rainbow, even if I do have to wear orthopedic shoes. I swim and work out at the health club every week, and have had a variety of fascinating volunteer jobs and drive a car, which neither Nettie nor Dorothy were able to do. My life has been easier and healthier than that of the earlier grandmothers too. I always had enough to eat as a child, and did not have to drop out of school to go to work but continued on through university. I married at a time when I had a choice about whether to work for money or stay home, and I honestly did enjoy - most of the time - looking after your Moms and Don and Janet. Like my mother and my grandmother Helen, I too love to dance, but like them, I was fated to marry a man who couldn't keep time to music.

I have been fortunate to be able to travel. My mother used to travel between Hamilton and Chicago on business, and she took my grandmother to England to visit her son's grave - he died at the age of 17 while serving in the Royal Flying Corps in World War I. My grandmother Helen was lucky to have been able to go to Toronto occasionally. My mother yearned to travel, and, in the years before she died, sailed up the Saguenay and went to Vancouver a couple of times. Granny realized her dream of returning to England, and also included a bus trip through Europe. She went west, and took bus trips to Florida and Texas and the Maritimes. But me - I have been across Canada, lived in Tanzania for three years and visited Kenya and Uganda and Ethiopia. I have been to China and Russia and Cuba (which has been enough to label me as a communist in my part of rural Ontario), New Zealand and a dozen European countries, Jamaica and Guadeloupe and Barbados, Iceland and Greenland. There are still places I want to see.

I have read you stories, played games with you, gone swimming with you, taken you shopping, and even helped you with your homework! I love visiting with you, or having you come to Picton. I am so fortunate to have the four of you, and to live close enough that I can see you several times a year. Grandmothers have all the fun of grandchildren with little of the work or responsibility.

What kind of grandmothers do you think your mothers will be – or you yourselves? Helen was born 142 years ago into a very different kind of world. Nettie and Dorothy lived through two world wars, and I grew up during one of the worst economic depressions the world has ever known. Helen and Maggie lived in two different centuries, as I hope to do, and maybe one day when they were little girls, someone asked them to find out how old they would be in 1900.

A LETTER TO ALLAN AND MICHAEL

David Brown
Dundas, Ontario

Dear Allan and Michael,

You may remember that last year I wrote to you about how I learned to ride a bicycle in England after our school had been evacuated at the beginning of the Second World War. In this letter I would like to tell you what happened to me after that.

Because everyone was afraid we might be bombed, people built air raid shelters and we had to carry gas masks with us, but in the beginning there were no air raids. Eventually France was captured which made it much easier for the enemy to fly their bombers over England and my parents (Parky and Gran) decided.that it would be better if your Auntie Jan and I were sent to somewhere safe.

One weekend when they came to visit us at school, they asked what we thought of going to Canada. I was seven at the time and, although I didn't know very much about Canada, it sounded exciting. Auntie Jan, who was only five at the time, was ready to go anywhere I went.

I remember going for a medical check-up and then the day came at the end of July 1940 when we were ready to leave. Parky and Gran took us to Liverpool where we spent a night in a hotel, but in the middle of the night the air raid sirens went and we all had to go to the air raid shelter. I don't remember if any planes came over, but if there was any bombing it was not near us.

The following day we went on board the ocean liner Duchess of Richmond. In those days airplanes couldn't fly across the Atlantic, so the only way to go was by ship. The big transatlantic liners were like cruise ships. I shared a cabin with other people but the dining room was like a large restaurant with lots of different kinds of food to choose from. The first day out to sea, Auntie Jan and I felt a little sea-sick, but a sailor took us for a walk out on deck and that made us feel better.

There were lots of enemy submarines in the Atlantic trying to sink the British ships, but the sailor explained that because our ship was so fast, they hoped to be able to out-race any submarines. They did, however, have a gun on the back deck in case of attack and the lifeboats were always kept in the ready. It was just as well. Although we got through safely, the next ship carrying children to Canada was torpedoed. Fortunately most of the people on board were saved, but after that they didn't dare send any more children to Canada.

I don't remember a lot about the journey except that as we got close to Canada we began to see icebergs and whales which was very exciting. Later, steaming down the St. Lawrence River we got quite close to a small but very beautiful blue iceberg.

We stopped in Quebec City for a couple of hours while they took off the mail. Since there were no airplanes that could fly across the Atlantic and there was no telephone cable, the only way people could keep in touch was by sending letters by regular mail. That was why they made the ships so fast, so they could get messages across the ocean as quickly as possible.

Eventually we arrived in Montreal. We all waited in the lounge of the ship until our name was called and we were introduced to our new foster parents. Auntie Jan and I were met by Mr. Luke and for the next four and a half years I lived with him and his family. Instead of being the oldest child in a family of two, I was now the youngest in a family of four and was always beaten up by my bigger foster brother, Morley (who now lives near Ottawa). Auntie Jan lived with another family several miles away so we didn't see much of each other until the end of the war when we were once again able to go home.

My love to you both,

Grandpa Brown

TO MY DEAR DAUGHTER – LYN

Terri Campbell
Ancaster, Ontario

Think of your love for Amy and Neil
That's how I love you
Think how their pain would make you feel
I feel that way for you.

I gave you life and watched you grow
How was I supposed to know
Your life would be ruled by pain
If we could only begin again.

I would give my life to bear your pain
And give your life back again
To see your smile each day
Before the pain came to stay.

If God is good and hears my prayer
And lets us have more years to share
Then I would go happy to my rest
Knowing your life is truly blessed.

With all my heart and love,

Mum

February, 1998

ASHLEY

Terri Campbell
Ancaster, Ontario

You were grandchild number three,
a lovely baby for Stuart and Cheree.
I knew when I held you in my arms
that I'd be slave to your charms.

You wormed your way into my heart
right from the very start.
I wish you health, happiness and joy.
Don't use it as a toy.

May life be everything you wish,
served up as your favourite dish.
May you take it as you need.
Use it wisely it will keep.

Only good things will life bestow
and through life you'll bravely go.
Health and success be your friends,
my prayer for you to the very end.

To Ashley with fondest love always.

Gramma, 1974

THE PEEPING TREE

Ruth E. Putt
Hamilton, Ontario
(Submitted by Helen Coomber)

The old willow tree had a secret. It grew in the wilderness on the southeast side of the island. This magic tree looked like all the other willow trees – gray rough bark, bare twisty branches with tiny green buds breaking out of their winter coats.

Out walking on a cold winter day, Sammy and Grandma saw a hole in the willow tree. It went way down inside the tree where a branch had broken off a long time ago.

"Peep peep," said the tree. Yes it could talk! Grandma put her ear to the hole and listened. Then she said, "Peep peep yourself." And of course the tree answered, "Peep peep."

Sammy knew trees could talk. Grandma said, "Let's go and sit on a log, Sammy, and watch to see who makes the tree peep." They sat very still and quiet and soon a red-winged black bird came and sat on a branch. She had a piece of bread in her beak and do you know what? She flew into the hole with the bread and when she came out the bread was gone!

"Land of Goshen," said Grandma, "I've seen some strange things and funny trees but this tree is the strangest tree I ever did see. It not only peeps but it eats bread too!"

Can you explain this mystery?

SAMMY AND GRANDMA

REACHING BEYOND THE 20th CENTURY

Kathleen Kemp Hayes
Dorchester, Ontario

Dear Katie, my only granddaughter,
named for me, close to my heart.
I remember well your first few days
in my arms, since your mom was sick,
you came home to my dresser drawer
because I had no crib for you.

I would like you to know more about me
but time has always been so short.
Second of four in the Kemp household,
my English Father, a Canadian soldier
during the war when I was born,
a war I know only second-hand.
I was a troubled teenage girl,
lived on a farm, quit school at seventeen,
was a Girl Guide, went to World Camp,
worked for three years as a filing clerk.

Married Harry, the love of my life,
Had three children, your Mom the first.
Life has not always been very easy,
a teacher's salary has not always been vast,
earned a B.A. in part-time study,
have four grandchildren I'm proud to say.

I believe that life should be fair;
that every race, colour and creed
should have the same opportunities,
that women should have equal rights,

that war should never replace the need
for negotiations with peaceful ends.
I fervently pray your generation
will carry the torch of human rights
and stop the mindless growth of hate
that's been such a part of this millennium.

My Mother's family pioneered this land,
and I hope that you will pioneer too,
in believing in everyone's cultural worth,
in respecting all the people of the earth.

You have blossomed ever since the month
you slept in a drawer beside my bed.
I hope the 21st will fulfill your dreams
and that I will have more time with you.
I hope you all remember me
as someone who tried to live a sane life
and loved you all unconditionally.

MY YELLOW-HAIRED GIRL

Marie Sedor
Dauphin, Manitoba

You were only three
when, so precocious, you explained spittle-bugs to me
in serious demeanour, leading me to tall firewood to show this marvel.
That soft little hand and whispery voice tugged at my heart.

You examined the pink peonies for ants and knew they were there
for the sweetness and not the beauty.
In your frilly dress you hoisted the plastic watering can half your size
and watered every plant in sight so nothing would feel left out.
And always that silky yellow ponytail.

By four, you had drawn me enough pictures of flowers, ladybugs and
monsters to fill a desk drawer.
Discarded envelopes, cereal boxes and cardboard were your canvasses;
crayons, yarn, glue and charcoal from the campfire your creative tools.

At five you began to read.
You wrote letters and stories and sang and mimed.
In Kindergarten, you were helpful and brave.
You said you liked dentists and went willingly.
With a frown you declared your hate for witches.

Your room's nooks were filled with books, papers,
clay creations, dried bouquets,
and an old purse crammed full
of chocolate-covered marshmallow bars which
Gramma often gave you and which you didn't care for

but took politely to spare her feelings.
And always the yellow bangs that would not hang straight
because of a cow-lick.
Your family moved away.
Though I saw you once each year, I sorely missed your growing-up
until you were
A young lady of twenty-one and came to visit on your own.
And still that yellow hair.

A WOMAN OF THE WEST

Mary Behrens
Gold Coast, Australia
(*Submitted by Marjorie G. Smith*)

This is a true story for my Behrens-Peterson grandchildren and their mates.

My girlfriend Margaret, married Geoff, one of the "Rats of the Tobruk," an Australian serviceman who was fighting overseas for many years during World War II. Though they managed a huge grazing property "Out West," Margaret, a trained nurse, was called to every crisis in the district. This part of Australia is so hot that even Margaret's lipstick had to be kept in the cooler.

When the matron from the town's only hospital was desperate for a break, Margaret took over. She dropped everything when the Flying Doctor needed her to board the aeroplane to nurse a patient and to fly enroute to the large hospital in the city of Brisbane.

On this occasion, a local woman had given birth to a premature baby who was very ill. Humicribs at this time were very primitive. Margaret and the babe were loaded on to the local ambulance where she tried desperately to keep the humicrib cool by draping wet nappies over it. Geoff dragged all the ice from their own ice-chest to use on the way, and off they went heading down the hot dusty road, to the nearest hospital many miles away.

You may not know that in the outback of Australia, everyone at the time hung a canvas water bag from the back of their vehicles (trucks, Sulkies, saddle bags, etc.) Margaret was known to all the locals, so she stopped every vehicle coming towards her ambulance, grabbed their cold water bags - (the Esky was not invented then -) and tipped the contents over the crib nappies which were cooling the poor sick baby. The ambulance called into every homestead enroute and Margaret ran to their Coolgardie Safe or primitive icebox, and used all their ice to continue the cooling process. This went on in the searing heat, until Margaret and babe reached the hospital. Here - God be praised - the baby's life was saved.

Margaret's name is now engraved on a plaque in the Hall of Fame in Longreach, Queensland. This wonderful woman, now aged, was herself lying ill in a city hospital many years later. Can you imagine her joy, and the wonderful feeling her husband and family felt, when who should walk into Margaret's hospital room ready for nursing duty but that same premature baby she had saved many years before? A baby who had grown into a healthy adult and was now a trained nurse ready and willing to serve others.

JUSTINE

Margaret Westhouse
Hamilton, Ontario

As I watch my two-year-old granddaughter move about I ask myself was I ever that energetic? She seems to have unlimited supplies of "Get-up-and-go." Mine has got up and done!

She loves to climb. On, off, over, under, through, around. Often her father is her climbing post. At 6'4" there's ample to climb. She never remains at something for very long. A sign of her age, I suppose. She must explore everything at once. Here, there, this, that, so much to investigate. I must admit I admire her curiosity and need to explore. There are times that she retreats to the safety of Mommy and Daddy but only temporarily, and then she's off again.

I hope she retains her sense of wonder as she grows.

MOTHER AIME

Mary Florence Huang
Hamilton, Ontario

She was my best friend when I was in India, but unfortunately, she passed away before I went back for a visit.

Mother Aime was born on January 17, 1894. She came from Roppenzwiller, Alsace, France. She had served our Lord for 74 years. She was a Religious Sister in India. She practiced as a general practitioner when she was a young lady. But, when she became a nun she changed her profession. She became a doctor of homoeopathic medicine. Homeopathic doctors don't touch patients.

When I came to know her, through my brother, she was a teaching nun in the convent of Our Lady Queen of the Missions, which also has a dispensary. The sick and poor people were not charged for medicine. For the rich people, she gave prescription so that they had to buy their own medicine. If you were very ill, she would treat you then and there with the first dose of homeopathic medicine. One day when I was pregnant with my fourth daughter Helena, I almost had a miscarriage! She came to me in my house with my fifth brother, Henry, and told me to have complete rest, otherwise Helena would not be in this world today.

After two and a half years, my oldest son Alexander was born. He was very close to his father, my husband Samson. One day my husband went to Bombay to see his friend. Alexander missed his father. He stopped taking his food. When he was too hungry he drank one or two mouthfuls of milk but threw up immediately, even a sip of water. Finally when there was no food to digest, he started to pass bile. Then my second brother, John, took us to see a baby specialist because the vomiting and diarrhea did not stop. He was very weak. Later the same day, my brother John rushed us to see Mother Aime. Mother Aime came down with Mother Superior because it was close to their bedtime. Seeing Alex seriously ill, Mother Superior allowed Mother Aime to stay up. Mother Aime watched Alex's movements. She found Alex at the time asking for water. But when he drank a sip of water he brought it up immediately. Nothing could be retained in his stomach. Mother Aime went to the kitchen and brought out "a tiny" glass of Brandy with a teaspoon of sugar mixed in it and handed to me. She told me that if Alex asked for water to give him the brandy instead. Sure enough when he asked for parny (water in Hindi) I gave him the glass of brandy. Because his mouth was so dry he took a big sip of the brandy then pushed away the glass. Mother Aime found that the sip of brandy did not come up so she said, "Yes, there is still a chance for him to live. Here are some globules for him. You must start now. Two globules now then after five minutes two more. After ten minutes two more after fifteen minutes two more and so on till you finish the rest of the globules." Thank God Alex did not bring up anymore. The next morning my husband received the telegram from my fourth brother, Alfred. He came back immediately. When Alex saw him, he leaped up from my arms to him. Since then he took his food nicely and didn't need any more medicine. He was well again.

FROM ME TO TRAVIS

Betty Stubbs
Burlington, Ontario

This September was a big step for you when you started Junior Kindergarten at a school close to your new house, where you will be moving in October. You must be excited with all the new experiences you will have at your school and the new friends you have met in your class. Mom has been driving you to school until you move, but afterwards maybe Mom and your sister Michaela can walk with you to and from school.

Did you know you will have lived in three different houses before you are five years old? Can you remember your house in Bradford? You arrived at the New Market Hospital on January 16, 1995. I remember driving to Bradford shortly afterward with Grandpa to see our new grandson. We were able to drive to Bradford many times to visit your Mom and Dad and you. In April 1996, we came along with Nana and Poppa to look after you while your Mom and Dad were on a trip to Australia and New Zealand. Your parents called often by telephone to check how you were doing without them, and you and your grandparents were getting along just fine together.

In 1996, you moved to Pickering. Grandpa and I decided that the traffic was too heavy to drive from Burlington through Toronto to Pickering so we travelled by Go Train. We could see the heavy traffic from our train windows as we travelled along the track. You liked coming to the Pickering Go Station with your Dad to pick us up and take us back to catch the train.

Your house is quite close to a park where you loved going to play on the slides and swings or just chase Mom around the evergreen trees. You know all the streets near your house and could direct me back to your house when we were together.

On April 2, 1997, your baby sister arrived and life at your house was a little different. You couldn't have all the attention from your parents because Michaela needed their attention too. However, your Dad and Mom have seen that you learned to swim well, are a good ice skater, can ride a two wheel bicycle and your Mom has taken you to many library activities, gym activities and many other things.

Now you will soon be moving to a brand new house. You will be exploring your street and those nearby. Maybe there will be a park close by or maybe someone in your school class lives close to your new house. Grandpa and Grandma will be anxious to see your new house when we come to visit all of you.

All my love and kisses,

Grandma

IF LIPS WOULD JUST BE KIND*

Bernice Price
Hamilton, Ontario

If lips would just be kinder,
How much better it would be.
If folks would just be blinder
To faults they try to see.
If ears just wouldn't listen
If lips just wouldn't tell,
How this old world would glisten
With love and joy as well.
If lips would keep from speaking,
When what they hear is ill —
And not go seeking, seeking
Some darker story still.

If lips would just remember
Some gentle word to say,
The sighings of November
Would seem the songs of May.
For day will lose its glory
And have its darker hours
When someone tells a story
That poisons all the flowers.
But life would bloom with
splendour,
And joy we all would find
If hearts would just be tender
And lips would just be kind.

*   *Penguin*:   Published monthly by the Halifax Flying Squadron, The Dartmouth Flying Squadron and the N.S. Women's Service Corps. Halifax, N.S., April, 1942. Vol. 2, No. 11.

A CHILD'S HOLIDAY

Maureen Carroll
Burlington, Ontario

Living in a small village where social events consisted of Jumble sales, a flower show and/or dancing round the maypole, the prospect of the traditional annual week's holiday at the seaside was always exciting for me.

The holiday, which left me with particularly vivid memories was the year we stayed one block from the beach, at a Bed and Breakfast in the small town of Weymouth on the south coast of England.

Weymouth developed as a town mainly due to George III, who made it popular by taking his large family there each year. It is still old fashioned now, in spite of new homes being built on the outskirts. The beaches of white sand stretch for miles, with the tidal water being shallow and therefore safe for children.

We travelled there by train and settled into our homes for the week. After a meal, and a walk around the relatively quiet narrow streets looking at shops, it was early to bed for me.

The following day Weymouth was no longer the sleepy little town we had seen the previous day. The soldiers had arrived from Dunkirk. It was May 1940.

The front doors of the houses along our street, opened directly on to the pavement, and when I went outside I immediately had to step over rows of legs. The men were sitting with their backs to the front walls of the houses with feet pointing towards the street. They had been ordered to sit this way, in lines, to make full use of the space available for more incoming troops. The air was full of noise, mainly voices shouting orders, vehicles and army boots on the cobbles.

The landlady of the B & B, together with the holidaymakers staying there, brewed tea and made sandwiches of any supplies she had on her shelves in the kitchen.

B & B owners were allowed extra rations to feed their guests, so the larder was in fairly good shape. I was roped in to carrying trays and plates outside, and told to work my way along one section of the pavement, while my Mother and Father started at the other end.

Every house on the street contributed something, and as a "guesstimate" I think we must have had approximately three hundred soldiers along our street.

When the food ran out, my Father and I were sent to buy something of use we could find in the shops nearby. He suggested to me before we left that maybe I would like to use my sweet coupons for the month, to buy something for the men.

Full of national pride I agreed and bought the number of small chocolate bars I was allowed. I was 10 years old at the time and even at this much later date, I can remember (being a chocoholic) how hard it was to hand them over. I also gave out toothbrushes, toothpaste, biscuits, soap, cigarettes, postcards and stamps, and the few other treasures we had managed to round up.

After the cards were written to loved ones, telling family they were safe in Weymouth, we mailed them, as the soldiers were not allowed to leave the street.

By later in the day the volunteer groups were organized and food became more plentiful, together with blankets and gallons of hot strong tea.

My Mother, who had been a nurse in the First World War, went to the church hall at the end of the street, where a triage station had been set up for the wounded. They accepted her offer of help and I didn't see much of her for the next two days.

My Father and I then walked to the docks to watch the boats of all shapes and sizes, arriving with more troops. They were wet and had nothing except their helmets and often their guns.

They were led to the beach in groups and sat down on the sand while the officers went amongst them, trying to find members of their own unit. The French were sent farther down the beach with their own officers.

As the day wore on, more and more military vehicles appeared in the area and the wounded were taken away by ambulance as others arrived by boat. These boats sailed again as soon as they were unloaded and refueled.

My aim that holiday had been to learn to swim, which I did, and added to that was a small increase in my knowledge of geography, as I now knew where to find Dunkirk on a map.

350,000 soldiers were taken off the beaches of Dunkirk that week, and landed at all the ports along the south coast. How many came into Weymouth, I do not know, but the streets were packed for three days.

I do know that whenever I have been in Weymouth since that holiday, I can still see young men in uniform coming ashore and sitting along the pavements.

I hope the few who ate my chocolate ration enjoyed it.

THE CHESTNUT TREE

Florence Brown
Burlington, Ontario

A stately gray two-story house is partly hidden by a huge chestnut tree. A rope swing with a wooden seat hangs from the tree - actually one swing on each side - for my sister and myself. The swings, it seems, were always there, yet I remember my grandfather Zwicker, (Puppie) putting them up. Sometimes our grandparents (Nannie and Puppie to us) came out and sat in the shade with us and visited.

Many a hot summer afternoon was spent swinging or just sitting on the swing. From our swing we could see our house down the hill and could try to imagine what Mom was doing. We could also take in the view of the South Mountain. We saw mostly trees but also in the clearings the homes and farms of other people in the area. Every once in a while we could see a horse and wagon passing on the road and in July we might see a hay wagon go by. Of course we knew every horse and wagon we saw.

From the swing we could also observe the comings and goings of our few neighbours. If we saw a mother and children with pails we knew they were going for berries. If they appeared to be dressed up we knew they were going to town (a one-or two-mile walk) and if the kids were by themselves they were probably going to the brook for a dip. We were never allowed to go.

If we tired of swinging and watching the world go by, we could pick up the chestnuts - green or ripe depending on the season - and see who could find the most and then make up a game. Interestingly enough, I do not remember us ever throwing them at each other or at the tree.

Time has passed and our grandparents have died. The house had been vacant for a long time; it became an unsafe structure so my cousin had it demolished. The cellar was filled in and the site was landscaped - but the tree is still there. It seems naked and lonely without the house and the swings, but the view of the South Mountain is still there. When I visit, I can still reminisce about the days of our childhood.

REMINISCENCES OF A GRANDMOTHER

Wynita Ray
Burlington, Ontario

To be added to, "A BOOK OF MEMORIES FOR MY GRANDCHILDREN"
(Excerpts will be given to my grandchildren on their birthdays.)

July 25, 1999

Ding, ding . . . dong
Someone's at the door!
Guess who?

Yes, it's one half of my family. Son, Scott, and his children have arrived from Etobicoke. Cindy wanted to get caught up with some household chores when she was alone so decided to stay at home.

I decided to hide in the kitchen and I could hear the calls, "Hi, Gramma. Where are you?" It was then that I poked my head out and replied, "I'm here!" As soon as shoes were off, it was kisses all around, then the squeezy hugs. I'm always so happy to see family members. It's so lonesome without Gramps and it's wonderful when we get together.

It was lunchtime and the table was already set. What do you know? Dad had brought potato salad . . . a generous treat from Mom. He had picked up other goodies at the store. Austin (two), you just nibbled on your peanut butter sandwiches. I guess you had a late breakfast! Lauren (nine), and Jessica (seven), you ate veggies and sandwiches and seemed to enjoy the weak tea I made. Of course I knew it tasted so much better served in my mini teacups. You know the "Little Boy Blue" one was part of a set I was given when I was very young. Dad and I did justice to the chicken, bean and potato salads. Dessert was fresh fruit and jello. Remember, I reminded you how thankful we should be to have this delicious food. Not all children are so fortunate here in Canada and around the world.

Austin, you soon found your favourite toys in the den. You started playing with the yellow Matchbox dump truck that had belonged to your Dad and Uncle Steve, many moons ago.

Lauren and Jessica, you cuddled up together in my Lazyboy chair and became engrossed in a nature program on TV.

It wasn't long before I sat down in the armchair by the window. I had picked up books that would put an added sparkle in your Dad's eyes. The first one was *A Fly Went By*, by Mike McClintock. As shown on the flyleaf, Gramps and I had given it to Scott at Easter 1961. Imagine it's thirty-eight years old!! Soon Austin snuggled up to me and listened attentively as I re-read the story for the umpteenth time. Your Dad was reminiscing too, as he quietly slipped from the room and reappeared with my camera. It was a precious moment that was recorded. How delightful to bring back the memories of those bygone years! I felt like forty all over again.

Jessica, you wanted to join the read-along so I produced the second book, another Mike McClintock classic, *Stop That Ball*, a gift to Scott at Christmas 1960. You curled up on the chesterfield and Dad joined you with Austin nestled in between. You and Dad took turns reading. This time I picked up the camera and did the honours. My heart skipped a beat as I watched from the armchair and a tear moistened my eyes.

Lauren, you were somewhat tired from being out late at a friend's house the night before, so you listened from afar. I snapped you enjoying the coolness of my condo. It seems you folks had lost your air-conditioning temporarily last week and you were relaxing.

Soon it was time for hugs and kisses again as we said our, "So long until the next time," farewells.

I sat back after you had gone and thought how fortunate I was to have such a loving, caring family. A smile came across my face as I reminisced over the day's events.

Thank you for giving precious moments of sunshine to an aging grandmother.

OCEAN VOYAGE

Ethel Hayward
Montreal, Quebec

For my grandsons Colin and Gwilym

As you know from our trip last year, I love water, as in rivers, lakes and oceans. When I was a child, younger than you are Colin, my mother took my sister Hazel and me to England on a passenger liner. My aunt Harriett went with us.

The ship was the "Duchess of Bedford" – not as big as the "Titanic" but the same kind of vessel. In those days air travel across the ocean was rare, so we had to go by sea. It took us a week to go from Montreal to Liverpool.

In those days when a passenger ship sailed from a port, friends would go to say goodbye. They were allowed on the ship for a short time, then a gong would be sounded and the call "All ashore that's going ashore" would be heard. The visitors would gather on the dock and the passengers would be at the rail. Paper streamers would be thrown between them, then as the ship moved out the streamers would break.

We sailed down the St. Lawrence past the places we drove through last year, Quebec City, St. Jean-Port Joli where we picnicked, Riviere du Loup and Rimouski. Then we followed the North Shore past Anticosti Island and on through the Strait of Belle Isle. That is what separates Newfoundland from Labrador, the water at l'Anse aux Meadows.

We had a cabin with four bunks – two up and two down, a sink with hot water and cold water, a clothes closet and room under the bunks for luggage. There was a round porthole for a window, but we couldn't see much as it was high up. The bathroom was just down the hall.

Although it was summer, it was cold. I have a picture of my aunt on deck in a coat with a big fur collar. Inside the ship there was a children's play area with swings, a slide, and best of all, a big rocking horse. They also held a children's party with paper hats, balloons, games, cake and ice cream. My mother played the piano and several boys and girls sang, danced or recited poetry.

There was also a room with writing tables, and chess and checkers set up. A very nice gentleman taught me to play chess, but I was quite insulted when he asked if I was "American." "No, I'm a Canadian."

The dining room was like a beautiful restaurant, and you could order anything from the menu. Of course, being me, I had to fall down the stairs to the dining room one day. No damage!

We came back home on another ship. The "Montcalm" was not quite as big or elaborate as the "Duchess", but very nice.

It was late summer, and like this year, the river water was very low. From Quebec City we prepared to leave the ship in Montreal – our bags were packed and in the hallway, the beds were stripped, and we were out on deck. The ship moved so slowly there was hardly a ripple. Word went around that there were only six inches of water between the keel and the river bottom. It grew dark and we could see the lights of Montreal. We were concerned whether we would reach the harbour and be able to dock in the dark. As we passed Auntie Harriett's street in the east end, she said if she could get off the ship she could be home in two minutes.

Eventually we did dock at about ten o'clock, to our great relief, because we had no idea what we would do if we had to wait until morning – no beds, no food. My father, your great-grandfather, was there to meet us and take us safely home.

HAPPY BIRTHDAY

Marion Nelles
Brantford, Ontario

It was three o'clock in the morning
When I woke because I was snoring
I tossed and turned at length
Then remembered this is the eighth
The eighth of December
And a milestone day
Cause you are "legal" in every way
Since I don't want to lead you
To the brink
Of drink
On this auspicious day
But must celebrate it in some way
I'll make a cup
And take a sup
While I sing Happy Birthday.
So close your eyes and open your ears
Laugh until you are in tears
If you like – just don't curse
While you imagine me singing THE verse
Happy Birthday to you
Happy Birthday to you
Happy brrrrr-thday Dear Sarah
Happy Birthday to you!!!!!

xxxxxxxxxxxxxxxxxxx

And one to grow on . . . X
Think I got nineteen kisses in there.

With love from Nanna Marion

LETTERS TO MY GRANDSONS, MYLES AND BENJAMIN

Helen Tyrrell
Hamilton, Ontario

Dear Myles:

After 48 hours of suspense – you finally decided to be delivered.

Well no wonder there was a delay, for you weighed 7lbs, 14oz!

You were a hefty baby boy. You were beautiful, rosy with plump cheeks and you studied us as much as to say – so you are family – la-de-da!

It was amazing to see you staring at us with such a wise look about you. You were so pink and beautiful, we could not stop staring at you.

Everyone was so thankful you finally were born and such a picture of health, even if your Mom had a pain or two.

We have watched you grow and mature and become so intelligent. I sometimes feel, because of your knowledge, that I know so little.

It is amazing how wise and knowledgeable you are and you continue to develop and become more interesting every day. You have been a pillar of strength to me as well as an inspiration.

You play the piano beautifully and also play hockey with almost a professional flare and we absorb the excitement of your hockey games as well as the joy of witnessing a goal or two.

You are a conscientious, eager, sentimental and kind grandson, very loving and just a beautiful person.

God bless you and Benjamin that you may continue to grow in strength, wisdom and love and be successful in all projects and endeavours as you progress and mature in your daily lives.

You are both the greatest blessing that can be bestowed on a grandparent. Too bad Grandpa did not live longer to see you grow up.

May you always shine and succeed in whatever you undertake. Also respect your teachers as they contribute so much to the moulding of your character, outlook, knowledge and progress of your life, as well as the care of two beautiful parents, Catherine and Gary.

Love and Blessings,

Gramma Tyrrell

Dear Benjamin:

We awaited your arrival with great happiness, anticipation and love, just looking forward to cuddling and holding you. Great! You arrived in such a hurry and in fine fettle, a dear little redhead, but sleepy so we had to wait to see your eye colour – a day later.

You will never know how happy we were to have you born safe and sound.

The whole family was elated over your arrival and your Mom and Dad called you Benjamin David – two beautiful names that suited you perfectly.

You were a hungry little fellow but you nursed well and slept a lot and still had your active moments and watched us all when we stood and admired you. You looked us over as though you wondered what we were all about. The years have passed by so quickly and we have treasured every day – enjoying your progress and growing up to now – age 7.

You are a bright, happy, witty, quick-as-a-wink boy with personality galore and energy that puts us all to shame.

You blossomed in kindergarten and had such a beautiful teacher – Mrs. Mendellson – a gem of a teacher for sure. She was so full of love and admiration for the children of her class – she truly loved each child and through her you gained great love and knowledge and enjoyed every moment in her presence. You were well prepared for school and your future. We could never express how wonderful Mrs. Mendellson is. So sorry – we did not have many like her.

As each grade comes and goes, we eagerly pore over your work with great pride and admiration, amazed at how well you are doing.

Benjamin David, you are the apple of our eye and we look forward to each day as you progress academically and grow in strength and stature.

You are a very busy grandson, with piano lessons, playing, and your hockey team keeping you very busy. Again, these extra chores are of great interest and strengthen you and add so much to building confidence.

Keep in mind you have beautiful parents, Catherine and Gary, who have your success at heart.

Love and Blessings,

Gramma Tyrrell

THE GIRL WITH SIX GRANDPARENTS
A "MODERN FAMILY" TALE

Pat Dickinson
Millgrove, Ontario

This is a modern day tale. There are no "Once upon a times" or good fairies, or bad monsters. The "happily ever after" remains to be seen since this is a "here and now" tale. And the only magic is the magic that occurs in every day life.

The little girl in the story is called Jennifer. Jenni for short. Jennifer was born, appropriately, close to Valentine's Day, a much loved and much wanted child. She is a child of many firsts:

FIRST CHILD to her proud MOM AND DAD;

FIRST GRANDCHILD to SIX GRANDPARENTS;

FIRST GREAT-GRANDCHILD for FOUR GREAT-GRANDPARENTS (and much loved by her fifth great-grandparent);

FIRST GREAT-GREAT-GRANDCHILD to ONE GREAT-GREAT-GRANDPARENT.

The "six grandparents" part is what makes this a "modern family" tale. Two of Jenni's grandparents had divorced and remarried. All six grandparents live close to Jenni. "How will she tell us apart?" they wondered.

"Will you have Jenni call us names like Grandma and Grandpa D?" they asked Jenni's parents. "We'll let Jenni work it out," her parents said with a wise smile.

Jenni became the centre of her Mom's and Dad's world, and they became the centre of hers, in no time at all. The six grandparents all waited patiently and watched Jenni and her Mom and Dad form these important bonds, during the cozy months after she was born.

Then summer came and Jenni and her mom and dad began regular visits to the homes of the six grandparents. All the grandparents planned carefully for Jenni's visits.

At one grandparents' house she always got to jump on the neighbour's trampoline, or "bouncy bouncy" as Jenni called it.

At another grandparents' house she was always greeted with a happy somersault and a "whoop de dooh."

At another grandparents' house, there was a slide in the backyard. Each time she went down the slide the grandparents said "whee."

One day, Jenni's mother was driving to her parent's home. She told Jenni they were going to Grandma's house. Jenni asked "Grandma Whee?" or "Grandma Bouncy Bouncy?"

From then on these two sets of grandparents had a name. Soon after Jenni extended the names to include Grandma and Grampa "Whoop de dooh!" Jenni is now nearly four and she retains these original names, correcting any who are unaware or who slip into the "generic" form of an undesignated Grandma or Grandpa.

One Grandpa, whom she called Grandpa Whee, is actually called Papa. This is probably because he did a lot of babysitting when Jenni's Mom first returned to work.

All the grandparents seem to remain equally distinctive in Jenni's eyes. This is probably because her parents wisely sense the importance of balancing her time and attention among all SIX grandparents.

This story suggests that there are many positives in the lives of modern families. Perhaps the term "broken families" could be changed in these cases to "enriched families." Jenni seems to be gaining much from the richness that her multi-grandparented world brings to her.

One Thanksgiving weekend when Jenni was two and a half, we were driving Jenni to a campground where she would stay with us overnight. I explained that this was going to be a SIX GRANDPARENT weekend!

In response to Jenni's puzzled expression, I said, "You are going camping with Grandma Whee and Papa tonight. Tomorrow afternoon your Mom and Dad will pick you up and take to Grandma and Grampa Bouncy Bouncy's for your first Thanksgiving with Grandma and Grampa Whoop de dooh."

"Wow!" Jenni replied. "That's wonderful!"

Indeed it did seem that we all had each other to thank on this special weekend for the gift of Jenni to us, and for our ability to ensure that Jenni continues to benefit from the richness of experience and love that we are collectively able to bring to her. Perhaps that is the magic in the "modern family" tale.

MY GRADE ONE

Sybil Shaw-Hamm
Steinbach, Manitoba

For Sharyne Hamm, granddaughter

I started to school when I was almost seven. When I first went, the school seemed far, far away from home. It wasn't really far away.

Our town was small. It had five streets running one way and three streets running the other. Nothing was far from anything.

But . . . in those long ago days, there was no daycare for little kids to attend, no kindergarten and mothers stayed mostly at home. I had never been away from my mother before starting school. I was scared.

To me the school looked very large - tall and square. The outside walls were made of yellow bricks and rows of windows. It was very old. My mother and father attended the same school when they were young. That was long before I did.

The back wall of the school had no windows. It was solid brick. Big girls used the wall at noon hour for bouncing balls. They had special ball-bouncing games that they learned from each other. Probably our mothers played the same games when they went to school there.

The school was divided inside into four classrooms, two upstairs for the high school kids and two on the main level for grades one to six. In the basement, there were two bathrooms, one for girls and one for boys. There was a light switch at the top of the stairs but some of us were too short to reach it. Some grade one students I knew would rather pee their pants than go alone down the steep, dark stairs. Mostly we peed at recess when we could take someone else along with us.

On top of the school was a tower. Inside the tower was a bell. At quarter to nine each school morning the bell rang and kids poured out of houses, laughing and shouting and running down the middle of the road. This was in 1945 and there were very few cars on our streets. Some kids came to school in horse-drawn wagons in summer or sleds in the winter. These kids were from the farms. Town kids had to watch out when farm kids came by.

At first, my schoolroom seemed dark and crowded. Six rows of desks. Seven desks in a row. One kid in each desk. Two rows for grade one. Two rows for grade two. Two rows for grade three. So many rows! So many kids!

Mostly, I wanted to cry. Everything was too strange, too crowded, too blurred. I was too small. Everything around me was too big.

On my second day, I began to notice other things. I counted five windows along a wall. If I turned my head sideways and looked out the nearest window, I could see the top of the sky. Seeing the sky made me feel bigger.

On my third day I noticed the blackboards. They covered two walls. Later, we made a circus with pictures of clowns and elephants and balloons and balls and monkeys, and pasted them along a paper that the teacher attached above the blackboards. It must have been a very long piece of paper because it covered the entire length of both boards. It was a long circus parade. The room felt happier with a parade.

At the back of the room there were two doors. One door opened to the hallway and the other opened to the cloakroom. ("Cloak" was a word once used instead of "coat.")

In the cloakroom each pupil had a hook for hanging up sweaters or jackets. On the floor we piled rubber boots if it rained, or winter boots if there was snow. The farm kids left their lunch pails in the cloakroom too. (I had no lunch pail. I never stayed for lunch - not one day of my whole school life.) The cloakroom always smelled of wet wool scarves and mitts. The smell was still there even if the scarves and mitts were not.

I didn't like the cloakroom for getting dressed in. Usually someone pushed you or stepped on your toes. But . . . it was also the "time out" room, although we didn't say "time out" back then.

"Go sit in the corner," the teacher said when you misbehaved. This meant you went and sat in the cloakroom. I liked to be in there alone. I counted the coats. I named the owner of each one. Sometimes I'd cuddle in a warm corner among the overshoes and go to sleep. (We called boots overshoes because they slipped over our shoes.)

In grade one, we were supposed to learn to read. The teacher gave us thin blue reading books with a picture on front of a boy and a girl and a dog and a cat and a baby sister and a red wagon. Right away I wanted to know who they were and what they were doing. Soon I learned their names: Dick and Jane and Spot and Puff and Baby Sally.

One of the best things about school in the olden days was how you got to hear stories from grade two and three readers. It was lovely to lean back in your desk and listen to big kids read their stories aloud.

By the time spring arrived, I decided one of the other best-things-about-school was recess. At recess we played in a big field around the school. Each of the four classrooms had their own corner to play in and we were expected to stay there.

Sometimes in our corner we played a tag game called Pump-pump-pull-away. In that game, the littlest kids were "It."

In summer, when it didn't rain or the bats didn't break or the ball didn't get lost we played softball.

Each Friday afternoon, our classroom was divided into ball teams. Everybody had to be on a team, even if you cried and said you didn't want to play. The biggest kids got to be Captains. Captains picked the teams, name by name. The grade one kids got picked last.

At first recess on Monday, the ball game began and we played every recess until Friday when we added up the scores on the score sheets and saw who won. Then Teacher named new Captains and the new Captains picked new teams. At first I was no good at all at playing ball. I'd swing the bat and never hit the ball. Later I did hit it and even managed to run around all the bases and make runs.

More important to my parents than me learning to play ball was for me to learn to read. Somehow I did learn to read and also to add numbers. I never did figure out how that happened.

My teacher's name was Mrs. Cutler. She had a very gray-haired bun on the back of her head and the loveliest long neck I ever saw. I always wished for a long neck like hers. My Mom and Dad thought Mrs. Cutler was the best teacher in the whole world. I had to grow up before I agreed.

In 1956, I finished school and left my small hometown for the city and studied to be a nurse. One day a letter came from my mother. It said our old school had burned down. All that was left was a pile of bricks. I was very sad.

Then, in 1994, I was invited back to my hometown for a party. Everyone who had attended the school was invited too. Such parties are called a reunion.

By then I was 56 years old. My grade one teacher was 101 years old. She lived in a Nursing Home and couldn't walk well enough to come to the party. So two old pals from grade one went with me to visit her. When she saw us she said our names as if she were doing roll call for attendance back in school. We talked to her about the old brick school, the classroom, the cloakroom, and the circus parade. Then she said, "I hope you girls remember the most important thing I taught you. Do your part to make the world a better place." It was then I knew what my parents meant about Mrs. Cutler. She was the best teacher a kid could have.

TEETH, YOURS TO KEEP

Anne Dunlop
Toronto, Ontario

Dear Rudy, Nicole, Jocie, Steve, Dan, Em, Andrew, Jeffrey & Joseph:

This is another letter prompted by S.H.A.R.E., McMaster University's volunteer research group that encourages those of us "over-age-60" to share what we've learned from our long lives. Rudy may remember that Grandma Anderson introduced Uncle Jim and me to S.H.A.R.E. and that in 1997, I wrote Rudy a letter on "Early Words" for his tenth birthday.

If you are already at or over the age of six, your smile is meant to last you for life – and you all may live to 100+. Keeping your teeth clean is hard to do, and no one else can do it for you. You have to do it every day and more than once a day. If you make it a habit and do not fight it, or make excuses for not doing the best job you can of cleaning your teeth, it won't be so bad. Just do it. Your biggest reward will be problems that you DO NOT have, such as toothaches, puffy bleeding gums that hurt and give you bad breath, and thousands and thousands of dollars for tooth repair. (I think of how many times I could sail around the world with all the money I have spent on my teeth!)

First I'd like to tell you what made me become especially interested in teeth. After I finished my university studies, I worked as a nutritionist in a clinic at the Forsyth Dental Infirmary for Children in Boston, Massachusetts. At Forsyth, people looked at the "whole child," so children were seen by dental hygienists, dentists, orthodontists (for "straightening" the teeth), biochemists (who studied saliva in mouths and its effect on teeth), other health-care people, such as doctors and nutritionists, like me. That is where I learned how bad sugar is for your teeth.

In 1955, I married a dentist and moved to New Hampshire, just north of Boston in the U.S. I lived there for the next forty years. I worked in the office, attended many meetings on better health and dentistry, and brought up four children.

I learned how to teach people to clean their teeth. It is true that you usually don't learn from just one lesson. The average person has to have five lessons before they get the message and then you need check-ups to see if you are doing things correctly. Your dentist's office can best show you how to clean your teeth, but here are the basic ideas:

1. BRUSH your teeth after every meal. Place the brush on the gum above your teeth and brush down. (Brush up from below your lower teeth.) Do this all around your mouth, on both side of your rows of teeth. Get behind your molars. Use a small amount of toothpaste if you wish. Brush a good two minutes (two seconds on the inside and outside of EACH tooth) even if you use an electric brush. Rinse your mouth and brush some more – a couple of brush swipes over you tongue is a good idea - then brush and rinse again. However, brushing does only HALF the job.

   If you miss the many colonies of bacteria in your mouth, they will eat their way down under the gum line. If this happens, you will have pockets between your teeth and gums, which you cannot clean out. Then the bacteria can go down far enough to make your teeth get loose in the jawbone, and even the bone starts being lost. Your teeth can actually fall out. That is why you need to get rid of plaque starting now. (This kind of tooth loss is NOT what happens when your baby teeth fall out; baby teeth are pushed out by a normal process of your permanent teeth erupting through your gums.)

2. FLOSS your teeth *every day* – to get off as much of the remaining plaque on your teeth as you can. Flossing also moves away food particles that stick between your teeth. Wrap it in a "C" shape around one of the teeth as close to the gum as is comfortable, and move the floss up in a

sawing motion to scrape away the plaque. Do the same with the second tooth. Repeat this all around your upper and lower teeth. Then carefully use a tiny perio-brush. Rinse your mouth well, swishing the water between your teeth.

The reason you brush after every meal is that no one is perfect, and what you miss at one brushing, you may get at the next. Also, after every meal you have food that needs to be moved away, along with colonies of bacteria that you previously missed.

Most people do have to do a good and faithful job of brushing and flossing. You also need a good diet with a minimum of sweets (including sugary gum and soft drinks).

I will end this letter with a few short stories about teeth that I have heard over the years:

1) Evidence of tooth decay has been seen in mummies from the tombs of Egypt.

2) Before Europeans came to North America, the aboriginal people used twigs to scrape the plaque from their teeth – today there are all sorts of toothpicks – like tools to use in cleaning teeth. However, the Europeans brought sugar and white flour to this country, and soon the native people began to suffer from tooth decay and gum problems.

3) Toothpaste is abrasive. To illustrate, if you have a water spot on a wooden table top, you can gently rub it off with a little toothpaste on a cloth. Several years ago, two groups of dental students in the U.S. were assigned an afternoon of brushing teeth extracted from dental clinic patients. All used toothbrushes, but one group used toothpaste and the other did not. At the end of the afternoon, the group using toothpaste found that much of the enamel (the shiny covering of the teeth) had worn off. The group using no toothpaste still had shiny enamel on the teeth they brushed.

4) Before the dental profession realized, as a group, how important "Prevention" (of dental problems) was, even some dentists did not brush and floss as they should. At a dental convention in the 1960's, the people attending were offered free dental checkups. One 49-year-old man, who had never had a cavity in his life, decided to have a checkup. The dentist who saw him told the man that he just had one chance to save his teeth, and that was to care of his gums by flossing and brushing with great care. The man had periodontal disease, meaning gum disease. The dentist asked the man what he did for a living. The answer was "Dean of a Dental School." This shows you how "silent" gum disease can be. If you look, you can see people who are teenagers and older with teeth that do not show decay, but with gums that are red and puffy.

I have spent hundreds of hours in the dental chair – including one in Denmark while visiting in 1953. The dentist went to the University of Copenhagen when my father did. I still have most of my teeth, thanks to great dental care and many dollars for operations on my gums, fillings, caps and a couple of bridges that hold a replacement tooth between two capped teeth. But I do want to save you the pain, misery and dental bills I've had, so keep up that BRUSHING and FLOSSING – and always see your dentist regularly.

WORLD OF MYSTERIES

Elizabeth Whitehead
Hamilton, Ontario

Davey stirred in his bed as the summer air breathed through the open window and tickled his sleeping face. Although still in dreamland, the ten-year-old was aware of "that Saturday feeling" and snuggled deeper into the comfort of his pillow. The stream murmuring around his feet as he sat on its bank, warm and playful at first was becoming increasingly agitated. The murmur, now a load roar, was loud enough to shake the bank and Davey jolted into wakefulness to find it was his mother shaking him.

"Davey, get up and dress quickly," Mrs. Lamont ordered. "Your father needs your help in the basement." "What's going on, Mom?" Her groggy son had successfully manoeuvered only one leg of his jeans over his sun-tanned legs.

"One of the pipes near the laundry tubs has broken and Dad is down there bailing out the basement. The noise of running water woke us, and your father found several inches of hot water soaking everything on the floor. The plumber will get here as soon as he can, but in the meantime we must get our things out of the area so they can dry." Mrs. Lamont had to stop to catch her breath.

Now fully awake, Davey descended the stairs two at a time and veered through the kitchen and down to the basement where he found his father in hip waders chasing floating debris.

"That huge trunk of your mother's was sitting right over the front drain and the drain at the other end of the cellar was somewhat clogged so the water has built up to nearly four inches." Mr. Lamont looked like a bedraggled little boy searching for tadpoles in a creek. Davey stood on the bottom step and started rolling up his pant legs.

"Oh, no you don't, young man," his mother warned. "You are not going to wade around the basement floor in your bare feet." Mrs. Lamont had picked up Davey's rubber boots from the back hall in readiness for his watery job. "You could hurt yourself quite badly if you tread on nails or any other sharp objects lying on the floor if you walked around with no boots on." His father's arms were full of jars of homemade jam rescued from the bottom shelf of Mrs. Lamont's basement pantry. "Oh dear, the hot water has removed the labels from the jars. I can't tell if the strawberry is the end of last year's batch or this year's produce. In fact it's difficult to choose which is raspberry and which is strawberry without a really close look." The distraught lady retreated to her kitchen to unravel the mystery. The main problem for Davey and his dad was the removal of the trunk from atop the front drain. Father and son took firm hold of the handles at each end of the obstacle, planted their feet solidly on the floor and strained to lift the trunk.

"What's in it, Dad? Let's open it and see." The boy started to release the large fasteners holding the lid tightly shut. "Look, it isn't locked."

"We'll empty some of the contents to make moving easier. Exploring will have to wait." Mr. Lamont's stern voice was betrayed by a smile and a wink at his curious son.

Lifting the lid, Davey's excitement quickly died as he peered inside. "Books," he exclaimed, "nothing but books."

The two removed some of the contents, stacking them on the workbench in the corner. "Let's close the lid and try again Davey." This time their efforts were not in vain. Their burden although lighter was still cumbersome. "Where to Dad?"

"Only place to go is up. Do you think we can get it through the kitchen door to the back porch?"

"Sure. We make a great team." Father and son lifted, pulled and pushed that big, old trunk to its temporary resting place and made a mess of the kitchen and hall floors in the meantime. Mrs. Lamont was more concerned for her men's safety than her added housework however.

"Why don't you just leave that old trunk down there?" We could just throw the whole thing away later."

"Aw, Mom, I want to see what else is in there. You never know, there could be hidden jewels and pieces of silver." Davey gave Mrs. Lamont's apron strings a playful tug as he skidded past her on his way back to the water-filled basement.

Floating debris was becoming "land locked" once again as the freed drain allowed the water to run slowly away.

"Hello, may I come down to play too?" a jolly voice boomed down the stairs from the busy kitchen. The voice belonged to a rather rotund, red-faced Joe Thomas, the plumber.

"If you call this playing, then I won't expect a bill," joked Davey's father. "Well now, Tom, let's not get carried away," chuckled Joe Thomas as he sloshed his way to the offending pipe and then to the uncooperative drain. "We'll get rid of this water first and then fix the pipe so as to get the water turned back on as soon as possible. Don't worry it's not as bad as it looks. I've seen plenty worse than this." Joe Thomas shook his head in remembrance of real calamities he had witnessed. "You have the biggest problem cleaning up."

As the morning wore on Mrs. Lamont busied herself preparing lunch of sandwiches, soup and milk. "Are you men ready to eat? It's just gone noon," she called down the basement stairs. "There's plenty for all of you." "Thanks Sarah," her husband answered. "If you can hold off for another hour Joe will be finished and you will have hot water again."

"Wonderful." She breathed a sigh of relief. The rest of the day was spent cleaning and drying. Fortunately the messy incident happened during a summer day, enabling the Lamonts to open all basement windows until the area was back to normal. The sun and Davey rose together the next morning keeping each other company as the boy once again opened the lid to the trunk. The contents were not "just" books as Davey had first thought, but photo albums and scrapbooks full of mementos belonging to his grandfather. Boxes of old photos showing stern-faced men in stiff poses and unsmiling ladies in long dresses were among other pictures of a more recent past. The albums that had been piled on the basement workbench were added to the collection as the boy dug deeper into his treasure chest.

Those lying on the bottom of the trunk were suffering water damage and young hands made sure they were put to dry. Wetness had crept beneath the metal covering and entered the cedar-lined interior leaving a four-inch tidemark along the bottom of the trunk. Only time and the summer heat could cure the problem, and Davey decided the best place would be under the south window in his father's den. The decision solved one problem and produced another. Mrs. Lamont had stated she wanted it thrown out.

"I must convince Mom to let me keep the trunk and Dad to make room for it in his den." Davey decided to present the case for his treasure chest at breakfast. Pouring milk on his Rice Krispies he asked his father, "Why can't I keep the trunk in the den, Dad? I promise to clean it up really good and once it's dry it will look swell in the corner beside the window. It won't be in anyone's way. Please, Dad, what do you say?"

"Well it seems to be in good shape." Mr. Lamont paused over his glass of orange juice as he pondered the situation. "Why the sudden interest?" he peered at his young son.

"Grandfather's scrapbooks of all the travelling he did are in it. So are his trip diaries and you should see all the photographs of back in the olden times. They're super!" His mother had to stop Davey from gulping his orange juice. "I'd never really paid any attention to the trunk when your Grandfather left it here," Mrs. Lamont said. "If it was in the den we could all enjoy looking through the contents."

"That settles it then." Mr. Lamont wiped his mouth and folded his serviette. "As soon as it's dry we will move your treasure chest inside, my lad."

"Thanks Dad. Thanks Mom." An excited Davey finished his toast and jam and rushed upstairs to get ready for another summer day. By the weekend the appointed corner in the den was ready to receive the trunk, which was once again filled with its interesting memorabilia. Davey spent many hours poring over scrapbooks whose pages held postcards and pamphlets, souvenirs of his grandfather's extensive travels. The diaries covering some twenty-five years detailed each trip and Davey glimpsed the world through his grandfather's eyes as he immersed himself in the accompanying photograph albums.

The aged photos of Davey's ancestors particularly fascinated the boy. "I can't believe how clear these pictures are," he told his mother. Sitting cross-legged on the floor near the trunk, he was unaware he was intruding on Mrs. Lamont's house cleaning. "These people seem to stare right through you; they look so stern. In these posed photos they look stiff, as if they were starched." Davey chuckled at the idea.

"Those are portraits," his mother told him, "and you must remember some of them are eighty years old. They had a different way of doing things in those days including posing for photographs."

"I didn't know they had cameras way back then. Look at this old lady in the long dress with the ruffles around the wrists and neck. Boy, she looks angry at someone. I guess she died years ago and, who knows, maybe she's haunting someone right now." Davey gave an owl-like hoot at his mother who shooed him out of her way and busied herself with the vacuuming. As the days drifted by the youngster was enticed by the summer sun to abandon the trunk and join the team on the baseball diamond. He returned to the lake for swimming and splashing with his friends in the time left before the routine of schooldays once more beckoned. After an active day outdoors, Davey found sleep a welcome visitor and was on to dreaming of hot fudge sundaes topped with cherries the size of baseballs.

Suddenly he was awakened by the sound of voices coming from downstairs. Checking his clock on the night table he found it was very late and decided to investigate the disturbance. Mr. and Mrs. Lamont looked up from the kitchen table as Davey padded into the room rubbing his eyes. "What's going on?" he yawned. "I couldn't sleep and came down for some milk." Davey's Mom shot a look at her husband. "Is something wrong?" Davey thought his Mom seemed upset.

"We might as well tell him, Sarah." Mrs. Lamont nodded her head and her husband turned to Dave and continued. "I haven't said anything but for the last few nights I have been hearing some strange noises. Tonight your mother heard them too, while she was getting something to drink." "Strange noises?" Davey, suddenly wide-awake felt the hairs on the back of his neck bristle.

"Yes I heard, well I can only describe it as, a sort of scratching noise. Oh, Tom you don't think we have mice do you?" Mrs. Lamont shivered at the thought.

"I don't think so. We would have noticed them before now. Mice are attracted by bags and boxes of food and the kitchen garbage can would be an enticement. We haven't seen any signs of nibbling or, for that matter, the waste they leave. Have either of you seen any of these signs?" Both mother and son shook their heads no, while pondering an alternative explanation.

"You've heard the noise too, Dad?" Davey asked.

"Yes, son I've heard what I thought was the rustling of leaves while I was sitting at my desk in the den, and again when I was reading my newspaper in the living room. After tonight I tend to discount that theory. Your mother called me when she heard them just a few minutes ago and I stood here and the two of us experienced the same noises at the same time." He followed the direction they were apparently emanating from. Leaving the kitchen he crept down the hall that led past the basement door towards the front of the house. On his right was the den, while across the hall stood the living room and dining area. Now the mystery deepened as both Davey and his Dad entered the room where the "scratching, rustling sounds" were the most evident – the den. Turning on the lights, boy and man entered the room and slowly looked around. On his father's direction they started to search in corners and around windows, peering under furniture. They even went so far as to lift the large oval rug covering the highly polished floors. Nothing! Not a sign of anything amiss. Yet the noises persisted.

Was there something in the walls? Here again Mr. Lamont discounted the idea. "The noise is too loud to be inside the walls."

"What are you doing Davey?" Mrs. Lamont had joined the search and watched as her son concentrated his attention on his grandfather's trunk.

"This is no time for reading son," his dad said half joking.

"Dad, the noises are the loudest right here around the trunk." He looked up from his crouching position by the chest and, making a ghoulish face, said, "Maybe the ghosts are trying to get out."

"Stop kidding around, although I do agree on one thing. The scratching is loudest here." So saying, Mr. Lamont opened the trunk and the next half hour was spent emptying and examining both contents and the interior of the container. A thorough search turned up nothing. Absolutely nothing. The noises had stopped in the meantime and he suggested everyone go back to bed.

"It's very late and I have to get to work in the morning. We all need our rest and we aren't accomplishing anything now." After promising further investigation, if and when the mystery continued, Mr. Lamont shooed his family back to their beds.

The early morning sunshine somewhat relieved the anxiety of the previous hours and the family went about their daily routine albeit rather subdued. Davey wandered into the den deep in thought and stood staring at the trunk. He noticed a newspaper lying on the lid. "Mom," he called. "Dad forgot the morning paper."

"Oh, he must have been having another look 'round in there before breakfast," she said, "I don't think he will miss the morning news for once." Mrs. Lamont went upstairs to make the beds and Davey got the lawn mower out of the garage. "Might as well get this chore over with," he told himself. The morning passed quickly with completion of chores coinciding nicely with lunchtime. Afterward Davey found himself once more in the den confronting the trunk. Suddenly it happened. "Mom, come quick. Mom!" he shouted unable to contain his excitement. Mrs. Lamont dropped the book she was reading in the living room and rushed to where her son was jumping up and down, gesturing at the trunk.

There on the lid, the newspaper was moving! Actually the paper was shivering more than moving. "The window." Mrs. Lamont rushed to close the window, although she knew the movement she witnessed was not consistent with a breeze blowing a paper. The newspaper continued its little "dance" with no apparent cause, but now it was accompanied by the rustling noises previously heard. Davey placed his hand flat on the surface of the lid beside the newspaper and pressed lightly downwards. The slight pressure left an impression on the metal covering of the trunk. Quickly the boy repeated the action on all four sides as his wide-eyed mother stood by, unable to move. Davey pressed down and then released the area covered by the newspaper. The rustling, both noise and movement ceased momentarily and then recommenced. The youngster was now crouched eye-level with the top of the trunk and suddenly he shot up straight shouting, "That's it! I've got it, the mystery is solved."

"Look Mom, the hide of the trunk is uneven all over. It should fit tight which it did once." His eyes were shining with excitement. "When I first started using the trunk the outside was nice and smooth." He paused trying to catch his breath. "When the basement flooded, the hot water seeped into the bottom of the trunk. It would also seep between the metal covering and the interior. The hot weather has dried it out completely over the last three weeks or so and the metal is in the process of separating from the trunk itself, a little at a time. That is the "scratching" or "rustling" noises we have been hearing. Metal peeling away from the cedar-lined interior."

"Then the newspaper was resting on a part of the covering as it was loosening and it started to rustle too." Mrs. Lamont was caught up in her son's excitement. She looked at Davey and gave him a congratulatory pat on the back.

Although feeling satisfied over his success at unravelling the mystery, the young detective also felt let down. The excitement of the unknown was over.

"I'm proud of the way you used perception and common sense to figure out how the noises were made," Davey's father told him at dinner that evening. "You know the world is full of mysteries to solve, the world your own grandfather travelled around and wrote about."

"Grandfather left me a real treasure which I would probably have never known about if it hadn't been for, of all things, a flooded basement." Davey got a faraway look on his sun-tanned face. "How do you suppose that hot water pipe really broke?"

A STORY FOR SAMANTHA

Dolores V. Gignac
Hamilton, Ontario

This is the story of two little girls. One of them is now the grandma and the other girl is seven years old. Well, when grandma was young she loved playing house with her dolls and having tea parties with her friends, and all the other things young girls do. But she was a little bit lonely playing alone and wished and prayed everyday for a little sister to share her games and dreams. As she became older, she began to realize that there would never be a sister for her to play with, so she began thinking ahead to the time she would find her Prince Charming and they would get married and then she would have a darling baby girl. What fun it would be to dress her in lovely dresses and play games with her!

Well, the Grandma grew up, met Prince Charming and they had a lovely wedding thinking of the future time when she would have a baby daughter of her own. After a time, the grandma found out that a little baby was coming to her and Prince Charming, and she was very excited and happy getting ready for this baby to arrive. Now imagine, that baby turned out to be a beautiful small baby boy to love and play trains and ball with. Grandma was very happy and just thought next time a baby came it would be her little girl. Two more babies came to the grandma and Prince Charming—both happy, funny sweet baby boys and they all had a wonderful time and lots of fun growing up together and the grandma forgot for a long time about playing with a little girl.

After a long time, the boys grew up too, and one of them met a young and lovely girl of his own he wanted to marry and have a happy life with, and so he did. Now, after a time, they told the grandma the happy news that there would be a new member being born into the family and everyone was happy and excited and made lots of plans and bought lovely things for the baby. It was so exciting thinking about and planning for a baby that the grandma didn't think too much about it being a girl or boy, but was just happy about the big event that was going to happen in their lives.

Would you believe that when the time came for the baby to arrive, and she was told it was a lovely healthy, chubby baby girl with big brown eyes and no hair to put ribbons in, it was the most excited grandma in the whole world? She ran out to tell her friends and buy dolls and pretty dresses. What a happy time it was for everyone who kept waiting for hair to grow. Santa will bring hair for Christmas, we all thought, but it was not there for Christmas. We will have hair for Easter we said, but not then either. However, eventually the hair came in a wonderful reddish colour and in beautiful curls.

Now, this wonderful friend and playmate for Grandma is already seven years old, beautiful and can do many things which makes everyone very proud and happy—especially the grandma when Samantha comes to visit and they play and talk together just as the grandma imagined it would be a long time ago.

Love Forever,

Grandma

A LETTER TO JEREMY

Dolores V. Gignac
Hamilton, Ontario

Dear Jeremy,

It makes me very happy to have such a wonderful grandson like you who is so happy, smart and handsome. Your bright smile brightens my day so much when I am with you. We have a wonderful time together playing your favourite games of dinosaurs and cars. You have taught me so much about dinosaurs because I did not know all their names or who was a plant eater or who was a meat eater. Now I know all about Tyrannosaurus Rex, the biggest and meanest of them all and who are his friends and enemies.

I love it when you sing your song about the Lone Dinosaur.

We have such a good time when we go to the park and play on the swings and slides and fly our kites.

The times we spend reading your favourite books are precious to me and you enjoy teasing me a lot too.

I look forward to the times when you sleep over and I get to tuck you into your little bed and you give me lots of hugs and kisses.

I am a very lucky grandma to have you and your sister to love me.

Love always,

Grandma

ON THE MOVE

Helen Brown
Burlington, Ontario

When my son Craig informed me that he and his family were leaving Toronto for Scottsdale, Arizona to take a position with his company there, I was selfishly devastated.

I thought back on all the wonderful happy times my husband, J.C. and I had spent in Toronto with his family. Walking only a few blocks to Bloor Street was an education all of its own.

Just to see the different age groups from different various ethnic backgrounds was an experience we will remember. We enjoyed the stores with food from different nations. I realized how fortunate we were to be able to enjoy their cultures while having all the opportunities this country has to offer. We would wonder where all the people shopping came from. No matter what time of day, it seemed every other store had containers outside filled with fresh flowers. Walking in the evening, we felt quite safe as there were always so many people strolling, enjoying the seasons.

Usually I would take my grandson Allan in the stroller when I went out for a walk. It was strange how each time we reached Bloor Street the stroller would make a right turn with no effort on my part and automatically enter Baskin Robbins. The family would have never found out about my secret vice had not my grandson who was too young to talk, had a tantrum when he was with his parents and they tried to turn the stroller left on Bloor Street. I wouldn't like to say that I was there often, but my son said that they had named a "Flavour of the Month" after me. (I have to admit that I did enjoy "Helena Nut.") I had suggested that when I die they could scatter my ashes in Baskin Robbins and instead of visiting me at a cemetery they could just have a double scoop cone, enjoy it and think of me.

My sister's son recently bought a home in Toronto. He asked if there were any places she would be interested in seeing. She replied, "Yes, I would like to see the Baskin Robbins that was your Aunt Helen's old stomping grounds." I was disappointed to hear the building had been torn down. "But there was a plaque there with your name on it," my sister jokingly told me.

My son Craig and his wife Katey have a very romantic love story. Her father John and J.C. were overseas together with the Canadian Air Force and formed a lasting friendship. After the war, we continued to keep in touch. As our families grew, we spent many happy times together. It seemed every time we had a son, they had a daughter. We had three sons, and they had four daughters.

Those were the days before babysitters. With the many family dinners, the seven children bonded. We lived very close to each other so we visited most weeks, but time and circumstances had a way of putting distance between us. Our dear best friend John took a position in Chicago, but we kept in touch. By now our children were all teenagers and we were all very much involved with our own families. One summer my friend Mary asked me to drive down to Chicago for a visit. Since my son was home from university, he said he would drive me there. My friend asked if we would drive her daughter home as she was visiting an aunt close by. As my son had not seen her daughter for a few years, they became reacquainted on the trip. After many phone calls and letters, they became engaged. They have been happily married for twenty years and are the proud parents of two wonderful boys, Allan and Patrick.

LETTERS TO AUNTIE LESLIE
UPDATING ANECDOTES OF YDN/ODG
(Your Darling Niece/Our Darling Granddaughter)

Marlene Rogers
Hamilton, Ontario

These are some of the many tales that I had documented with the intention of keeping them for our granddaughter, Ashley, as a remembrance of the love and joy of laughter she has brought into our lives. The tales originated as emailed updates of her many antics to our daughter, her Auntie Leslie, whose career as an animator has taken her far away to what Ashley used to say "The Vancouver." The acronyms have changed over the years from SLB (sweet little baby), NEDB (nail everything down baby), SCITW smartest child in the world) all now lovingly embraced in YDN/ODG (your darling niece/our darling granddaughter).

I believe that there is only one word in the English language that conveys every nuance without the embellishment of an adjective. That word is 'love,' and that is what was brought into our lives on May 13, 1994.

BABY-SITTING THE "SPRAINED ANKLE"

Dear Auntie Leslie:

On Monday evening, in some mysterious fashion (that has not been told *in toto* to me, because 'it will upset Nana' – probably something she shouldn't have been doing in the first place) YDN/ODG sprained her ankle – quite severely, and spent the evening in the hospital. At 11:00 p.m. your father and I were called into duty as babysitters (note: plural) for the following day.

So, the next day, we were up bright *and* early to dispose of any miscellany in preparation for the arrival of our darling. She arrived swathed in winter garments (an overprotective penchant from Mommy) although the fall season had yet to wane. Mommy came armed with "sugar pops" (soothers for the day) under one arm, and "crunches" (crutches) under the other. Once the layers were peeled away, we all staggered to ensconce her "cocoonly" for the day on our newest living room acquisition, a spanking brand new recliner. And so, our day(s) began.

Your Great-Aunt Eva's cherished Dresden plate quilt, was draped lovingly over the spanking brand new acquisition, the body was tenderly and gently laid on the same, feet elevated, afflicted offending foot gravely positioned on the cushion, whereupon we were informed by our darling that "*you will have to do everything for me, you know.*" Not once, during the ensuing two days, was the house quiet. I had forgotten, Auntie Leslie, how much a five-year-old can talk, talk, talk, ask questions, laugh, *eat*, drink – and fight sleep.

However, furniture re-arranged, her blanket, crayons, books, papers, pencils, stickers, jewellery, coins, TV, the choice-of-the-day stuffed animals, and food, food, food, were at hand at almost every command; and verbs – covered, coloured, read, cut out, drawn, stuck, tried on, wrapped, watched, played with, and consumed – duly addressed.

The day proceeds joyously, with me out on the front lawn, to find the nicest fallen leaves (on the overnight rain-soaked lawn) to press into a book, totally disregarding the fact that the neighbours would see what I actually dressed like behind closed doors (versus makeup applied, hair patted into semblance, and matching garments when presenting myself to the world). Trailing the leaves that stuck to my slippers back into the house, the joyous thought that had prompted this bonding moment was gone in just that – a moment. Well almost! It only took about 5 minutes AND THAT WAS DONE.

How were we ever to get through the day? Navigating the stairs to the bathroom took quite a bit of time, and only came close to disaster once or twice when we both teetered on the stairs. That incident only brought joyous peels of laughter from YDN/ODG, but brought to the front of my mind that which had been on the back of my mind – funeral arrangements – not yet 't' crossed and 'I' dotted. Shouts of " *I gotta, Nana!*" "*I really do!*" made me feel our darling had a serious bladder problem, until I realized how much she enjoyed our "revised" returned flights. These found me dashing down the stairs to play catcher as she careened down on her rump, putting both our lives and limbs at further risk. The physical energy expended in moving "her" from point A to point B was yet another reminder that my "times" were once again being ravaged. The attempt at using the adorable miniature crutches was somewhat helpful, but couldn't get our darling around as fast as putting her full weight on me, and hopping around – "she" on purpose, and me accidentally. You can bet that was great fun.

However, even with YOUR father taking off with YOUR brother for a couple of hours, the day wended Leave it to Beaver "Cleaverly" along until preparations for dinner began. As soon as the aroma hit the nostrils of YDN/ODG, I was plagued – yes plagued – with "Is the food ready yet, Nana?" Your father and your brother return, Mommy now home from work – all sit down to dinner that had taken me two hours to make, and only five minutes to see disappear.

Mommy, now in command for the rest of this day, re-swathes our darling and with crutches in tow, they are (mercifully) homeward bound. I collapse among the disarray of the day, hearing YOUR father say, "Of course, bring her back to-morrow. She can't possibly go to school on that leg." (totally disregarding "both" of mine).

I pleaded to God to let me stay in bed the following aching morning, but YOUR father bounced out of bed, even after I said he would have to stay home ALL DAY to help. His last words, before further bouncing downstairs was to remind me that he had to go the store to replenish our larder after yesterday's foray (my words – not his).

We repeated the morning of the day before (with the exception of leaf pressing), had "ummmmh" lunch, and took off on a "counting of who had the most pumpkins on their side" ride. Shouts of glee were offset with pouts when she had more or less pumpkins than I (me?). Gasps of "Oh! Look at the beautiful colour of leaves over there" prompted me to tell YDN/ODG of the delightful story that you might remember your Nana made up about your *other* brother (my son, YDN/ODG's father). I hastened over this part of family genealogy as I could see the look of confusion on her face, and proceeded with the tale of how he (your *other* brother, our son, her daddy) would get up early in the fall and paint ALL the leaves. Omitting the silent "Oh sure, Nana" the 5-year-old skeptic asks one of their universal questions, "*How*, Nana"? I didn't recall if you, my children, had been smart enough to ask that question, and if you did, I could not recall your Nana's clever response, so I "responsed" as well as I could. My "could" was obviously not that good, for after only a few moments of cogitation, I just made out her almost inaudible aside "Well, he must have gone home looking like a rainbow." Well, so much for tales of yore. However the "leaf" conversation was not quite over, when YDN/ODG asks "Who makes the leaves, Nana?" "God, does," I matriarchally reply as I pat her head, to which she adds, "and, He made bumpy roads, too, didn't He?" The reverent moment dispelled, the "Department of Highways" comment is ignored, and on we go.

Our "pumpkin" ride continued with shouts beyond that of any known decibel to man of "Stoooooooop" as we approached red lights, giggles ensuing and further shouts of directions (after once again determining which hand is right and which hand is left) of "turn left Grampy," or "turn right Grampy" as we journeyed along our curvaceous country roadways.

Grampy highlighted our "pumpkin" ride with the purchase of candy and popcorn that made me wonder when I had forgotten "his" rule of "NO FOOD IN THE NEW CAR!" I guess the small print should read "NO FOOD IN THE NEW CAR WITH THE EXCEPTION OF YDN/ODG." Oh well, the vacuum cleaner will take care of the dropped salty popcorn, bits of hardened chocolate can easily be peeled off the upholstery of Grampy's new car, and mommy can wash the rest. "Her" big chocolate smile, however, did not make up for the chocolate smudge on my white jacket.

Somewhat somber (somewhat, I say) from all the shouting at the onset of our "pumpkin" ride, fatigue finally taking over, I actually saw beautiful long eyelashes fall on someone's fat cheeks as they fought off sleep on our "Thank God, we've gotten through another afternoon" ride home.

No dinner offered this day by an "old" Nana, the layers of clothing re-applied, I hear YOUR father saying once again "She really shouldn't go to school this week, at all." I'm not sure that this was heard by Mommy as I quickly closed the door, but you know something, Auntie Leslie – our house is *very, very* quiet today, and should the phone ring for yet another stint of sprained ankle baby-sitting, you can bet that Nana and Grampy would be ready to gird their loins, gulp down a shot or two of geritol, re-re-arrange furniture, re-pull out Disney video's (seen for the umpteenth time), etc., etc., etc., to welcome *WITH OPEN ARMS*, YDN/ODG.

Love, hugs and many kisses,

YM (Your Mommy)

P.S.   YDN/ODG is on the mend – I am on the mend – your father has been forgiven, but I am thinking about buying a new telephone with caller I.D. (just in case). As YDN/ODG often says after a whopper "Just kidding, Nana", "Just kidding, Auntie Leslie".

P.P.S. The expense of two-day's baby-sitting: the Mother Hubbarding of our cupboard, and *two and a half rolls of toilet paper, have been PAID IN FULL with a plethora of hugs and kisses.

*   You remember, Auntie Leslie – the small "toidy tune" gizmo that fits inside the toilet roll (that drove you crazy on your visit home last summer) that plays music each time the roll is rolled – ergo the 2 ½ rolls of paper. I never thought the tune played ironic until this

110

extended visit. It is "It's a *Small* World" that has been promised by the manufactures to cease after 3,956 rolls. So, Lesson 129 reads: never leave an inquisitive visiting child (be they "grand" or not) of one, two, three, four, five (and probably six) year's old alone in your bathroom. (I'm sure future lessons will cover other rooms).

THE "REWARD"

Dear Auntie Leslie:

I don't know if you remember me telling you last year about the "drawing" incident during YDN/ODG's pre-kindergarten year (1998 AD). Bear in mind, Auntie Leslie, that school had barely started, and bear in mind how *very* precocious our darling can be. Well, Mommy knows better than anyone how precocious her darling can be, and one lovely early "fall" day, having just picked up our darling from school, and wending their way to their car, the school door bursts open with a Ms. Clark (teacher of our darling) yoo-hooing for Mommy's attention. "Oh, my gosh," thinks Mommy. "What has she done *now*?" "Just look at this!" shouts Ms. Clark, waving a large piece of paper at Mommy. "Look what Ashley has drawn!" "Oh, my gosh," Mommy further thinks. "School has only begun, and she's only in pre-kindergarten. Don't tell me she's going to be expelled already!" Bracing herself for the worst, Mommy is shown a picture of a large bear with two smaller bears that our darling had drawn. The excited Ms. Clark, *knowing talent when she sees it,* asks Mommy to let her enter it in next year's local fall fair. Mommy, now able to un-brace herself, and the quick facial adjustment from "I'll see that she never does anything like that again" (although beads of sweat remain) to a tish-tossily look says "Oh, she does that all the time," and proudly cedes to the request.

The months ensue, with varying degrees of good school days, trips to see Christmas lights, scary animals at the Lion Safari, coming home with the "biggest, Nana" pumpkin from the patch, her 5th birthday (a resounder at

McDonald's with school mates), and bad days – too few to mention – and, all of a sudden, it is a lovely early "fall" day in 1999.

And do you know what, Auntie Leslie? Do you? Do you know who took third prize? No? Neither do I. Do you know who took second prize? No? Neither do I. Do you know who took first prize? No? Well, I do! This year, it is a Ms. Hardington, who yoo-hoos Mommy to tell her that "our darling" had taken first prize at the 1999 Fall Fair! Bear in mind again – our darling is a mere four years old at the time of this artistic achievement.

Our darling's "reward" consisted of a ribbon, which was immediately set aside while diving into the more important accompanying large bag of goodies.

It is a mystery, Auntie Leslie, where this talent has come from, but it has alighted on you, my darling, and our darling. I just wonder if it has anything to do with the fact that you are both left-handed? Now that I think of it, this should not have come as a complete surprise. I recall the day, while busily preparing her favourite lunch (Kraft Dinner), the "lack of noise" coming from the front room prompted me to call out "What are you doing, sweetie?" "Nothing, Nana – just drawing. " All marker and crayons are always supposed to be kept under lock and key, so what could she be drawing with, and worse – on what? I stop stirring, and run to see what damage has been wrought, to find our darling, now standing aside to reveal the nicest picture of a little girl with long curly hair that she had free-handed – *in the dust of our TV screen.*

What more can I say?

Many hugs and kisses.
 Love,

YM (Your Mommy)

LIFE IN THE CONVENT

Cornelia T. Grenier

Freelton, Ontario

The convent was located in a small, flower bulb-growing town named Noordwijkerhout in the Netherlands, close to the North Sea. It consisted of two large buildings that were separated by an alleyway. One building had the nuns' quarters on one side, the children's on the other plus kindergarten and up to grade six schoolrooms on the lower levels. On the top floor were the dorms. The building on the other side of the alleyway held the rooms for grades 7, 8, 9, and 10.

Children from the town attending the school came in through the alleyway from outside the wrought-iron gates surrounding all of the convent.

On the ground floor were two homerooms for the children who were living in the convent; one from kindergarten age up to twelve years of age, the other from twelve years up to fifteen.

Homerooms had wooden floors and tables and chairs for eight persons per table. There was one large cupboard in one corner with shelves. One of these shelves was a spot for every girl, about one foot wide and two feet deep, to keep their schoolbooks, knitting and sewing baskets. There was also a black, pot-bellied stove to heat the room in winter, a bookcase and another cabinet containing some candies, medicine, etc. The latter was always locked.

Both sides of the room had large windows, one side faced the back yard, the other, the hallway. No privacy there.

The beds we slept in on the 3rd floor were referred to as "cigar boxes." They were narrow, wooden structures with half moons cut out of the sides to get in and out of bed. When lying down you couldn't see anything but the ceiling, some part of the wall and the inside of the bed.

Talking to your neighbour was not allowed, and quite impossible as long as Sister was up sitting in her chair, since your head would pop up to do so and you'd get a warning. The bottom of these beds had wooded boards and a straw mattress on it; something we'd sink right into. A little sticky in summer but nice and warm in winter. Sometimes a straw would poke through the cover and prick your skin.

The floors were wood also, knots and all poking up here and there. Rather unpleasant for evening prayers on the knees by your bed before teeth brushing etc. Following evening prayers, dear Sister always added a sermon mentioning (without names) all our sins and trespasses of that day; this seemed like eternity with knobby knees on knobby floors. Often Sister-dearest would scare the liver out of us by saying something like: "I hope and pray God will not take your soul tonight for you're sure to go to purgatory or worse." This worked very well for the girls who'd not confessed to whatever they'd done wrong that day. They couldn't sleep out of sheer fright of being struck down dead during the night and eventually would knock on Sister's door shaking and blubbering to confess.

At the far end of the dorm was a double bathroom with a partition wall between for privacy. Having a bath was a once-in-a-while happening with just enough warm water in the tub to cover the thighs.

Our daily ablutions consisted of standing in front of a bowl of cold water and washing face, arms and neck with a cloth. Before sprouting breasts, we also stripped down to our panties and washed our torso as well. Nudity never took place in full view; we always wore undies and at night p.j.'s on top.

Washing hair took place now and then, with many girls hanging their head over the same tub of water.

Summer weather in Holland was always moderately cool and comfortable around 70 degrees Fahrenheit. Winters were quite damp and cold with the always-present wind blowing off the North Sea. Our dorm windows were open year round and if you were the unlucky stiff straight across from one (I was), you'd wake up many times during the night, shivering. There were never enough blankets on the bed but we were allowed woollen bed socks. Without them you'd pop into bed and rub your legs back and forth to warm up the icy cold sheets. We were certainly not coddled in that place.

Most of us decided to become nuns since we already lived like one and considered ourselves well trained for it, if not for all the prayers alone. Our wake-up call by Sister was a prayer; she'd start: "In the name of the Father," right then you'd get up and answer her with: "and the Son and the Holy Ghost, amen." If you didn't, you had to do it all over again by yourself out loud.

Before breakfast we always always went to mass at the church, prayed before and after each meal, before and after each school session, in the chapel before bed and then once again on our knees in the dorm before sleep. That's 14 prayers per day! Prayers like that are meaningless, mind-numbing mumblings, habitual routine, no more.

After our morning prayer and a quick wash and dress, we marched off to mass at the church. A couple of girls always fainted while on their knees in church on an empty stomach, especially when the priest was swinging the incense burner – "in the name of the Father, the Son, and the Holy Ghost." These girls were allowed to sit down, but not until their faces turned ashen. I tried to look ashen just to get off my knees, but never mastered that so far. After church, we went back to our homeroom for breakfast. On tin plates there'd be two slices of bread with "scraped on" margarine and on one, a slice of cheese or a gob of peanut butter. Sticks to the ribs, see? In a tin cup we'd have weak tea with milk, no sugar. We were never hungry; Sister would come around a few more times with bread and tea. Lunch was our hot meal for the day; lots of potatoes with gravy, some veggies and, by Jove, sometimes a meatball. Porridge for dessert to fill us up. Supper; same as breakfast. Fruit was available only when a local farmer donated a bushel of apples or pears.

Candies donated from home were locked away in a cupboard with our name on the container. Every Sunday we all received a few. Mid-week there'd be another couple of candies handed out, but this time *only* to the girls who were good and well behaved. I was outta luck there.

I was definitely a rebel; mouthy, clowning around by making rude and crude noises during quiet times, for example, during meals, in the hallway on the way to church etc. The girls nearest me would burst out into helpless, hysterical, rip-snorting laughter, trying very hard not to make noise, tears streaming down their convulsed faces, some of them choking into their scarves or other. Some had the misfortune of audibly passing wind. Well, that was really rewarding. My younger sister would find out and come to me crying, "what did you do this time?" I wasn't always caught but nobody ever snitched on me, because we were having too much fun.

In hindsight, it must have kept me sane, for these five years in there seemed like eternity with some of their ridiculous rules, regulations and incredibly monotonous routines.

After breakfast, we were allowed to play outside until the school bell rang, except when it was your turn to wash or dry the dishes and sweep the floor after meals. After lunch, we all went down to the cellar and sat on wooden benches on both sides of a long trough full of potatoes. Sister would tell us stories from a book while we peeled potatoes, nice and thin or else the peels would be served to you the next meal. That was pretty disgusting to us then. Nowadays people *pay* to eat them 'skins' in a restaurant! I remember once having to do an enormous mountain of potatoes all alone in the cellar for being mouthy again. I think I drove all the sisters to drink with my shenanigans.

After supper, we'd play outside until dark, then go inside to knit, repair clothes, darn socks, do homework or other. Pleasure reading was allowed on Sundays only. It was the same with board games or any other leisure time activities. All our mail and books, coming and going, were censured. There was no radio, no newspapers or magazines from the outside that came our way (bad influence). We were not allowed to whistle or to sing pop music we'd hear at home during the holidays; "they were full of silly notions and may give us bad ideas."

Saturday was "cleaning day." The tiled floors throughout the buildings' lower level were scrubbed with cold soapy water and long-handled brushes, then rinsed and dried with a heavy, rough cloth. That was backbreaking work. Schoolrooms were dusted and mopped, windows washed and polished, toilets scrubbed etc. Any work done with water was always a chilly one, since there was no hot running water. In the wintertime, it was awful and chill blains on both hands and feet were common.

During the week I remember helping the sisters with their ironing; great big nightgown-like undergarments the sisters wore and the collars and cuffs were starched as stiff as cardboard. In summer, that "ironing room" became as hot as a sauna, leaving us all red-faced and wringing wet.

Sunday, after High Mass with all the Latin chants, lots of incense burning and fainting girls, we'd have breakfast and then had free time to play with dolls, board games (never cards!) or read the same old books again.

I had started to write stories for my friends, mostly about castles with secret passageways and other kinds of mystery stories. I often used to put together a little skit or copy a play I had seen in school or other and was director, producer and all. When there were special occasions coming up like Christmas or Easter, one of the sisters would have a play for us to put on and I was right in there. Same with the choir or folk dancing. Anything to break the monotony and to act out.

After Sunday's lunch, parents were allowed to come for a visit. I believe it was once a month. For most parents it would be a long trip by train and/or bus. Our visitors would be ushered into a special visitor's room and the sister in charge would come in to call out your name. The minute this sister walked into our room we'd all stop dead in our tracks hoping the call was for us. With our visitors, we were allowed outside the convent and often went to a nearby coffeehouse that had tasty snacks and a children's gym outside. Heavenly!

The rest of the girls, who didn't have visitors that Sunday went with two sisters for a long walk, weather permitting. We walked two by two with a sister at the front and one at the back. It always reminded me of a gaggle of ducks waddling to the pond.

At the end of our stay in the convent, it was time to go back home for good. We were in for a rude awakening to the real world. Going back to the city of Amsterdam at 15 and going to work full time was tough. You could say we were in shock, scared and numb for a while. Often my sister and I cried during these lonely evenings when mom had gone to work. We missed our little friends and the protective security of what was to us "family" for five years. It had left us very naïve, vulnerable and not at all experienced or worldwise.

But, over time we did adjust and became more and more independent and self-sufficient.

EXPERIENCES OF WAR

Bernard Sutton
Buckinghamshire, England

The following is an excerpt from my Uncle "Bun's" autobiography. I rarely saw him when I was a child growing up in England and Canada because he traveled so much. Following his retirement, he and my Aunt Betty settled in a small village in Buckinghamshire. Following my Aunt Betty's death in 1996, he began to look for 'a project.' We suggested that he get a computer, which he promptly did – through the mail. Because he had always told such interesting stories about his life, and because he was our mother's only brother, we suggested that he begin to write them down – for my children and for my nephews

Within a year he had mastered the computer and most of his memoirs - with many transatlantic phone and email conversations. The next few pages are from Chapter 2: Experiences of War.

Ann Kinmonth

The three years 1941 to 1943 were a strange mixture. I was part civilian and part serviceman. I seemed to be forever charging from one thing to another. Perhaps it was just as well, since death and destruction were a daily occurrence and it did not give me time to think about it. We still contrived to keep our music band together and now we were in much demand. People wanted to dance the night away in an effort to forget the war for a short time.

In June of 1942, the War Office 'offered me a post in the Royal Signals.' I shall never forget that phrase; I have often wondered what would have happened if I had said no thanks. So it was that I arrived at Catterick Camp in Yorkshire carrying my suitcase and seeing for the first time the enormous notice "The only good German is a dead German." This was a basic training infantry unit and I was to start training to kill Germans. It soon became obvious to the powers that be that I wasn't going to be very good at it. The main purpose of this training unit was to instill blind obedience into every soldier. To this end, the senior N.C.O.s treated the conscripts with contempt; the Commissioned ranks treated us as the lowest form of life on the planet. The need for blind obedience became apparent to me in 1944 during the Normandy campaign. I witnessed on one occasion, (when I was at a battalion HQ), three dead infantrymen being carried back on stretchers from a forward post. They had been killed by mortar fire, which was still continuing. The sergeant major yelled to three men to replace them. They went forward immediately, without a moment's hesitation.

I endured 6 weeks of this training, which included assault courses, route marches, and other fiendish methods designed to destroy one's spirit entirely. Sneers and insults from the N.C.O.'s accompanied the whole nightmare. We would much rather have killed the N.C.O.'s than the Germans. However, at the end of it, I was 10 pounds heavier and so fit that I felt that I could have done anything. It was at this point that I was transferred to the Royal Corps of Signals – a rather splendid title – and life became much more civilized. Instead of looking like a bag of potatoes, I could dress in a uniform, which fitted and had been pressed. We still slept on the floor, but you can't have everything.

They still paraded us each day – to show who was boss – and on one of these occasions, my name and number was yelled to nobody in particular and I 'fell out' to report to the orderly room. This was how I received news of my mother's (your grandmother's) death. The whole thing was so cold-blooded that it seemed unreal. They gave me a railway warrant and told me to go home for a week. If I required more leave I was to let them know. Betty, whom I had only known for a very brief period before reporting for duty, met me. The whole thing seemed like a dream, and I really cannot remember the funeral. I do remember it was delayed and that I would require more leave. I notified the commanding officer as required in order to attend the funeral. After it was all over, Betty and I went out one evening to try and restore some semblance of normality. As we strolled along in the city, we looked for somewhere to sit and have coffee. There didn't appear to be anywhere. I suggested that there would be coffee on a railway platform so off we went – it was not a good idea – Military police were everywhere and my pass was overdue. I tried to explain to them, but they were not interested. The result was that I was locked up for the night and Betty went home alone. They put me in a civilian prison, which was quite appalling. In fact, looking back, it was a disgrace for a so-called civilized country. I picked up the blanket with thumb and forefinger and placed it as far away from me as possible. I could still smell it, and it made me ill. I tried to explain about my mother, but no one was interested. Breakfast consisted of a slice of bread and margarine and a mug of cocoa with no milk or sugar. I tried again to explain about my mother and they said that they would ring my unit in due course. About midday, the warder said to me "Come on, you have been a good lad." I wish I could have strangled him.

I returned to my unit, and found that I was now a member of the 11th armoured Corps, a new unit that was evidently destined to be part of the invasion of Europe (in due course). I was taught how to read Morse and other signaling techniques. Leave consisted of rather frantic 36-hour or, if lucky, 48-hour passes. After various moves around the country, my unit eventually settled in a small country town called Swaffham, in Norfolk. Betty and I managed to see each other on these frantic weekend passes and finally, in August 1943, married (on another rather frantic few days leave). A sort of ceremony was possible; we married with a special license (7s/6p) and I returned to my unit after about three days.

The remainder of 1943 was rather bleak. Army life was tough but certainly challenging. The plus side was the comradeship, which developed when we were all struggling to cope. Some men enjoyed the life, but I cannot say that it was my 'scene.' Blind obedience, with no opportunities to use initiative, is not my idea of living.

I can't remember much of the early part of 1944, except that it was the army at war and consequently not particularly pleasant. There was training, strict discipline, and American 'K' rations, which were a typical bit of American ingenuity. For example, their bacon and egg in a tin was a remarkable concoction; it looked terrible but tasted exactly like bacon and egg. And the rain - it rained and it rained, except for May, which was a beautiful month. We were, of course, constantly on some form of exercise. On one occasion the whole affair became a shambles; whole units were lost, with a breakdown of communications. At one point, I found myself in the middle of nowhere in particular looking for somewhere to sleep. I eventually found a farmhouse and noticed a small outbuilding and wondered if I could find a corner without anyone worrying, but decided to enquire at the house. They invited me in and asked if I knew where I was. When I told them that I was lost, they sat me down and gave me a meal. When I asked if I could sleep in their outbuildings they laughed and showed me up to a spare bedroom - What luxury! The next thing I knew, someone was knocking on the door. I was given breakfast and the morning newspaper and eventually made my way out in search of the army. In due course an 11th corps truck appeared on the scene and took me to an assembly area where lads from all parts of the corps were to be found. In June we were transported to the south coast to a gigantic assembly area and, of course, it was raining. There was never enough shelter, although no one ever became ill. We were all far too fit for that. But one day, someone came along who seemed to know what he was doing - a Captain Nixon - whose job appeared to be to organize 'this lot' and somehow get it across the English Channel. I was allocated a place in a local command vehicle and in the black of night, we found ourselves together with numerous other military vehicles in an American LST (Landing Ship Tank).

The ship gradually inched its way out of the harbour (I learned later that it was Southampton) into the English Channel. It moved very slowly. It soon became apparent why; the harbour was so crowded that there were times when we were so close to other craft that it almost seemed as if we could have reached out and touched them. Eventually the ship began to roll, and as we increased speed, it soon began to pitch. I hoped that my companions were good seamen - in such a confined space. The seats in the LCV (Local Command Vehicle) were quite comfortable and we were soon asleep.

Some hours later, we were aware of a new sound - the clatter of mess tins with an American voice shouting, "chow." We lined up for breakfast, and to our surprise, in the grey of very early dawn, we were each given a TRAY - YES, a TRAY! And SERVED orange juice, a "cookie" and cooked tomato and bacon (can you imagine!). I was so pleased to be on an American ship.

There was no evidence of enemy action, but we took nearly 24 hours to cross the Channel. I was able to examine the radio equipment in some detail. It was a typical 'intercept lay-out' and I was quite familiar with it all from earlier training. Each table contained signal pads, logs and a list of radio frequencies to monitor.

The sea was full of ships of all kinds, all heading one way, and surprisingly, moving very slowly. The bombardment from battleships, which had been going on all night continued, with each of the huge shells sounding like an express train overhead. The damage they caused on shore was incredible, and not just to enemy gun emplacements, as we were to find out later. Everything from the beach to about 10 miles inland was smashed to bits and any cattle were slaughtered.

The landing craft ground to a halt on the beach and the whole of the bow of the ship was gradually lowered. The vehicles trundled on to the beach. We didn't even get wet, let alone shot at. It was difficult to believe that the initial assault had only been four days before. The whole operation was conducted with military precision (a far cry from the chaos we had been told to expect). My vehicle was directed to a point just off the beach, and there we stayed. What did we do? We made tea - what else!! It was now getting quite dark so we ate some of our rations and prepared to get some sleep. But not for long. Suddenly the whole place erupted with a mass of anti-aircraft guns hurling shells into the air and the German air force appeared. One plane dropped one bomb, but we were in far more danger of shrapnel from our own shells than from the enemy. Nothing else happened that night, and in the morning we were moved inland in convoy, moving through country lanes devastated by shellfire. Our infantry were in more danger from French snipers using shotguns than we were from the enemy at that time. The French hated us for what we had done to their farms and animals - and who can blame them? They didn't understand; they were just farmers.

Divisional headquarters was set up and we were all sited to the best advantage. It soon became apparent that our forward units had no idea of security. The company and battalion offices used the radio like a telephone. I made one entry in the log where a Brigade Major started talking about "the 43rd Division on our left"! It was difficult to understand how they could be so ignorant of the need for security. In spite of this, however, the Germans soon dispelled the idea that this was going to be a 'piece of cake.' They brought up the 21st Panzer division and then the 'fun' started.

Communications were soon a major problem, with telephone lines being destroyed almost as fast as they were repaired. As well, two of our radio jeeps were lost. The security vehicles were disbanded and the operators sent to Brigade and Battalion Headquarters to restore communications. I was sent to the 46th Brigade HQ and then on to the Seaforths Battalion HQ that I was told was "just over the hill." But it wasn't. All I found was a long trench with a number of machine guns and the gunners almost shoulder to shoulder. I asked for HQ and was told, "This is it." I then 'acquired' a Colonel who started directing me all over the place. Like so many, he had no idea about the radio and blamed me when it did not work, because he had not made the necessary switch. He was a fearless character and I soon began to regret having 'found' him. He eventually established HQ in a barn, but again there was trouble because the barn was a perfect screen, making the radio useless (my fault of course). The Colonel then decided to use runners between HQ and the forward units. When one of these came back with a message, saying, "I don't want to go back there sir," the Colonel told him to take a rest in the corner of the barn - much to my surprise. Just then tank shells blew the top off the barn and it became obvious why the Colonel had taken no action - the Sergeant Major was shaking with fear and completely out of control (the man responsible for discipline). All the Colonel had to say was "Demm those tanks." We eventually extricated ourselves - I don't quite know how - and in due course I sort of became the O/IC's driver/operator who liked to do a reconnaissance every morning at 4 am. I acquired a thermos from somewhere and the cook filled it each morning with something hot (I don't know what). It seemed as if the Colonel thought he was playing chess. He directed me into the most impossible situations quite fearlessly. All I wanted to do was crawl under the seat. I learned later that he was a professional soldier (ex Sandhurst) and that explained a lot.

The next two months were as near to hell on earth as it is possible to be; three great armies, British, American and German, all refusing to give ground. But eventually, the entire German 5th army were surrounded at

Falaise and pounded to bits by the air force. During this time, I was at the 46th infantry brigade HQ and at one point, enemy mortar shells were landing in the compound. At the time, I was operating the radio in the command vehicle and shrapnel somehow came from under the vehicle and through the brigade major's seat, then through the roof. "I've been hit! I've been hit!" the brigade major yelled. But he hadn't. His assistant, a dainty captain who wore a fur collar and insisted on having his meals off a plate, just stared at him with disdain.

Once during a lull, a captured German SS officer could be seen ambling about HQ looking with disgust at 'this rabble' that had had the audacity to capture him. In all this mud and general mess he was immaculately 'turned out,' with his jackboots gleaming. But, obviously, he was not as free as he appeared to be.

Another memory I have, is of walking along a country road on my 21st birthday thinking, "I hope my 22nd is better than this." But I can't remember where I was going.

We moved through Belgium quite rapidly, our main enemy being the weather. I traveled in the command vehicle keeping radio contact with other command vehicles. The supposed encoding system was so obvious, like having elephants for tanks. But the Germans were nowhere to be found. We eventually attempted to support 30 corps in their efforts to get to Arnheim, but like them, we spent most of the time digging ourselves out of the mud (nothing whatever like the film). But after the Americans captured the Eindhoven and Nijmegen bridges, the Germans beat a hasty retreat and we settled down near the banks of the Maas. Food was poor at this time but we managed. The 51st division then left us and we learned that the Germans had made a massive attempt to break through the American lines in the south and reach the river Meuse. Fortunately for us all, they ran out of fuel and like their 5th army earlier, were pounded to bits by the airforce. The war seemed to fizzle out then. The army set up a film unit at Nijmegen and I went to the pictures (the movies). Throughout all this we had a mixed reception from the civilian population. The French were hostile, the Belgians mixed, some friendly, others aloof, but the Dutch friendliness was overwhelming. They insisted in sharing what little food they had with us and made us very welcome in their homes even though many had had their homes damaged by us in the fighting.

And, of course, throughout all of this, the thing that really mattered was letters from home and Betty (my wife, your aunt) never let me down, although (as I learned later) she was having a very bad time herself. So that was the end of 1944. A traumatic time, but also an experience/adventure I shall never forget.

In the New Year we spent most of our time trying to keep warm and existing on very meagre rations. We crossed the Rhine by TRAIN on what appeared to be a Bailey bridge. These bridges are normally used by assault troops, so we all sat there with our fingers crossed. The train moved at about one mile an hour but we eventually made it to the other side. I suppose the army reasoned that if the bridge could withstand armoured vehicles and tanks it would be ok, but I suspect that the engineers were standing there with their eyes closed.

After the German defeat in the Ardennes it seemed that the war was virtually over and we settled down to a daily routine. We had an ingenious cook who had 'found' an enormous cooking pot and had thrown everything he could 'find' into it. We began to enjoy quite delicious stews but did not enquire too closely as to the contents.

We had in fact become complacent - the Germans were not going to just lie down and die, although it must have become evident by now that they could not possibly win. One day they appeared to assemble all the fighter planes they could find and attacked our landing strips. We were caught off guard and we learned later that a great number of supply planes had been destroyed on the ground.

The enemy left snipers behind and on one occasion our convoy was attacked by a group using a 'Bazooka.' One of these missiles hit a scout car and decapitated the driver - which sort of held us up for a bit. The snipers were very difficult to cope with since once they had claimed a victim, they immediately changed position.

Another episode, which stands out in my mind, was the sudden appearance of an ME 262, a jet-propelled fighter/bomber which the enemy had recently brought into service for the first time. It whistled over our positions near a crossroads, dropped one bomb and then vanished at high speed.   About 15 minutes later, a squadron of American thunderbolt fighters (traditional piston engine planes) trundled across the sky in the direction of the enemy plane without a hope of catching it.

By March, the German troops were surrendering in droves - just appearing from woods and farmhouses with their hands up. We had the job of searching them for weapons - not a very pleasant job. We were surprised to find so many Russians amongst them. One of our officers spoke fluent German but found that these Russians and other non-German troops didn't understand him. We supposed that they were just being used as a rearguard and in any event preferred the army to slave labour. The Russians, in particular, were dejected and had obviously been badly treated. Very few German civilians could be found. Those we did see were surprised that we were on their side of the Rheine.

We had only one more military confrontation - it could hardly be called a battle - when some fanatical SS troops tried to hold us up in a village on the main road. They had to be forced out of every building before retreating. We then found that they had a flame-thrower, which they used in an attempt to stop our advance. The result was that the whole village was destroyed.

When we reached Hamburg, we found the city completely destroyed and crosses stuck into piles of rubble where it seems that families had died in the air bombardment.

We saw a deserted concentration camp. The main gates were open and a scene of total devastation inside. I always remember this when later German civilians denied all knowledge of the camps.

Finally, we reached Lubeck on the Baltic coast. When we entered the city, every building had a Russian soldier at attention outside it. They conspicuously ignored us. It soon became apparent that they had taken the city and had no intention of leaving, so that night, we quietly disappeared.

Shortly after this, we were told that home leave was being organized. The war in Europe was over, but to us it was just another day. We did not feel like celebrating amongst the ruins. In due course, we were put aboard 3-ton trucks and started on the long journey to the channel coast. Upon arrival, we found ourselves in Ostend, which appeared to have been untouched by war. I remember strolling along the glorious beach and telling myself that one day I would return for a holiday.

We had a very pleasant journey across the channel where we were moved to a staging camp and given new uniforms and equipment. I had my better battle dress tailored to fit me (for a few shillings). I then bought all the trimmings like lanyard, badges, shoulder flashes etc. and went home on leave for three weeks.

Love to all,

Uncle

THE WEE ONE

Margaret Westhouse
Hamilton, Ontario

So delicate and fair,
The picture of serenity.
Sleep my pretty one,
Without a care.
Mommy and Daddy are here,
To answer your every need.

Welcome to our families,
Aunts, cousins, uncles, grandparents
Waited for your arrival.
At last you've come!
Expanding our family circle once more,
Giving us all another member to love!

NIGHTMARE

Inge Moll
Ancaster, Ontario

To: Aaron, The Magnificent and Alexander, The Great.

The following story happened in Holland, during W.W. II, 1944. Even though your great-grandmother, Paula Theunisz-Glatzel was German, she and your great-grandfather Joseph Theunisz, were part of the Dutch Underground. Jewish people and deserters from the German army were helped to escape from the Nazi's. Our house always had strangers staying there. Sometimes for a very short time, sometimes for days. My parents had a store, selling and repairing radios and all kinds of electrical appliances.

*   *   *   *

Suddenly, the little girl was awake, fully awake. She threw back the top of her comforter and the coldness of mid-winter hit her face. Her room was dark. Only the light of the moon shone through a slit in the small ice-covered window. She could see her breath turning to mist and floating away. The hollow in her bed was damp, warm and comfortable. She wanted to stay and drift back to dreamland.

Sounds in the house. Muffled footsteps, running down stairs. Mother whispering, "Gott, oh mein Gott." Calming sounds from father. Click of a lock, squeak of a door. More muffled sounds. Another click. Dead silence, eerie stillness.

Then there was noise; harsh voices, yelling, hurried feet, running in the street, three stories below. Dogs barking. Soldiers shouting. Hard boots with steel-covered toes and soles, echoing loudly. Running, over cobbled stone. Pounding on doors. "Nein, nicht hier," "muss doch, kann nicht." Conferencing. "Wo kann er . . . los!" Whistles, shrill, fear!

She slid out of bed, barefoot, icy-cold floor, shivering in her flannel nightgown, whimpering softly, "Mommy." In the dark, sliding down the stairs, pausing, shivering. Soft noises below, "Mommy?"

More loud noises, door-slamming, more yelling. Lights on full in the store, blinding lights. Father, frozen – unreal, behind the open L-shaped counter, facing the store entrance. A young hard-faced soldier square in the doorway, with two German Shepherds, pulling and sniffing, sniffing and pulling hard on the leash. "Ruhig!, wo ist er, wo, hier?"

Feet and shoes, sticking out from the back of the counter, next to father. Deadly-pale mother, with a little girl clutching her, silently watching the scene from the side-door, seeing the soldier, dogs and feet . . .

Voice from outside. "Wir haben sie, kommt!" At once, soldier and dogs are gone.

Note: My parents and I would have been shot, if the person inside the sales counter (storage for wrapping paper etc.) would have been discovered. My parents greatest fear was, that the little girl (me) would have said something. My mother always thought that she was going to have a heart attack, she was so afraid.

YOUR HERITAGE

Ethel V. Allen Hogg
Burlington, Ontario

To my grandchildren: Kaila, Jayme and David

I think that most of us during our lifetime wonder about our roots. We are curious about our ancestors, and from which set of parents we inherited certain traits, and sets of values. We know certain ones are learned, as it has been said, "we live what we learn." However, we know that many traits are passed on through the genes, as the DNA sets the complete pattern for every organ, and every physical feature in our body. We look around us, and wonder why some people suffer so many tragedies in their lifetime, and others seem to have received so much blessing. We as a family, for the past generations, seem to fall into the last category, as the Lord has truly blessed us as a family down through the years. This summer, while I was in Nova Scotia, I was doing a little research on my family tree, as I have become very interested in tracing my roots. I would like to share one of my findings with you, my beloved grandchildren. Many times I wish my parents had told me more about my forebears. I realize they were busy providing for their family, and then we, the younger generation, didn't show much interest, because we were too busy in our own little world.

I was reading a book titled *The Chignecto Isthmus and its First Settlers*, by Howard Truman. I had already known that my father, William Burton Allen, was a descendent of the Empire Loyalists, who came to the Maritimes in 1783 and 1784 from New England. They were driven out, without the choice of remaining, because of their loyalty to the Crown. They were said to be the right stamp of men, and have left their impress on the Province by the sea. They were a superior class of men, industrious, hardy, resourceful, and, above all, Godly men. It has been said that they were made of the right material, to form the groundwork of prosperous communities, and wherever this element predominated, it was a guarantee that justice and order would be maintained. Honesty and fixedness of principal made for righteousness, wherever they were found. They would certainly need all of the above characteristics to survive the hardships of the Pioneers in Nova Scotia, and what is now known as New Brunswick.

The work ethic was engrained in all of us down through the generations. You worked hard, shared what you had, not only with your friends, but the less fortunate (they were known as hobos when I was growing up). We never spoke ill of our neighbour, trusted everyone, and things haven't changed that much even today. Maybe that is why Nova Scotia is known as one of the friendliest places in the world to visit, or live. Many people are very proud that they are descendents of the Empire Loyalists. Once you prove it, you can get a little brass plaque to put on your tombstone. This never interested me very much, but your grandfather often teases me about getting my little plaque in place.

When I read excerpts from *The Chignecto Isthmus*, I learned that my other great-great-great-great-great-grandfather was one of the first Yorkshire settlers to emigrate to Canada, in 1772. His name was William Wells, and lived at Point de Bute, New Brunswick, formally part of Nova Scotia. The author said, "there is no question whatever, as to the value to Eastern Canada of this emigration of God-fearing, loyal, industrious, and progressive Yorkshiremen. They have been useful citizens, as contributing as they did, to the solid foundation of the upbuilding of a great people. These pioneers left so rich a heritage to their descendents."

This, my dear grandchildren, is a rich heritage indeed. However, I discovered you have a far richer heritage than that, your Christian heritage (I am speaking of what God calls a Christian, not nominal Christianity that we talk about today) which dates back to at least your great-great-great-great-great-great-great-Grandfather. William Wells was known as a Godly man, and a real man of prayer. The Bible says that God will bless, down to the third and fourth generation, and I think we are reaping the blessing of the prayers of that man of God, until this present day. I know that my grandmother, along with my parents, prayed for me. Their prayers were that I might come to know Christ as my Saviour, and honour Him in all my ways. It is not that I don't pray for good health, and success in your endeavors, but it is not the number one priority on my list. My prayer for you is that you may become part of the family of God, by accepting Christ as your Saviour when you are young, and go on to serve Him all the days of your lives.

John Wesley was an ordained minister in one of the Main Line Churches in England, but it was when he realized the value of the sacrifice of Christ that his life work really began. He wrote that beautiful hymn, "Amazing Love." The first verse shows his appreciation for what Christ had done for him, and I quote,

> "And can it be that I should gain,
> an interest in the Saviour's blood?
> Died He for me, who caused His pain?
> For me, who Him to death Pursued?
> Amazing love! How can it be,
> that thou, my God should Die for me?"

> One of the lines in the fourth verse says,
> "My chains fell off, my heart was Free,
> I rose, went forth, and followed Thee."

William Wells married Margaret Dobson, and they were among the first of his converts. I'm sure William and Margaret could say "Amen" to the truth contained in the above hymn, as they travelled around preaching the Gospel in all the surrounding areas. It was because they were so methodical in trying to reach every area that they came known as Methodists. William Wells built the first Methodist church in Thirst, England, and he built the first Methodist church in Canada, which was at Point de Bute, New Brunswick. Previous to William and Margaret's departure for America, John Wesley knelt in prayer with them, and placing his hands on their heads, commending them to God's Divine Protection. William led a class in his own house, at Point de Bute, frequently conducted public services, and performed burial services in the absence of the minister. The power of his exhortations and fervency of his prayers are

well described by the first provincial itinerant, and in his narrative of his own conversation. He died in peace in 1819.
(Excerpts from: *History of the Methodist Church*)

I want to be faithful to the legacy that was passed on to me, and I now pass it on to you, which is your rightful heritage. However, your most important inheritance will be when you make Christ the center of your life. It is then, and only then, that you become partakers of the inheritance in Christ. The following Hymn written by John Gowans, is my prayer for you.

WHAT SHALL I ASK FOR YOU

What shall I ask for you, what shall I pray?
Speaking to God for you, what shall I say?
Shall I ask influence, Shall I ask wealth?
Shall I ask happiness, Harmony, and health?

This I will ask for you: God, grant each day,
Wisdom to know His will, and grace to obey.

If I could see for you, what lies ahead?
What you should greet with joy, what you should dread;
I'd bridge the stream for you, fence every height,
Life would be beautiful, burdensless, and bright;
What ever the future holds, this is my prayer:
God who is with you here, Be with you there

This I ask of for you: God, grant each day,
Wisdom to know His will, and grace to obey.

GRANDMA'S SCHOOL YEARS

Palm Roberts
Stoney Creek, Ontario

To my grandchildren Amy, Katie, Paul, Joseph, Genny, Maria, Susan, Brian, Patrick, and Evan

During my many years at school, I have had a variety of teachers. Some I liked and would eagerly work for and others I would only work for out of fear, some teachers I didn't appreciate until much later in my life, when their words of wisdom made sense to me.

I attended private Notre Dame Convent in Glasgow, Scotland. My father had been killed in a car accident and the insurance paid for my education. As I look back, my brother Billy should have received these benefits. He was nine years older and smarter. He insisted on leaving St. Aloysius College, to help support the family. Someone should have taken time to explain to him the necessity and importance of a good education and not accepted the noble gesture of a fourteen-year-old grief stricken schoolboy. However, who thinks clearly when there is tragedy in your life - another lesson I have learned.

Notre Dame teachers taught the Madame Montessori method for our first 3 or 5 years. We started at four years old and finished junior school seven years later.

The headmistress of the Montessori school was Sister Thérèse Bernard SND, a tiny wee lady with horned-rim glasses and dark brown hair that peered at you from under her habit. Of course we never knew the colour of her hair. At first sign she appeared to be insignificant, with no personality, but believe me when you lived under her rules she was every inch the Headmistress of this progressive school.

She was in fact the kindest and most understanding woman I have ever known. She treated her students with respect and therefore received the same in return tenfold. Sister Thérèse was firm. The school rules had to be obeyed. On occasion she would turn a blind eye, when she felt her silence would be more effective than more words.

I spent quite a few hours in her room and tidying her library as a form of punishment. Her quiet voice always got my attention. She never judged me and took time to talk with me, always looking straight into my eyes.

No one told me my father had died, and I could not understand why he wasn't coming home. My behaviour changed and I became restless and rebellious at home and in school.

The classroom teacher meted out the punishment and you were only sent to the Headmistress room if she couldn't handle the situation.

Sister Thérèse always talked with you and allowed you to explain your actions. She listened and explained why the behaviour was not acceptable, the discussion ended with a punishment. She punished wisely. I used to feel that my behaviour had let her down. This was probably the beginning of my many guilt trips. Not that she imposed guilt; I just didn't want to lose her trust. She always gave you faith in your own capabilities.

I remember once kneeling in the hall, outside the classroom, where I spent a great deal of my time. She was busy bustling back and forth and ignored me. She knew kneeling there, for everyone to see, was enough humiliation.

Many a time she came to my rescue. I had an English teacher in highschool, Sister Aloyuise, who was not tolerant of my behaviour, and I still believe 'pushed my buttons.'

Once during an English exam my inkwell was dry, and she refused to have it filled. I sat for a while, then got up, and went to her desk. When she saw me approaching she lifted the lid of her desk, put her head inside, and ignored me. I felt I had done no wrong, so I took the lid of her desk from her, she looked up, I slammed the lid down and demanded ink, then proceeded to walk out of the classroom.

It was unacceptable behaviour, but it was the only way at the time I knew how to deal with the humiliation of being ignored and denied the right to finish my exam. The penalty was heavy. My high school Headmistress Sister Marie Anthony suspended me for several days with a warning I could be expelled.

The only person who took time to explain my inappropriate behaviour was Sister Thérèse. She made me understand that it was not acceptable for a young lady and gave me alternate methods of dealing with frustrating situations. I was then able to understand how badly I had behaved. Sister Thérèse knew her students individually.

Whenever I came back to Glasgow on vacation, I always went to visit. On one of these visits she was ill. I was allowed to go to her room. We were talking and her book dropped from her bed. I immediately took responsibility for the accident and apologized, even though I had nothing to do with the fall. Her response was, "Are you still apologizing for incidents that are not your fault?" Once again she made me aware of myself.

In later life she was made 'front door portress' i.e. she answered the convent door to visitors - a post she accepted with humility and dignity. Everyone, who came in contact with her loved, respected and admired her strength and her ability to get her message of love across. Her favourite saints were St. Theresa of Avalon and St. Francis of Assisi.

I loved her and made her a part of many events in my adult life. After my marriage ceremony, still wearing my wedding dress, I took my bridal bouquet to her. We placed them on the altar of the convent chapel. Every birth, I sent pictures and an update of the children and what was happening in my life in Canada. We wrote long letters every Christmas. How she remembered us all was part of her uniqueness.

After her death, a Glasgow newspaper wrote a long article about this great little Sister of Notre Dame who was a pioneer in the field of education. Although I was not surprised at what she had achieved in the educational field and the many honours that had been bestowed upon her, I was awed at her humility and her unassuming ways.

A kind, wonderful, generous woman who knew how to give love and dignity to all who knew her, and I hope my grandchildren will have the opportunity to meet, respect and have such a role model as Sister Thérèse Bérnard SND.

MY ELEMENTARY EDUCATION

Raoul R. Bouchard
Ancaster, Ontario

Dear Dennis,

As we have discussed often in our conversations, the chance to learn is one of the greatest privileges in life. Here is the story of my early education, which stimulated a lifelong curiosity to learn more. I am so pleased to see this trait in you and all my other grandchildren.
Love, Grandpa

*   *   *   *

My parents became homesteaders in the hinterland of Quebec. On our concession, children up to ten years old had never seen the inside of a schoolhouse. The year I was four years old, a one-room schoolhouse was opened and my Aunt Lydia was hired to teach for one year. Since I could read better than my older brothers, the three of us were enrolled.

The next year my family moved to a farm close to the U.S./Canadian border. We belonged to the parish and school system of Stanhope, Quebec. Seven miles away were the church, convent and small village of twenty families right on the Vermont border. The whole parish consisted of about sixty families of Catholic French-Canadians who had about thirty families of Protestant Anglophones as close neighbors.

I was enrolled in the nearest school, the always reliable one-room schoolhouse with five full grades. I was brought down one grade because, in the days before radio and TV, every time you crossed a stream or a range of mountains, you heard a different dialect of French, and, after all, we came from three hundred miles away. So, I was an alien, a new immigrant who had never heard of English.

All my early teachers were seventeen-year-olds, fresh out of Normal School. They delighted in a bright, very inquisitive pupil and trotted out their advanced books for me. I had much leisure to listen to all

139

the grades reciting. I soon became an excellent speller in both languages and more inquisitive than ever of all the ideas bandied about. As for pronunciation, I learned English by very strict French-Canadian rules that are still with me today.

The Pastor, Father L'Heureux, was also a member of the School Board. As he was greatly interested in the schools and had the leisure, he was a frequent visitor to the four schoolhouses of his widely scattered parish. In my one-room school house we had twenty-three students spread over five grades, plus two in sixth grade. In the grading system, out of a hundred points, there were thirty points for attentiveness, neatness and deportment. I often missed many of the thirty points while my rival, a good female student, invariably earned them all and once in a while ranked above me. In an effort to hold me below the boiling point, my devoted teacher threw at me all the extra material she could gather and had me assist with the younger grades. Father L'Heureux soon found out that the good girl student was so shy that she froze whenever he came to visit and missed many easy answers, while I could generally supply any missed answer in all six grades.

When I was ten years old and in fourth grade, the Sisters at the convent school were looking for a boy to live at the convent and run errands for them. Father convinced the nuns and my parents that I was the man for the job.

I came to the Sisters of Presentation of Mary on the eighth of December, a Feast day, that is very special to them. The spirit of celebration was so intense that I felt the whole convent opened its arms to welcome me. My first impression, and its impact has never lessened during all my years, was the graciousness, calm and absolute self-control of the nun who greeted us at the door and took my parents and me into the parlor. My parents were engaged in pleasant conversation, being informed of the joy that permeated the whole establishment on that day; an Anniversary of the founding of the Order, sort of everybody's birthday. As for my part, I was overwhelmed by all the shiny varnished surfaces and the smell of waxes and polishes.

Soon, Sister Superior appeared and thanked my parents for their confidence in leaving me in her care. Then addressing me directly, she told me that she needed a pair of "sturdy boy's legs" to run a multitude of errands around the convent, but more importantly around the village, where I would represent her. I must be intelligent, loyal and obedient. Then, she introduced me to Sister St. Honoré who would be my mother while at the convent.

That Sunday, after a delicious dinner, we all attended an evening of theatre where the French love of romantic adventure and the magic of teachers' and students' scissors and needles had created a make-believe world that I had hardly dreamed about. When I was finally shown to my room, I did not particularly care if it was in Avalon or the magic kingdom; I could have slept on a fence post.

I began to find out the many roles that my foster-mother played in that convent and what a remarkable person she was. Sister St. Honoré was probably the oldest nun, around sixty years old, I believe. She had been in missions in the Yukon and Northwest Territories, on the Mackenzie River, Great Slave Lake and such. Among her adventures had been dogsled travel over long distances accompanied by Indians or Eskimos; shooting rapids in longboats powered by Indians wielding oars or poles. She was Sister Superior's main counsellor on maintenance and construction projects, a resourceful handyman and a good judge of tradesmen's abilities and intentions. She was a safety officer with eyes in the back of her head and antennae in all directions.

My admiration for her knew no bounds and has only increased through my recollection of her personality throughout my life - the more so because she was involved in so many facets of the convent life. What concerned her, concerned me, either by her instigation or mine.

During that first week, I gradually learned the limits of my new domain. I already knew that the convent fronted on the main street of Stanhope, Quebec and also Norton Mills, Vermont. Now, I learned that the imaginary line that divides Canada and the U.S. bisected the building. The original part had been a large family mansion of two stories with a small part in Canada. To this had been attached a large section of three stories entirely on Canadian soil. So I had the unlikely task of visiting the U.S. and Canadian post offices daily for the convent school.

My relations with all the other Sisters were also a dream come true. Since all the teaching nuns had duties as housemothers for a small group of girls superimposed on their other duties, they were always in danger of being overcome by childish feminine problems. I had the impression that they enjoyed their short encounters with a "sturdy boy," who was not their responsibility. At any rate, the few times I got in the doghouse with Sisters St. Honoré and Constant, there was no shortage of nuns needing my immediate help, even if it was to dispose of a candy or two in danger of going stale.

My arrival at the convent of Stanhope marked such a watershed in my life and I have reflected so much on it that I don't know what I learned at the time or what became my opinion in later life. Realizing that I was there twenty months between the ages of ten and twelve, let us assume that the seed was planted in Stanhope and the harvest gathered throughout my life.

In my second year, I was riding a tidal wave of hints and suggestions about my future. Our local school system stopped at sixth grade, which was one year away. My teacher, Sister Constant, had a brother who was a priest in the Oblate community. He had written a book about his work in the Northwest Territories of Canada where the Oblates and the Sisters of Presentation collaborated in mission work among the Indians and Eskimos. This was the country where Sister St. Honoré had spent many years of her life.

The Oblate Fathers were opening a new prep school where they would offer classical courses based on Latin and Greek to prepare young men, who felt attracted to the priesthood, for seminary studies. My pastor agreed that I was as likely to hear the 'call' as anybody else the Oblates could attract at that age. My parents saw a chance for me to stay in school longer than they could provide. So, still "transported by the tales of heroics and derring-do" in the missionary book, I applied and was invited to visit the school at Chambly, Quebec, for scholastic tests and a week of orientation for prospective students. I was accepted to enter the next September and while there, celebrated my twelfth birthday. The next youngest was fifteen, and the average age in my class was sixteen.

Again, I discovered a brand new and much larger world, in many ways very exciting, but it was not a happy year for me. I was a very young backcountry boy who had been surrounded all his life by a loving family, friends of his family or by nuns who had treated him as a special person. Now, I found myself in an all-male environment of street-wise city boys. Because I was frank and naive, I revealed too much of myself in the early days and was left defenseless in the daily brawl for turf that is life in a boys' school. I soon discovered that I was not a spectator any more, but rather every rule and directive seemed to be aimed straight at me.

I took to Latin like a duck to water and within two months, I was borrowing Latin books in the library to delight in their adventure and mythology. Before spring, I was introduced to Greek and soon realized that these two languages were the true source of the French roots and history that I loved so much. I enjoyed Geography, Modern and Ancient History but learned nothing new in Math. I realized later that my adventurous early teachers had given me glimpses of algebra and trigonometry that I would not see again until years later.

For many periods of the day, our life was dominated by upperclassmen, young men as old as twenty who took the same classes and often struggled in courses that I breezed through. Naturally, they were not very patient with my daydreaming and antics. For the only time in my life, I developed pugilistic tendencies to combat my lack of sophistication and social graces. This was the exact opposite of qualities admired by the Oblates who must find men compatible to community living. A few weeks before final exams of the first year, I was given a passing grade for the seventh grade of provincial education, assured that I would be greatly missed and placed on a train to Coaticook with bags and baggage.

There the train dropped me at 4 p.m. without my parents, or anybody else, being notified that I had departed school. It soon got dark and I sat in the station waiting room without a better idea until daylight would reappear the next morning. By 9 p.m., an Immigration Inspector whom I had often seen in Stanhope happened to see me. After a few questions, that elicited my expectations of meeting some of our farm neighbors on the street the next day, he offered me a comfortable bed for the night where I was soon asleep. Imagine my surprise at daybreak the next day, to discover the door locked and bars on the window. I had spent the night in a temporary detention cell used by Immigration when they had a guest with an unresolved problem. Inspector Dupuis, who later became a cherished family friend, took me home for breakfast. He then helped me to find a neighbor for a ride home.

I don't know if my family or my pastor were given a satisfactory explanation, but everybody agreed that my "vocation" had been a long shot that had not paid off. I was satisfied. I was where I wanted to be and never gave much thought to the unusual circumstances of my travels.

It was the end of my education as a child. From now on, I was a workingman earning his living, as many of my age, not quite thirteen.

CHAPTER 2

CONNECTIONS FROM THE MIDDLE GENERATION

THE IMMORTAL

Laura Wang Arseneau
Grimsby, Ontario

1980, People's Republic of China

There are far more people here than I expected. Neighbours, relatives, even strangers are drawn to this event. It is a big event for such a small village. They gather together in groups under huge black umbrellas, dressed in the universal uniform of mainlanders – white cotton shirts and baggy dark pants. They peer out like ducks from under cover. They watch as the small marble box is lowered into the muddy earth, the box that holds the ashes of Wang Siu Ing, my father's father. Neither Immigration nor Customs questioned the battered cardboard box, tied many times over with string. Not even the Red Guard in China would be so unfilial as to deny the homecoming of a patriarch.

It seems like the entire village of Golangsu has come to see him off. They knew him before, in his younger days as a father, as a young man, perhaps even as a boy. When he left the mainland for the Philippines, he took with him my Pa, the only boy, leaving his wife and five daughters behind. I am told that he used couriers in the underground to send the money home, though the likelihood of it ever reaching them was slim. Now look at my mainland cousins. They are all adopting this serious expression on their faces, which passes for grief, yet not one of them really knew him. But then, did I? To them he is only a distant patriarch, this funeral a paying of homage to an ancestor. He became an exile when the Communists took over, a stranger in a foreign land, while the rest of his family was left to Mao. So I am the only grandchild he ever really got to know, my brother and sister being too young. And now we have brought him back home to be buried alongside his wife. I wonder what kind of reunion this might be, when their two earthly vessels meet beneath the earth, reunited after forty long years.

"It's been a long time, wife. My how you've changed. Sorry I missed your funeral." Or her, "You left me behind, you coward! Get away! Dig him back out you thoughtless children! Do you really think I want him here to disturb my peace?" Years of bitterness rising up from the grave.

I am suddenly overcome with tears, and in the Chinese way, quickly turn my face upward to the camouflage of rain. I have caught myself conjuring up my Ankong, from the depths of memory. I see him the way he was many long years ago, when he lived with us in Manila. He is a tall and handsome man, tall for a Chinese man. He is holding my two feet in his left hand and I am balancing upright, smiling, like a trapeze acrobat's junior assistant. Age six months. I know it's hard to believe, but there are pictures in my baby album of him holding me up high in the air like this.

Next scene, I am sitting on Ankong's knee looking up, fascinated by the mole on his chin that has one single hair sprouting from it. Our conversation took on a didactic tone of late – he knew he didn't have much time left to him. He began, in his slow, gravelly baritone. "Red is the colour of happiness, Gao Kia (the nickname of endearment in Fukienese, in rough translation meaning little dog child). So we wear it at weddings and at birthdays. Here, close your eyes. I have something for you." Ankong pressed a slim, palm-sized red envelope into my hand. It is for my fourth birthday.

"Ang Pao!" (A red money envelope, containing a denomination, always in the multiple of two.) I tore it open and fingered the glittering coins. "But Ankong, what does white mean?" I asked, now circling in loops the handkerchief snatched from his breast pocket.

"Oh white – that signifies death," he said with a weary solemnness that stilled my fingers. He shifted me on his knee and smiled. "Now *you*, you are the most beautiful colour of all. The colour of gold, the colour of the sun. Only the Emperor of China was allowed to wear Imperial Yellow."

"Now let me tell you a story." I sighed with satisfaction, knowing that this would come. "In this world, there are people of many colours. You know the American family who live across the courtyard? Now what colour are they?"

"They have no colour. Well, maybe pink."

"True. And remember the soldier we saw in the market the other day?"

"He was black as the earth!"

"True again. Now in the beginning, the Creator decided to make people. And he made them in batches, like baking cookies."

This made me laugh.

"When the first batch came out, it was taken out too soon and he saw that the cookies were pale and soft. These became the white race. When the second batch came out, it was left in too long, and these he made the dark people. But finally, the last batch came out and they were golden brown, just the right colour. Now our people, we came out just right, didn't we Gao Kia?"

I clapped my hands at this clever tale, laughing in delight, but I would not fully appreciate the story for many more years. We were sitting in the courtyard, the scent of the white sampaguita flower permeating the still air. He lit a cigarette and took my small hand in his, pulling me onto my feet to commence our walk around the garden. He slowed his steps to match the rhythm of mine and as we walked, he blew smoke rings like halos above my head. I tired to catch them before they disappeared. I thought that day, that no one in the world could be as strong as he - as wise. No matter that his hands were dotted with age or that they trembled when he tied my shoelaces. His head, bent before me, was spotted too, and bald though I greatly admired its handsome gleam, like a trophy to be displayed. His aged eyes looked at me through thick, black rimmed glasses which he wore to correct his failing vision, but he always managed to see more than I did. My most enduring vision of him is this: an immortal, eternally strolling among the clouds, the smoke rising up like incense around him.

That day ended like any Saturday, with the two of us watching a wrestling match on the black and white TV. I loved to see the opponents struggling with each other in that ring, building up to the thrill of the win, the anticipation of the victor. Which one would it be? Down to the last count and then the bell was struck. Rayy! As I leapt up from the comfort of his arms, suddenly I was the victor too, he laughing with such a pleasure in me.

There is a memory lapse now, a fast-forward. "How come Ankong has to lie down all the time?" An illness, they said. Cancer was not a word for five-year-olds then. Time passed and I watched as his once vigorous frame diminished with frightening speed into a shrunken form, scarcely recognizable under the faded blanket. I remember being too scared to touch him, scared that those hills and valleys jutting and poking through the blanket were where his knees, his hips, his chest should have been. Yet every day, his was the first room I would visit, even for a moment, on the way down to the hall to the bathroom. I would stop, watch and wait, holding my breath until I saw the painful rise and fall that signaled his presence. Then and only then, would I allow myself to look up into those clouded eyes.

Until one morning, I awakened to stillness. I called out for my mother and when she appeared at the doorway I remember saying to her, "Ankong's dead, isn't he?" And yes, he had died through the night. We wore black armbands for ages.

"This is where you belong now, Ankong." The earth is patted down on top of his box, with final blows of the shovel. A cousin busies himself repainting in vermillion, the characters carved into the monolithic headstone. The aunts are using stones to scrape the low walled sides of the concrete grave clean - the scrape, scrape, a steady and gentle sound underlying the patter of rain on umbrellas.

A tall, authoritative looking man is stepping forward to give the benediction. I catch a familiar profile, the balding head, the long patrician nose.

"Gao Kia."

"Yes?"

He raises his hand in blessing.

AT GRANDMA'S *

Diane Driedger
Winnipeg, Manitoba

In your kitchen
You rumble and swish
Buns and cookies
Flow from
The warm oven
Of your heart

I lurk in the
Corner
Waiting to run
To the treadle sewing machine
Ferret in its drawers
For hidden treasures

Oh dimes and nickels
There
For the taking
You chuckle grandma
At my glow
My disbelief
Your warm body
Pressed against mine
Hearth enough for me

* From Diane Driedger's *Mennonite Madonna* (Charlottetown: Gynergy Books, 1999)

BEARS OF THE TEENAGE VARIETY

Gwen Boettger
Hamilton, Ontario

You made me smile.
Watching you grow and change was entertaining, but joyful.
I wished for you only the best, good health and great success at what ever you put
your hand to. And that will always be my prayer for you. But it is a time of
change. You are entering the teenage years and all I can do is hold my breath and
pray that you get through this period of self-discovery. You are like the fuzzy,
land-bound caterpillar that struggles to put off the old and take on the new. Soon
you will be complete. You will fly. But I don't want you to forget what is
important. Maybe this little story will help you.

Bears of the Teenage Variety

"I don't think that we should be doing this," cried Sister Bear. She was getting scared and for good reason. She could see her breath. Gray clouds hung in the sky. The wind whistled through the bare tree limbs. Her mind was full of doubts and she wanted to go back.

"Listen, we talked about this and we each decided it was a good thing and now you are not sure. What is your problem? Are you or are you not going to do this?" Big Brother was ticked.

For as long as time itself, every winter when the winds blew cold, all bears would go into the Big Sleep. It was their way.

Now Brother Bear and Sister Bear wanted to change the way things were done. They had decided that they would be the first bears to stay awake during the long cold winter.

"But don't you think we should tell mom and dad what we are doing? . . . after all . . . "

"Oh, give it up," said Brother Bear, "I'm going to do this with you or without you. Now what is it? Are you with me or not?"

Sister Bear pawed at the ground for a minute. It was cold. "Oh, all right, but I don't feel good about this," she moaned. "I think we should tell mom and dad so they won't worry about us."

"Oh, it's going to be okay," Brother Bear assured his sister. "Remember, we know how to catch our own fish and hunt for honey and find all the juicy sweet berries in the meadow. I know we can do this."

"Yes, I guess so," said Sister Bear. But she wasn't convinced.

"Where have those two gone now?" demanded Mother Bear. She was putting the finishing touches on the winter den. She had brought in some fir boughs and had piled them evenly to give some added protection to the bears as they hibernated through the long winter months. She had also stored some berries and nuts just in case they woke up really hungry.

"Oh, don't worry Mama Bear." Papa Bear was trying to reassure her that the two cubs would be okay.

"They have probably gone down to the river for one last romp. You know, they could be a little restless. It will be a long cold winter."

"Oh I know that they can take care of themselves, but I would rather that they be here, safe with us."

But the two young bears had other ideas.

Full of confidence they went charging down to the river leaving their paw prints in the fresh snow. They knew the area well. In the summer they would stand on the rocks and wait for the salmon to swim by, and then they would grab the fat delicious fish out of the water with their paws. But something was wrong. As the two cubs approached the river they couldn't hear the sound of the rushing water. As they clamboured over the rocks, the water was gone. What was this hard glassy stuff?

Gingerly, Brother Bear stepped onto the ice. Step by step he moved out near the moving water.

Crack!

Brother Bear's front paw broke the ice and as he lost his balance, the ice disappeared from beneath him and he got soaked. The water wasn't deep. He quickly jumped out and headed for shore.

Sister Bear was scared.

"Now what are we going to do?" she cried.

Brother Bear shook himself off. He sat back on his haunches and caught his breath. "That was a close call," he thought. But he had to be brave.

"Oh don't worry," he wheezed, hoping that the fear he was feeling would not be heard in his voice. "We can catch some fish later. Let's go over to the meadow and find some nice sweet berries."

So off they plodded. They both were a bit quiet. They were not saying a word. But they were both thinking. Little doubts were beginning to form in each mind.

"Oh Papa Bear, it is getting late. The Big Sleep will soon be here. We have to go find them and bring them home." Mama Bear was past the point of patience. She could wait no longer.

"I think you are right Mama Bear. You go towards the meadow; I will go to the river. Those are the two places that they might be."

So Mama Bear and Papa Bear split up. The snow was softly falling and crunching under their padded feet. The sky was threatening. Soon the wind would change and the snow would really blow.

The two cubs struggled through the forest. The snow was cold on their feet and the Big Sleep was beginning to take over their bodies.

"I can't go on," whimpered Sister Bear. "I'm getting tired."

"Don't give in to it," Brother Bear coaxed. "We don't have to give into it, we don't have to do the Big Sleep. We are going to be the first to live through winter. Don't give up."

But Brother Bear was also getting tired.

"Let me sit down, just for a minute," cried Sister Bear.

"Okay, I will sit down with you."

Brother Bear could object no longer.

The forest was getting dark. Mama Bear plodded on. She was worried. If they didn't find the two cubs soon they risked their own lives. She had to find the cubs and get them to the safety of the den before the Big Sleep overtook her body.

She was coming near to the meadow. A cloud moved past the full moon. A shaft on light fell on the ground. It was a rounded mound. It wasn't a rock.

Mama Bear's heart pounded in her throat. She ran as fast as she could. It was them. She let out a loud Roar. Papa Bear heard her. He turned towards the meadow. He helped put Sister Bear on Mama Bear's back and then struggled to lift Brother Bear.
The journey back to the den was difficult.
But they made it.

Dropping the cubs on the firs, they crawled in together and snuggled up to each other to keep warm. They fell asleep. There was no time to be thankful.

A HIDDEN TREASURE *

Jocelyn Boileau
Winnipeg, Manitoba

I write this to honour my grandmother, Beatrice Watkin, circa 1885-1960, who lived most of her life in a silent world. This story, as seen through the eyes of a child, is of the Grannie I now wish I really knew. But there is no one to ask. And so I also offer this true story as a gift to my three sons. Perhaps to be stored away with the old camel ornament and curling yellowed photos, against the day they too may ask.

From the time I first knew my grandmother, until the day she died in 1960 I never had one serious conversation with her. From my earliest school days I knew my Grannie was different. My first silent prayers were for her to be made well. You see, I wanted a Grannie like all my friends' grandmothers.

Grannie Watkin lived in a world of her own, completely isolated by her deafness. I don't know when she became deaf, whether it was before or after losing her second child. Randolph was only a toddler when he fell to his death from an upstairs window. It was the early 1900's and Granddad was in India serving in the army.

But my Grandmother's subsequent isolation was not solely on account of her stone deafness. There was also the other . . . in those days unspeakable family secret.

It was 1994 that I returned to visit Wales for the first time in over 21 years. From that trip I brought back an old silver-plated ornament depicting a camel in full-fringed trappings under a palm tree. A lady sits sidesaddle on the camel looking down on a diminutive servant with outstretched arms. The ornament is one of a pair of candlesticks Granddad bequeathed to my brother and me, one each, in 1970. Richard kept them tucked safely away in his attic awaiting my visit; insisting I choose. And so the heavy camel, wrapped in bubble plastic, accompanied me back to Canada. It rode in my carry-on baggage through the high-tech airport security without a peep.

Once home in Winnipeg – armed with Silvo, rags, and an old toothbrush – I tried to polish the tarnished silver-plate. As I brushed and buffed I noticed faint traces of red in the crevices and splashes of red under the base. Then the memories of my grandmother's erratic behaviour came flooding back. This ornament was one of the many things she painted red.

Amid a strong smell of turpentine I recall watching Granddad painstakingly remove the red paint. Later he'd lock up the statue. Keep it out of harm's way. But if any ornaments were left out when Granddad went to work, then Grannie would paint them red. She liked red.

There were red lampshades, red chair, red pots and red "brasses." All hand painted with a one-inch size decorator brush and a can of oil based vermillion, the brightest in stock. Even her hair was red.

Yes, your great-grandmother, my Grannie, was off her rocker. Completely bonkers. She spoke to unseen images. "You dirty chandler. I know what you are up to." She would shout in a high-pitched tremble, while tossing a spoonful of sugar on to the coal fire to watch it burn and see who was trying to poison her.

Most of the time she appeared to be happy, at least from a child's point of view. She often made my brother and I laugh.

I would watch her sewing. Short, short skirts (in days before the mini-skirt) and way out tops that looked strangely orange after her attempts at dying the fabric.

I remember mother telling me that Grandmother came from an upper-middle class family who lived in a large white house on the island of

Guernsey. She had a very genteel upbringing. After her breakdown her language changed. Grannie swore.

As I polish my camel I wonder whether Grannie was happy in her madness. She was certainly afraid of the 'dirty chandler' and other unseen presences around her - afraid of being poisoned. She spoke to thin air and to the fire.

It was Grandmother's habit to rest the oak leaf of the gate-leg table precariously on the corner ridge of the piano (instead of pulling out the extension's support) and proceeded to lay a fine table on a red linen cloth. She filled the electric kettle and placed it on the hot stove to boil. She might call us to lunch at 10 a.m. or to supper at three. She was known to dress up and arrive at church on a Saturday or a Monday, much to the consternation of the vicar.

Grannie was fun. She bought us Pontifract cakes (little embossed licorice disks) and sent us a big Christmas parcel in October or November. This was in the days before postal services urged one to "mail early for Christmas." Often the parcel arrived falling apart and full of fascinating surprises (not always appropriate), which we were allowed to open straight away.

On Christmas day Grannie travelled with Granddad to our house in Holyhead. All the family had to watch that she didn't wander off on her own because she wasn't known in our town as she was in her own little village of Port Dinorwic. There everyone was used to Mrs. Watkin. The locals looked out for her and were good to her. Granddad could go into the hairdressers to settle the bill days after she'd had one of her impromptu perms. He'd thank the hairdresser for the transformation. The pleasure of seeing gentle gray curls, knowing full well that in a matter of days he'd face again that wiry shock of orange.

The camel candlestick reminds me of my grandparents in an intimate way. If it were in mint condition, it wouldn't be the same. It is special because it bears the scars of life. Red scars. A reminder of blood and pain, love and joy, the enduring qualities of life.

As for Grannie . . . deprived of hearing the melodies of this life; experiencing the horror of finding her baby boy lifeless on the flagstones beneath a broken French window . . . my Grannie . . . It is only now that I wonder, "Did God give her a kind way out from anguish too great to bear? Is this, perhaps, the answer to that childhood prayer?"

* Also appeared in *The Western People Magazine* under the title "Grannie's World" as part of a Mother's Day theme in May 1995.

A POD OF LOVE

Jocelyn Boilieau
Winnipeg, Manitoba

November 1963

Dear Gran,
I remember the Riddle you used
to tease . . .
"How many peas make five?"
You'd laugh. We'd count. Little
fingers working out
4 and 1? Or 2 plus 3?

Beneath, an ancient answer lay.
Lost In depths . . .
A potting shed. Dusty webs.
Like a faded
Fallen
Packet of seeds.

With a long lost love,

Gwynettie

February 1993

Dear Grandmama,
Your question rang down halls of
time
While I sang to babies of my own.
"How many, how many, how
many peas?"
Like a curled up seed in a palm
divine
. . . No answer to the rhyme.
Until. In an old book my lover
sees
That dubious riddle . . .
"How many peas . . . ?"
Now with affection, in contrition,
he says:
  "So you and your Grannie.
You're not so crazy."
Then the mystery is revealed:
    "Two peas
        two half peas
      a pea and a half
        and half a pea."

In fondest memory,
  Your Gwynettie

"GO, LOVELY ROSE"

(Title by Edmund Waller)

Ellen Jaffe
Woodstock, Ontario

For Rose Albert (June 26, 1895 – May 19, 1988)

Bloom of my childhood
Grandmother
Today everything bursts into
flower
Green, pink, white
While you wilt softly
In hospital nursery
Glass and tubes around you.

Rose, bloom of my childhood
Dressing up in your clothes,
Your high-heeled shoes
(on my last visit, I
peeked in your drawer like a
curious child,
found nests of gloves white and
black, neatly folded
waiting for occasions . . .
a lady is never without decorum).

We came to your 90th birthday
party
You came to my 43rd,

A surprise planned by my son
You wore a paper hat
Over your newly-done hair
Elegant – as always.

I remember
Your rose-painted nails
And nestling in your feathery bed
When I slept over, you gave me
Cantaloupe and ice-cream
Balloons and kisses
You were never old to me
(even now, even now)
and I am not really grown-up, it is
all an act
still dressing up in your clothes,
putting on plays.

Rose, bloom of my childhood
Your light goes out
Your scent will remain
In our hearts.

THE PASSAGE OF TIME

George Appleton
Burlington, Ontario

"En roulent, ma boule, a roulent."

The song seemed very far away. Every few minutes it would increase in volume, then a flash of pink would twirl past her open door and it would fade.

"En roulent, ma boule."

There it was again. This time Lillian Carr could see blonde hair flying as the pink flowered dress spun down the hall. Then her coughing returned. She closed her eyes and held a tissue to her mouth and prayed the spasm would pass quickly. The prayers didn't work any more; it made her chest ache and the world around her disappear.

An eternity later it stopped. Lillian felt drained. Slowly she opened her eyes and looked up from her hospital bed. Standing in the doorway of her hospital room stood a young girl.

"Hello my dear, my isn't that a pretty dress? I had a dress something like that when I was eight, or nine. It was pink like yours, with small burgundy flowers and piping. My mother made it. That was such a long time ago." She closed her eyes, shook her head and asked, "Do you want to see my special treasure?" The girl nodded, took a couple of hesitant steps into the room and stopped.

Lillian rolled onto her left side opening the drawer of her bedside table. When she pulled out her hand it held a small square box covered in dark blue velvet. The old woman looked down at her trembling hands as she pushed a small brass button releasing the lid. Inside lay a white cotton bag with the name J.G. Graves, Sheffield, printed in black. She ran her fingers over the letters. The girl's eyes were wide as she inched her way toward the bed.

Lillian wriggled the index finger of her right hand into the puckered opening of the bag. She turned it upside down and brought it to her chest. Her left hand had been broken in a fall three years ago. She refused to see a doctor and the fractured bones knit at new angles leaving the fingers hooked together with little mobility and even less strength. She used the back of the thumb on that hand to pin the bottom of the bag to her chest. The entire effort seemed too great for her body. She paused, attempting a deep breath and instead finding a deep, wet and painful cough. With the spasm a silver pocket watch dropped into her good hand, its chain and fob spilling across the pastel green blanket covering her lap.

Lillian turned her head away from the girl toward the window. Outside, the hospital's parking lot was beginning to fill as Sunday afternoon visitors began arriving. The maple trees around Burlington's Joseph Brant Hospital were shedding the last of their yellow leaves. The sun fought for room in the sky with clouds that were thick with dark promising rain, or, if the temperature were to drop a scant few degrees, snow.

"I'm all right. It's just a cough. It comes and goes. Come up so you can see." Lillian patted the bed and the girl climbed up on the mattress. "This belonged to my grandfather and my father. Granddad was a conductor on the Flying Scotsman. Dad was a conductor on the Canadian. They were very important passenger trains. What's your name?"

"Ainsley," was the reply.

"What a lovely name. I'm Lillian. How old are you Ainsley?"

"I'm going to be seven on the twenty-third of November."

"My, my. Seven years old. Can you guess how old I am?" Ainsley shook her head.

"Let me see. With a little luck, I'm going to be ninety-three on January second." Lillian pulled a handkerchief from the sleeve of her housecoat and wiped some saliva from her thin lips.

The girl didn't know what to say. She thought the old woman seemed nice and she did want to see the watch. Lillian turned it over. The back was covered in spiral hatching. Before the pattern could reach the middle, it disappeared behind a crest with three small lions surrounded by what looked like a belt. Lillian pressed a thumbnail behind the large ring that fastened the chain to the watch. The back popped open. Inside, there was a small hole leading into the dark interior and its mechanical secrets. Lillian cradled the watch in her damaged hand and drew the square links of the chain between the fingers of her right. At the end was a small funny looking tube with a square hole in one end and a large ring on the other. Ainsley stared at the translucent skin on Lillian's hand as the old woman grabbed the ring. She slid the other end of the tube into the hold in the back of the watch and with great care turned the winding key ten times.

"You must be very careful," she said, "to never wind too tight. Ten turns once a day. My Granddad and my father used this watch to make sure the passengers on their trains were safe. There were no digital watches back then, no wireless radios. The conductor had to know the exact time every minute. A minute out here or there and they might have had a very serious accident."

Lillian held out her hand, offering the watch to the girl. Ainsley looked up not believing her luck. When Lillian nodded, she reached over and her small fingers closed around the watchcase. "It's heavy." She said. The chain trailed back across the bedding as the young girl pulled the watch to her lap.

"That watch was made in 1887, one-hundred and eleven years ago. My granddad had just been promoted to conductor on a small train that ran from London to Sheffield in England dear. Do you know where that is?" Ainsley said yes and told her new friend about her studies in school. Lillian watched and smiled as Ainsley stroked the stainless steel timepiece and its thick crystal. She talked about her grandfather and spun some of the tales he had told her about his adventures on the Flying Scotsman's long runs between London and Edinburgh.

Her father was a big man. Lillian remembered sitting in his lap when she was seven. If she closed her eyes even now she could feel the rough tweed coat he wore and smell the spicy aroma of his Balkan pipe tobacco. He too loved the watch and it kept him company on many runs of the Canadian Pacific passenger liner, The Canadian. It ran coast to coast back when people considered train travel the best way to see Canada. The watch was to have gone to her brother Ben. However, he was killed in a car accident in the early nineteen-fifties. So, when her father retired five years later, he gave the watch to her. Now Lillian was the only one of her family left alive.

As the afternoon crept on, Lillian showed her new friend more of the watch's secrets; how to open the front cover and press a spring latch that allowed the works to swing forward. That delighted the girl because she could then see the tiny machinery inside move. Ainsley began to talk about her life. Her mother was a single parent who volunteered at the hospital each weekend. Since they couldn't afford a sitter, she came with her and sometimes helped. Today, she was on her own and had decided to visit some of the older patients.

For most of the afternoon Lillian let the girl hold the timepiece. Lillian met Ainsley's mother and the three had supper together. At the end of the day, Ainsley promised she would return to visit next weekend.

She did and she came for many weekends after that as well. Soon their birthdays came. They exchanged small gifts. Then it was Christmas. Ainsley decorated Lillian's room with crafts she and her friends had made after school. Then one Sunday, early in January, Ainsley was surprised to find Lillian's room empty. She walked to the nurse's station to find out where she was. One of the nurses opened a drawer and pulled out a small navy blue box containing Lillian's watch. She said, "Lillian had to go away but she told us she wanted you to have this."

Ainsley popped the catch and opened the box. There inside its white cotton bag laid the watch. "Thank you, but when will she be coming back?"

"I don't think she will honey, but she did leave this note for you and your mother. Take it to her and she will read it to you."

Her mother was just down the hall helping a patient. Ainsley was amazed that the wonderful watch and its history were now hers. She walked slowly carrying it with both hands held in front. She found her mom putting flowers in water for a man who looked almost as old as Lillian. She waited in the doorway until he invited her inside. Her mother introduced her to Mr. Williams. He was being treated for pneumonia, the same sickness that had put Lillian in hospital. Ainsley handed her mother Lillian's letter. Mr. Williams asked what the girl was carrying. She replied, "Do you want to see my special treasure?"

REMEMBRANCE DAY

Susan Evans-Shaw
Hamilton, Ontario

November 11, 1999

Dear Gran,

Today is the day you hated. Dad told me how you loathed attending Remembrance Day ceremonies, but you went out of a sense of duty. He said that Remembrance Days were the only time he knew you to cry. Eighty-one years, seventy-two days ago, Jim died, shot by a sniper on September 1, 1918. We don't know the time of day, but we do know the place, 10 miles southwest of Arras, just east of the Cagnicourt-Dury Road, while preparations were in progress to break the backbone of enemy resistance at the Queant-Drocourt line. Not that you cared. Jim was dead and you had the next fifty years to live without him.

Thirty years have passed since you died, but it seems appropriate today to write you a letter. We used to communicate more often by letter than we did face-to-face or by telephone. You lived in Winnipeg; I began life in Sudbury, and then moved to Port Credit. Of course you visited; you and Aunty Gwladys travelled every year for your holidays in that little Morris Oxford of hers. Over the years you two toured from coast to coast, Halifax to Nanaimo, the Dakotas to the Alaska Highway.

You died in South Peel Hospital in the upstart city of Mississauga, Ontario, far from your home in Manitoba and even further from where you were born in Mold, Wales. You often talked of Wales but you never went back after Jim died. In January 1919 you packed up your belongings, your three young children, Frank, Gwladys and baby Eric, and returned to Miniota, where you felt you belonged, close to your sisters, within the community where Jim had chosen to make a home.

I haven't heard you speak in a long time. I haven't heard your tuneless whistle as you worked in the kitchen, preparing meals, baking scones, and making cookies or as you dusted and Bisselled the apartment. I remember your last days when you sat neatly on the sofa, your hands folded in your lap, your ankles crossed, your feet barely touching the floor. I was 24 then, and on a visit to you in Abbotsford, to help Auntie Gwladys because you had become forgetful and tended to wander. You, who took care of so much and so many, needed care yourself.

It was your quiet hands that seemed wrong, and your sitting so quietly. In the Winnipeg years, your quiet time would be the afternoon when you would stretch out on the sofa with a book. After an hour or so, you would remove your glasses and close your eyes.

When family came we sat at the kitchen table, a cup of tea in front of us – I remember one occasion with Peggy, Debbie, me, Auntie Ciss, Eira, Gwendda – family and friends always seemed to gather in your kitchen. You made tea and passed around cookies and scones. Dad likes to tell us of the days in Miniota after the war when your living room became the social centre for the local teachers. They would gather around the piano while you played old favourites and everyone sang.

I've been thinking a lot about you lately. I stepped into the past, the past that you and Jim shared, and edited his letters for a book. I know you never stopped missing Jim. You said so in those last months. Before that, you seldom mentioned him, or perhaps with a child's self-absorption, I never asked. I remember once I tried to guess how old you were and you said "Yes" when I got up to fifty. How Dad laughed when I told him. I didn't know you were already 64 when I was born.

Dad told me whatever stories he had heard about Jim. Dad was too young to remember his father, so Dad's stories came from his brother, his sister and his aunts. Only in very old age did you allow yourself to visit the past. By then you were beyond longing and regret, overwhelmed by the loss of your home, your security and your daughter to marriage with a man you thought unworthy.

I have Jim's letters to you but not yours to him. Your letters are lost. Perhaps it was you who destroyed them. Perhaps you only wanted to hear Jim's voice, not your own. Jim's words reflect your love and your spirit.

He made demands – get my watch repaired, send my books, buy a razor strap, send my summer suit, you forgot the button fasteners. He needed ask only once, except for photos. He could never get enough photos of you and the children and you seemed unwilling or unable to get them done. Perhaps you hated to be photographed.

I wish your letters had survived. How I would have loved to share in your love, your quarrels, the news and the gossip! The summer of 1915, when you took the children on a holiday to Vancouver, when Gwladys and Frank learned to swim, you learned with them. You were 35 at the time and Jim was so proud of you. He would have been even prouder to know that you continued to swim the rest of your life. I remember you in your black bathing suit, your white head moving through the waters of Lake Winnipeg. You swam the breaststroke, gently, sensuously, with barely a ripple.

I never saw your tough side. To me you were small, plump and cuddly with masses of fine white hair done up with hairpins. I probably passed your height by the time I was in grade five. We, Debbie and I, saw you about once or twice a year on visits. Either you came to us or we went to you. I paid my first visit to you before I was four months old when I went to Winnipeg to be baptized. For years, Mum and Dad took us by train to see you, but one landmark year Debbie and I travelled all the way by ourselves on the CPR to spend two weeks with you and to meet our west coast cousins, Peggy and Gwendda, Frank's daughter whom we hardly knew. We five Evans women squeezed into your two bedroom apartment. Debbie and I, still pre-pubertal, got a first glimpse of adolescent angst.

Peggy and Gwendda saw you more fully as a woman and mother. When Frank, your oldest, died of encephalitis and Aunt Helen had to go back to work to support the family, you and Gwladys took in Peggy and Gwendda. Peggy wasn't quite six and Gwendda was just 2 ½. For the next several years, you were their parent and Peggy remembers those very qualities that must have enabled you to carry on after Jim died. Carry on you did. When the shock and grief had subsided, you had returned to Miniota, where you made a warm and happy home for your children.

It was a hard life and you hadn't much money. At first the army would only allow you a Captain's pension. That was the rank Jim assumed in order to escape the safety of England, where he taught musketry, to serve at the front. You reminded military officialdom that Jim had been promoted to Major in 1916 and the lower rank had been a temporary measure. You fought and you won. You got a pension as a Major's widow, and retroactively too!

In 1921, at the age of 15, Frank won an IODE scholarship to the University of Manitoba. A year later you decided it was cheaper to move to Winnipeg than to pay Frank's room and board. You found rooms in an old house on Carlton Street, and for the next forty-six years you remained on that same street. Eventually you sold the house in Miniota. It was draughty and expensive to heat by coal and your base had become Winnipeg. For the next several summers Dad returned to the farm and worked for Uncle Jack. Frank had gone to university, a step hitherto unheard of in Miniota, and Dad and two other village boys followed suit. Like his brother, Dad intended to become an engineer, but a summer job introduced him to geology. Gwladys always regretted the unoffered opportunity and in the light of later events, we can't help but think how different her life might have been. Instead, she took a job at the Prudential, and remained at home with you.

Then in 1967, Gwladys married. She married the man who had been courting her for thirty years, a man you never liked. Your memory began to fail and you couldn't be left alone in your apartment at 45 Carlton Street. Eric and Gwladys agreed to keep you in their respective homes, six months each, like a child of divorced parents. Even before the wedding, your anxiety overcame your intellect. You had lost Jim in 1918, and for the sake of the children, carried on. You lost your oldest son in 1943 and became a parent to his children. In 1967 you lost your home and your independence and there was nothing to live for.

So long you've been silent, Gran. For ten years I've been reading and re-reading Jim's letters to you while you remain silent. Today I opened an old brassbound doll's trunk I'd kept, filled with letters and childhood detritus. I found three of your letters. How proud you were of us, and how supportive when I failed out of university. How you loved and shared. Reading your letters after all these years I see another legacy I have from you. We write alike – large, sprawling and loopy, except I write a backhand and you wrote a forehand. As writing is so important in my life, I'm happy to have this link with you.

You were the tolerant and accepting grandmother. I have no memory of you making a fuss over any of us. You accepted us as individuals. I can read it in your letters about Frank, Karen and Bruce, your great-grandchildren. There isn't a hint of adoring babble but your affectionate delight in them speaks volumes.

My teenage years with Mum were turbulent, full of passion and conflict, and many times I thought of running away from home. My imagined haven was always in Winnipeg, Suite 16 the Monterey Apartments, where I knew love would be unconditional.

A few years ago I accompanied Denis, my husband, whom you never met, to a meeting in Winnipeg. We took an afternoon to walk over to Carlton Street and all the familiar places of thirty-odd years before. The Monterey Apartments still stand and Carlton Street looks much the same, except smaller. Only the wishing well has disappeared. If it had been there, I would have dropped a coin to make a wish for you, a wish that somewhere, on Remembrance Day, you and Jim are together again.

Bundles of love (as you used to close a letter),

Your granddaughter,

Susan

A CHILD'S HOLIDAY REVISITED

Patricia Whitfield
Victoria, British Columbia

In early morning as I am moving through my sun salutation on my yoga mat, visions of my Grandmother and a young blonde-headed girl with freckles, riding the shuddering streetcar towards the adventure of shopping at Eaton's, pop into my mind. Thus this account.

When I was six, my family moved from Mount Dennis in Toronto to a village north of Bracebridge that boasted a population of approximately ninety. My father and Mother had purchased a fifty-year-old pioneer home complete with surrounding verandah alongside the old village general store, where they would spend the next few years struggling to make a living, while offering the many cherished benefits of country living for my brother and myself.

In the latter part of summer to coincide with the Toronto National Exhibition, I would travel by train to the city to spend one glorious week with my grandparents, and one of these days was to shop at Eaton's for school/winter clothes and other items for our family such as long underwear for Dad and flannelette sheets, to ward off the cold in our uninsulated house.

On the appointed day of departure from the village station, at the age of seven, I enthusiastically boarded the steam train by myself, waved farewell to my parents and then turned to the friendly, familiar black porter, who would be my guardian for the next couple of hours. I would plunk myself down on the desired seat and sit by the window gazing out at the speeding countryside, while clouds of black smoke billowed past, partially obscuring my view of lush fields, little inlets and the towns of Washago, Orillia and Barrie as we wound our way southward to Toronto. What an adventure, to escape the quaintness and serenity of village life, and to embark upon the sights and sounds of a thriving metropolis! I loved the old green coaches with the worn, firm benches, the travellers whose faces were creased with joviality, the smiling porter in his cap and crisp uniform, manouvering down the jerking aisles, checking train tickets and conversing with the passengers as he punched their cards, the haunting blast of the whistle when we crossed numerous roads, and the incessant clacking of the shiny wheels hitting the joints in the rails as we sped along, resound in my memory still.

When the train slowed its journey into St. Clair, I would eagerly grab my belongings and with steam hissing and billowing from underneath as it squealed to a full stop, I disembarked, bidding goodbye to the grinning porter whose extended hand assisted me down the portable steps. There standing patiently on the wooden platform was my Grandfather, wearing his proverbial cap, wide-legged cuffed trousers, and a soft smile. Short in stature, he would bend down, utter a few kind words of greeting and give me a gentle hug. Then we walked a short distance and loaded my bags into the trunk of his cherished green Ford. From the station we would wind our way along heavily trafficked streets, my eyes marvelling at the tall gardens in Mount Dennis, the place where my Mother had spent a privileged childhood. Through a narrow laneway that exited from another neighbouring street, Gramp edged the car into the old black garage, an old wooden structure that smelled of oil, tar and earthly garden tools, the tiny casement windows covered in thick layers of dust and cobwebs.

In haste and excitement I would skip up the path, passing soft, green asparagus ferns waving in the summer's breeze, straight rows of lettuce, onions, radishes, and ripe tomatoes, to reach a white trellis laden with aromatic pink roses. From under this arbor, a stone walkway that was bordered by green lawns led to the back of the old family home. On my left was a circular rose garden, lush with varieties of prized blooms and flanked by the perennial flowers that edged their property while the snowball trees reached high to the neighbour's shed on the other. Standing on the stoop, her tiny spectacles perched on her nose, the bibbed bright-printed apron surrounding her generous girth, my Grandmother would call out my name, and laughingly surround me with an embrace of love and delight as I reached the upper stair.

Eagerly, I stepped into the familiar summer kitchen, spying her huge, gleaming stove with its warming oven that stood on the polished linoleum floor that had been laid years ago, but bore few scars and wounds of endless treading. Assorted large aluminum pots graced the black elements, poised for another meal. From this room hundreds of sugary-brown, crisp apple pies, a variety of preserves from their garden, assorted cakes, and mounds of mashed potatoes had been prepared for family gatherings and church suppers. Always a beehive of domestic activity, this place held the comfortable ambience of nurturance and contentment.

Past the old chiming wall clock and up the walnut stairs I would traipse, my hand fondly passing over the embossed green wallpaper that was a favourite pattern, and then turned into the front bedroom where a patchwork quilt, which my Grandmother and her quilting friends had lovingly completed years ago, covered the double iron bed on her fall wall. This was my comfortable sanctuary for the next week.

The anticipation of tomorrow's excursion would prevent me from sleeping that first night as I anxiously would await the clanging of the dishes, the smell of coffee and the voice of either Bob Hesketh or Gordon Sinclair on CFRB as breakfast was being prepared. Outside the window from the neighbour's orchard, the din of flocking birds heralded the approaching autumn, a reminder that the cessation of my daily swim at the lake and a return to the first central school in Muskoka were fast approaching. Undaunted, I hopped out of bed, quickly washed and ran down the stairs to greet the morning.

Gramp would be already sitting at the table and Gram standing near him, wearing her bibbed apron, another one of her sewing feats, and I would be warmly greeted with, "Well, here she is. What would you like to eat?" A substantial breakfast was important in this family, so usually this included juice, porridge, eggs and toast with homemade preserves from her larder that was packed with food for the winter. Gram had lots of energy so she would prepare the meal effortlessly and then finally sit down to the table that was covered with a fresh white linen cloth over the regular one. The old fashioned spoons of intricate and varied designs in the spoon jar always fascinated me and I would take great care in choosing the right one for this particular meal. During breakfast, while listening to the radio, we would discuss our plans and purchases. A hasty retreat to clean teeth, make the beds, and comb my hair into pigtails secured with elastic bands followed, and then we were ready to set off.

To reach Weston Road, we would walk along their tree-lined street, Astoria, past dark brick homes built in the early part of the century and then we would wind our way toward the bus stop. Along this route there would be someone we would inevitably meet and the greetings and quick catch-up news would ensue before we proceeded. In the early fifties, the community was vibrant and people were connected through regular church functions and neighbourliness; folks knew each other and a friendly chat during a stroll was the norm in this less busy time. As a child I didn't appreciate this diversion from my focused plans and would restlessly poke the sidewalk with my shoe, which my Grandmother sensed as impatience, and shortly with a cordial farewell, we would continue our way along the street.

Finally, reaching the stop near the Salvation Army building, we would wait for the red trolley and eventually its broad face would appear far down the street corner of Weston Road and Eglinton. I was always fascinated by its antennae edging along the high wires creating sparks intermittently as the bus lumbered toward us. With several steps along the route, past the Swift Packing plant and the Toronto Stockyards, where pungent smells wafted through the open windows, it would wind its way to the Junction, and here we would transfer to the Dundas streetcar that would take us into the core of the downtown. Sometimes its wrenching and swaying on the tracks would create some nausea, but the anticipation of this day warded it off.

With her glasses sitting demurely on her nose, her purse hanging from the gloved wrist, Gram would sit beside me and relate a few stories to pass the time and point out places of interest that had changed since her last visit. During the conversation, she would brush her lap to soothe out an imaginary ripple in her skirt or smooth a curl that was out of place. Then as we neared our destination, her eyes peeled out for landmarks (she was very observant and quick), she would announce with certainty that we had reached our STOP, poke me to get going, and head for the doorway of the streetcar.

With list in hand, a shove on the heavy rotating doors and a brief pause to gaze at the bronze statue of Timothy Eaton, we would head off into her familiar territory of the ground floor. Amongst the surging crowd of coiffed heads, my eyes were drawn to the bustling figures in suits or bright coloured dresses, slim white gloves, straw hats, and stockinged legs of avid shoppers. A word of direction and Gram would steer me toward the escalators, their grinding sound audible over the hum of the store, and I was momentarily apprehensive of those fearsome black teeth on which I would have to place my two little feet. Would they be caught and swept underneath to obscure, dark depths? I gingerly stepped on, grabbed the rail, and until I safely reached the top, hung close by her, and then quickly jumped onto a welcoming, firm floor.

Our first stop-off was the dry goods and notions department where Gram would guide me to the stacked bolts of material that she closely examined with an eagle eye, and then moved on to choose matching thread for use on her old treadle Singer machine. Asking pertinent questions of a helpful employee, she scrutinized the cotton being carefully cut and folded on the long cutting table. The snip-snap of those awesome black-handled scissors slicing the desired length, to this child, was fascinating. Purchases completed, we then marched along and upward into the Children's Clothing Department for a much-needed warm winter coat that would combat the frigid Muskoka temperatures.

The multi-coloured selection of long and short coats suspended on many racks overwhelmed me, but with Gram's urging at choosing the correct size, I would try on several and parade in front of the full-length mirror, gesturing with my arms extended, and twirling in a dance, to check out the fit. Then the examination began. How close was the stitching; was the hem secure and was the lining adequate for frigid weather? Was it a good value for the dollar? After narrowing the choice and growing hot from the exertion, I would finally decide on one that was sure to be used for two winters, and with satisfaction, I carefully scrutinized the procedure of it being wrapped in paper, placed in a sturdy box, tied with cord and passed into my hands.

By then, Grandma was getting a little weary, and at her suggestion of lunch, we would head to the waiting elevator, step inside to brush against other hungry bodies while I watched the gloved attendant push the brass button and crisply announce, "Going up!" The crossing gates that clicked across the doors as we began to move ensured us that we were indeed, on our way, and in a few minutes, they would collapse shut, and after a gentle rise, at the call of our floor number, we would be dropped off at the Georgian Room.

Here the tantalizing smells and a wide selection of foods awaited our craving appetites. Waitresses in prim black and white uniforms and caps buzzed around the restaurant and to me, they resembled auto matrons. Always cheerful, they patiently made suggestions and would scratch the items for our orders on their pads. One time I recall eating succulent deep fried chicken and was told that I could not pick up the bones for the last few morsels. "Humph! A waste," I thought! This behaviour, which was standard in that era, was strictly enforced.

The remaining afternoon's visits to other departments are hazy in my memory, but the return via TTC, the trudging homeward, loaded with boxes and bags along streets that had seemingly increased in distance, and the relief of setting them down on the kitchen table with a sigh, are clear in my mind's eye. I was happy to be home, satiated with shopping, weary, but content. Following a fresh cup of tea, Gram would regain her energy and begin her preparation for supper.

This entailed Gramp and me walking around to the corner fish and chips store, a little family run business, "a hole in the wall" that reeked of hot cooking oil. Those bubbling vats of grease intrigued me and I would fervently watch the dipping of the fish into the creamy batter and the lowering of the homemade chips taken from pails underneath the counter, and plunged into sizzling oil. After turning into a rich golden brown, the food would be dumped from the wire basket onto brown paper and then wrapped in newsprint tied with string. Oh, the smells and anticipation of this enticing meal urged me to walk a little faster but Gramp seemed to enjoy my anxiety to hurry and would deliberately slow his pace to tease me. After a quick wash of hands, we would sit down at our set place with Grandma as keen as us to 'dig in.' Smothering the chips in Heinz ketchup and vinegar, this sumptuous meal would be readily consumed. Few words were spoken. What a treat to complete a productive day!

The remaining week included an exhilarating trip to the Exhibition, where Gramp allowed me ample time to experience some of the rides at the crowded Midway, which echoed the screams of excited groups of thrill-seekers, or to attempt to win some useless stuffed animal at the game counters. My hands and face sticky from devouring a pink sugar cone, we would then head off to sample dozens of foodstuffs at the Food Building, where we waited in long line-ups. He enjoyed this part of the day and Gramp would patiently chide me on my restlessness if the wait was excessive. Hmmm . . . I don't believe that this attribute of patience was passed on to me.

Our stomachs brimming from samples of soup, cheese, juice and assorted other foodstuffs, we would then saunter down toward the waterfront in late afternoon. Here we sat on the benches or grass in refreshing shade and listened to the music of the big brass bands at the band shell, a pause from hours of exploration and wandering. Following the traditional snack of a cool honeydew and hotdog, we headed out from the grounds, exhausted and grimy, and boarded the crowded streetcars along with other weary visitors who were too tired to converse. En route, the jerking and heat of the street car would lull us to sleep and at the clang of the bell and call at our stop, we would jerk from our reverie, slowly rise and descend the steps at the back of the bus to trudge homeward.

The week flew by, and before long I was reboarding the train for the north; my holiday concluded. It is with such fond memories that I recall this period in my life when the gifts of love and attention from both my grandparents were bestowed upon me. I feel a deep gratitude for their teaching that friendship and humour are possible in an intimate relationship and that connection and communication in community are rewarding. In moments of reflection and contemplation from my past, I feel them reaching out, enveloping me with love, that amazing essence that is an integral part of our earth's mysterium.

MUM

Carolyn Marie (Snow) Schreuer
Stoney Creek, Ontario

This lady walked on Earth with grace
With charm, finesse, and feminine taste
Her love she shared nearly 90 years
Saw many changes, wiped many tears

She loved two husbands to their end
She was a nurse and mother and true friend
As the embrace of her love grew
She raised three lovely children too

As if to add more love to this
Eleven grandchildren brought her bliss
The years passed and her family grew
She loved ten great-grandchildren too

A social butterfly, we would say
As she loved tea parties and Bridge to play
She would never miss a social event
It was certainly time well spent

It's so hard to say good-bye
To a lady who's been our loving guide
We wish her peace. We still wish her fun!
To the mother, grandmother we call Mum.

May 8, 1998
A tribute to my lovely Grandmother, Vivian Marie Lunney Mallette, who passed away
on May 6, 1998, a few weeks before her 90th birthday.

THE CRICKET VIOLINISTS

Karen Moore
Caledonia, Ontario

As soon as we got to the farm, Gramps would take me outside to listen to the crickets. Then we'd head down to the dock hoping that the loons would call. Not that we'd hear them every day. But you could always hope. When I heard those hauntingly beautiful yodels I'd show him the goose bumps on my arms. I always got goose bumps when I heard the loons.

In the winter when it seemed impossibly still outside, he'd take me crunching out over the new snow to sit by the lake, look up at the stars, and listen for the "music of the spheres" as he called it. Sometimes I was sure I could hear it, especially when the northern lights were dancing across the lake.

"I hear it, Gramps," I'd say, even though part of me said it must be in my head.

He'd hug me closer and whisper, "Does it sound like bells, violins, or flutes?"

"Bells," I'd say. "Glass bells," figuring that stars had to sound like bells if they sounded like anything.

I guess I got it right, because he'd laugh and say, "I knew you were going to have good ear, Caitlin, ever since you were a wee little thing. You always knew it was me from my footsteps. I could tell by the way you tipped your head up and smiled."

Now, crickets and loons are normal things to listen to, but Gramps even had me listening to cornstalks, crocuses, and lilies-of-the-valley. Cornstalks are easy when there's even a little breeze. They rustle and murmur like school kids when there's a supply teacher. And crocuses almost always buzz because the bees in late March are so happy to see them. But lilies-of-the-valley are quiet little bells. I kneel down and stick my nose in them because they smell so sweet. But I'm not sure I hear any music.

For a long time I wasn't sure I heard any music when I practised my violin either. I was sure I was hopeless and that the lessons were a mistake, but Mom and Dad had spent so much already. And Gramps would just sit there and listen like I was a child prodigy. Sometimes he'd even bring his recorder out and play along.

One day Gramps had me crawling though the grass listening to the ants, ladybugs, and clover. Another day I stood by an old dead oak tree listening to the bark. It's actually amazing how many little ticking and scratching sounds you can hear while listening to a dead oak tree - even when there's no wind. Then when the wind comes up there's a symphony of sighing and creaking that goes on. I noticed that myself.

In the early spring, everybody hears the spring peepers. But I also listened for the bullfrogs and those frogs that sound like somebody's scratching one of those old plastic combs. Gramps still had one around, one of the combs, I mean - and he showed me how it sounded like the frog.

All of this, though, was just a prelude to the summer of the cricket violinists. That was the summer I was twelve and was sent to stay with Gram and Gramps for the summer. Everything was secretive at home, and for a while I had the feeling Mom and Dad were trying to get rid of me. There was talk behind closed doors, and I heard Mom mention Gramps several times. I tiptoed around the house a lot and tried to smile encouragingly whenever Mom looked at me. But it was no use. Finally she pulled me to her and rumpled my hair like she used to when I was little. "How'd you like to spend the summer at Gram and Gramps'?" she asked. Like as if I had a choice. I love going up there, but something felt wrong.

The week after school was over Mom and Dad drove me up to the farm. They were quiet most of the way except for a few great conversation starters like, "So, I bet you'll have the best summer ever!" And, "Be sure to do extra stuff to help your Gram. She's going to have her hands full."

I don't know how many times I told them I'd be good, I'd be helpful, I'd dry the dishes, but when I asked, "Why is Gram going to have her hands full?" Mom just sort of mumbled something about Gram always trying to do too much.

Then we were on the gravel road, up and up the hill, to the farm with its small lake in back. The two huge oaks were the first things we saw, then the five maples along the lane and the neat white farmhouse. Gram and Gramps were waiting on the porch. The car scrunched to a stop on the gravel, and the porch creaked like always. When I hugged Gramps, I thought I heard a soft sound like letting go of your breath when you've been holding it. Maybe I hugged him too tight.

That night, after Mom and Dad had left, Gram tried to get Gramps to go to bed early. I couldn't believe it. It was only nine o'clock! But Gramps wasn't having any of it. "Caitlin and I are going to a concert," he said, all serious. And Gram had to give in. I wrapped up in an old black silk shawl of hers and felt very elegant. Evenings could be cool up there . . . and buggy.

Gramps held my arm as we made our way down the rutted path, fireflies twinkling all around us. "What kind of music do you think fireflies make, Caitlin?" he asked me.

"Jingle bell music?" I asked.

"That's it exactly!" He squeezed my arm.

The frogs were getting louder as we neared the lake. "It looks like the overture has already started," remarked Gramps. We sat on the dock and watched the fireflies. They may have jingled a little; though the frog chorus was so intense it was impossible to hear anything else. "Those green frogs are obviously playing banjos," said Gramps. I laughed. It *was* obvious. "What would you say about the others? By the way, those ones that warble are really toads, not frogs."

"Well that old bull frog is a bass viol," I said. "But the others - maybe dime store whistles?"

"Perhaps a hint of piccolo?" asked Gramps. "And in those big guys, don't you hear a didgeridoo?"

I laughed. The concert immediately quieted down except for one persistent chorus frog who must not have heard me. Then Gramps started coughing. I guess the cool night air was getting to him. When he couldn't stop, I realized we'd better not wait to see if the loons would sing. I helped him up and we trudged up the path toward the house.

The next morning, I paused at the kitchen door a minute and caught Gram fussing over Gramps, trying to get him to eat something. Gramps winked at me. He looked a little tired, as if he hadn't slept well. "Sorry the concert was so short last night," he whispered as Gram took out the muffins.

"No problem," I said. "Are you OK?"

He winked again and nodded toward Gram. "She's always worrying, but ignore her. Hey, I thought maybe we could have our own concert down by the lake. Serenade those who've been serenading us. Give something back to the wild. Whattaya say?"

It was a lovely idea but not so easy to do. I couldn't play anything that was worthy of a concert. We finally settled on my new piece, which needed a lot of work, and another that Gramps found up in his study.

I started practising every day. When I felt ready to smash the violin on the floor and jump up and down on it for good measure, Gramps would appear and help me go through the piece one more time. He'd bring his recorder, and we'd play together. Then it always miraculously sounded like real music, like I was actually getting somewhere. But I didn't realize how tired I must have been making Gramps until after one session he eased himself into the armchair and wiped his forehead. He seemed to be wheezing a bit.

I wanted to say something, apologize for tiring him out. But he winked. "Guess I'm getting slack in my old age."

"You aren't old," I started to say, but then I looked at him again. Certainly he looked older than I had ever thought of him.

Still, we spent quite a bit of time outdoors - down at the lake checking whether pebble splashes sounded like kalimbas, standing by oak trees listening to June bugs, or listening for trumpet sounds coming from the morning glories. "Won't do to have you up there practising day and night, girl," Gramps would say. "Gotta get out and listen to the summer, listen to the wind. That's where real music is made." And standing in front of those heavenly morning glories I became quite sure I was hearing the music of Purcell's Trumpet Voluntary that Gramps had been playing for me all week.

One windy day we took old bottles outside and put different levels of water in them. The wind hummed across them, making an eerie sound. We tried different chords until we got one that, as Gramps put it, "Sounded like the voice of the universe." The next day, we tried to duplicate the tone by blowing on the bottles ourselves, but it never sounded quite the same. We weren't as big as the universe.

As the summer passed from the frog prelude to the cricket violin chorus I started actually enjoying the time I spent practising the violin. I also found it a good excuse to go inside when I could see that Gramps should be resting. I kept telling him, "Gotta go practise now so we can have that concert before I go back to school."

He would go in with me and lie down on the chesterfield. Then I'd take my music stand outside under the big maple in back and play for the delphiniums and roses.

Mom and Dad called often. Mom was worried that I was getting in the way, not helping Gram, or tiring Gramps. "Caitlin makes me feel young again, not tired," Gramps would say.

I had assumed that our recital would be the last week of vacation to give us lots of time to prepare. I was surprised, then, during the second week of August to hear, "I think we'd better get it ready for this weekend, Caitlin." I glanced up from my music and realized that there was no arguing with Gramps on this. We were running out of time.

Friday night we headed down to the lake an hour before sunset. Gram and I made a couple of trips, taking folding chairs and music stands. Gram kept muttering about "foolishness" under her breath, but when I said, "We don't have to do this, Gram," she waved me on.

"Always would get his own way," she muttered. "Thinks he knows what's best." We arranged the chairs and music stands and then went back for Gramps. It was slower taking him down than carrying the chairs and stands.

"We'll just listen to their overture first," Gramps said, wheezing a bit. The crickets were tuning up. "Do you hear that little one over there playing first violin? Don't lose track of him. Watch how the other sounds are a counterpoint to him." We sat silent for quite a while, though sometimes I was sure that above the cricket sounds I was hearing Gramps wheezing. Then he was better, and for some reason the crickets took a little break.

"Shall we, Caitlin?" I stood and placed my violin under my chin. As I brought the bow down across it, the clear tone drifted across the lake.

Gramps came in on the recorder, and the two voices, violin and recorder, created an enchanted place and time. Everything else melted away, lake, dock, crickets, and Gram. There was only music and the evening sky. Music and the universe. If he'd asked, I would have had the answer. This is what eternity sounds like.

There were footsteps and voices on the path. Nobody had told me Mom and Dad had been invited. Dad was clapping as he stepped onto the dock. "That was lovely!" exclaimed Mom. She gave me a big hug, then hurried to Gramps and put her arms gently around him.

Dad clapped me on the back and hugged me, telling me how great I sounded, "Just like Perlman!"

On the way back up the path, Gramps leaned hard on Dad, but I don't think he weighed Dad down. He couldn't have, because when I hugged Gramps good-bye the next day, he didn't have any weight at all. Mom was staying to help Gram while Gramps went into the hospital for a few days.

"Hey, I don't want to hear any crying," Gramps said, as I sobbed on his shoulder. "You can never make a symphony out of that." He held me away a bit. "What is the sound of hope, Caitlin? Don't forget," he said as we climbed into the car, "last night we wowed the universe!"

I had been right. Our time had run out. Mom called early on Thursday morning to say Gramps had died in his sleep. I ran back into my room and threw everything on the floor and screamed. I didn't throw the violin though. Then I got very, very quiet.

I'm glad I didn't trash the violin. I needed it desperately that year to get me through the sad times. And starting that fall I made rapid progress on it. By grade ten I was first violinist in the school orchestra, and I knew then that I would go to music school. Now that I've finished, though, I realize that I want to compose. Strange, isn't it, how I just hear music everywhere? The music of the spheres, I guess.

We went up for the funeral, of course. It was one of those perfect end-of-August days when you swear you can smell September waiting in the wings to play its piece. I walked out under the sugar maple in back of the house. A few early leaves were already turning, and a yellow one drifted down in front of me. "What is the sound of a yellow leaf falling?" I

184

heard Gramps say. I almost turned around to look for him. I started sobbing again because I had thought of my own question - "What is the sound of life without Gramps?" I knew that no silence would ever feel deeper. But there was a second answer. Somewhere a cricket began to chirp haltingly, comfortingly. I walked over to the last of the lilies and listened as it played Purcell's Trumpet Voluntary. I swear I also heard a recorder playing along.

THE CHILD WITHIN

Dorothy Coates
Burlington, Ontario

Is it possible to love someone you have never met? I won't be seeing you for another three months and I'm already excited at the thought. I understand that about now you are approximately 13 inches long and weight less than 2 pounds. And your skin is delicate and transparent. I believe that if you decided to make an early debut you would have a reasonable chance of surviving.

I wonder how you will look. I have a mental picture of you and you have a tall strong body, your mother's beautiful brown eyes, your father's soft gentle features and blonde wispy hair.

I wonder how you will be. Will your personality be there when you are born, or will the way your parents nurture you make you into what you will become? Will characteristics of your grandparents and great-grandparents show in your looks and personality? So many questions.

In these days of modern technology your parents could easily have known whether you are a boy or a girl but they have chosen to wait until you are born. As for me, if you are a boy, I hope to love you and sometimes care for you as you grow up. I would like to introduce you to some of the passions in my life which include being with family, travelling, hiking, swimming, being with people, books and so on. If you are a girl I will do exactly the same, so it matters little to me. I hope that slowly I can share my life's experiences, my wisdom and my background with you and perhaps introduce you to my native England.

I think you are a very lucky child with stable loving parents who love each other and want you very much. You will have the material things in life, but more importantly you will receive love, understanding and patience as you grow. Your parents will tolerate your moods and your mischief, hug you when you fall and discipline you when you need it. You will be taught right from wrong, how to love and be loved, but most of all you will be encouraged to be the best that you can be, and love yourself for whatever that best is.

Some believe that we all have a purpose for being born and that each individual has unique talents and qualities. If that is true, I hope that you are able to find your purpose and talents.

Some who believe in reincarnation believe that we choose our parents before we are born so that each member of the family is able to learn and grow through the unique interaction with each other. If this is so, you are indeed a wise one.

Life will not always be wonderful. No amount of love can protect you from challenges, heartaches, loss of loved ones, and many other of life's difficulties, but certainly life will offer boundless joy and unfold many treasures.

Some researchers are saying that children born in 2000 will likely live a hundred years, and since life expectancy was only about 50 at the turn of the last century and is now around 80, it is probable that to reach 100 years will not be that unusual. If luck and good health prevail, I hope to have about 25 of those years with you. I cannot begin to imagine the changes you will see in your lifetime, in technology, in medicine, in world politics, in space travel and so on.

Perhaps it is possible to love someone you have never met. I feel that I love you already and along with my dear daughter and son-in-law, eagerly await your arrival.

TOO CLOSE FOR COMFORT *

Susan Ioannou
Toronto, Ontario

I dug my fork into the scrambled eggs. Behind, I could hear the water bubble in a big black pot on the wood stove.

"Mary," Grandma called, "come hold the door."

I pushed my chair from the breakfast table, ran around the heaps of dirty clothes, and pulled back the woodshed door. On Grandma's farm, everything was so different from our life in a city apartment. What was she up to now?

Squeak-eek, squeak-eek, Grandma rolled out the heavy washing machine. It slid along, a round green tub as wide as Grandma herself. Above the lid, two wooden rollers rattled and bounced until Grandma turned a knob on top and locked them into place. She parked the washing machine between the stove and the table.

"We have a good day." Tucking back a loose strand of gray hair from her bun, she nodded toward the window, where white clouds puffed across blue sky. "That wind will dry the sheets in no time." She folded back the sleeves of her dark blue housedress until her plump elbows showed bare. She turned toward the stove and the black pot. With two ends of a long towel, she gripped the pot's handles, eased around, and tilted. Boiling water streamed into the washing machine.

From a big jar on the table, she shook a handful of soap flakes into the water. The flakes just floated on top, until she bent down and yanked a lever on the machine's side. The water swirled and splashed. *Ka-chug, ka-chug* went the motor, a comforting sound like the sturdy wheels of a train. The flakes foamed into bubbles.

"Can I help, Grandma?" I wanted to pull that lever on the side, to make the water churn, stop, churn.

"You certainly can," she replied. She hobbled to the sink and from underneath lifted the metal pail. After half-filling it with cold water, she

188

crossed to the stove and added a dipper of hot. "I need a strong pair of hands to scrub Uncle Louis' wool socks. Here." She set the pail on a kitchen chair, and handed me a yellow block of soap. "I'll fetch the socks."

"But, Grandma," I cried, as she disappeared to the wood shed. "I want to run the washing machine."

"You'll use a special machine, all your own," Grandma called back.

"Goodie!"

A few moments later she hobbled back. Under one arm stuck a wooded scrub board like Mama's. In her other arm, she clutched a pile of Uncle Louis' socks. She dropped them in front of me on the chair.

"Ugh, these stink." I pinched my nose.

"That's why you need a scrub board to wash them." Grandma put a hand on my shoulder. "Why, that big contraption of mine just swishes the clothes around. These socks need muscle power to scrub them sweet and clean. That's too hard for an old lady like me. But a strong, young farmer like you . . . "

"O.K., Grandma." I pushed my T-shirt sleeves up to my shoulders. Once she explained the scrub board that way, I knew I could really help.

"Like this . . . " She scooped the socks into my lukewarm water and kneaded them up and down. She fished one out and handed it to me. "Now, push your fist right inside the toe." She unrolled the rest of the wet sock to my elbow. "Soap it plenty. Then rub the foamy part up and down the board's bumpy side, till all the dirt and smell are gone. When all the socks are clean, I'll help you rinse out the suds."

"I can do a really good job, Grandma." I bent over and scrubbed.

"Good girl, Mary." From the floor she gathered up a heap of dirty sheets and underwear and stuffed them into the washing machine.

When we both finished our first load, we piled the wicker basket high. I helped Grandma lift the heavy, damp mound and carry it outside, down the porch steps to the lawn. Behind us, across the grey floorboards, the drips left a little trail.

"Mary, you hang up the socks you washed," Grandma told me.

On tiptoe, I reached up. "But Grandma, the clothesline is too high."

Grandma winked. She walked down the lawn to where an old board propped up the middle of the clothesline. She yanked the board sideways and the whole line dropped a foot lower. "There, Mary, now you can reach."

As the knobby wooden clothespins tucked the socks along the line, we talked about how Grandma got born in a log cabin in the orchard. Great-grandpa didn't build the brick farmhouse 'til she was two. When she grew up and got married he let her buy the farm and built himself a house in town.

"Thum day," Grandma took the wooden clothespin out of her mouth and stuck it on a flapping pillowcase, "when I get too old to run the farm, I'm going to buy that house in town, and retire." As she worked her way down the clothesline, the fresh white sheets billowed and snapped about her in the wind.

Back in the kitchen, Grandma still had two more loads to wash in the big machine. "Next," she said, "before the water from the whites get too dirty, we'll put through our coloured dresses and Uncle Louis' shirts. Those smelly barn overalls get washed last."

Now that Uncle Louis' socks were done, I dragged my chair around beside her and munched on the rest of my toast and jam left from breakfast. I liked watching Grandma work the machine. She pulled the lever to the right to make the water swish back and forth. When she set the lever in the middle, everything stopped.

"What happens when you pull it the other way?" I asked.

"I'll show you soon," she answered, "after the clothes wash a bit more. First, we need clean water for rinsing out the suds. Here." She handed me a foamy pail. "Take this outside and dump it."

The pail swung more that half full. Across the porch and down the steps I lugged it. In the middle of the lawn, I saw the socks I pinned up drip, drip, into the grass, like slow rain from the clothesline above.

"Watch where you throw that dirty water," Grandma shouted out the screen door. "Don't empty it over the well. Go down by the orchard."

I puffed to the tall grass behind the outhouse. On my way back, I made sure to step around the well. This well didn't have a little pointed roof and a bucket you could crank down, like the kind in a park for wishing on a penny. Instead, double wooden doors lay flat on the ground, like the doors to the root cellar in the barn. Underneath, in the dark, hid the bricked hole where Grandma got drinking water.

When she was a little girl, the well gaped open, uncovered. Every morning, Grandma and her sisters dragged pailfuls of fresh water into the house. When Great-aunt Hulda was seven, she found a dead cat floating there. She screamed, and ran inside, and told everybody her brother Wilf threw it in. Great-grandma wrung her hands. One of the children would fall in next, she cried.

After that, Great-grandpa cemented the doors in place over the hole and set up a pump. It wasn't 'til after Mama left home that a pipe ran the water straight into the kitchen taps. You had to be sure you drank the water from the right tap. The other tap piped in rainwater from the cistern. The water made you feel sick to your stomach, but was safe for washing hands and clothes.

I hurried back into the house with the emptied pail. Grandma filled it with cistern water for rinsing.

"Are the clothes done washing?" I asked. I wanted to see what happened when Grandma pulled the lever on the machine the other way.

"Yes, but sit on the chair, Mary, and keep your hands back," she warned.

I perched beside the washing machine. She yanked the lever to the middle, and the wash stopped churning. Over the open water, she swung the two wooden rollers into place. When she flicked a switch on the side, one above the other, the rollers rumbled to a start.

Grandma pulled a wet shirt from the suds and fed the corner of the cuff between the rollers. Like wide rattling lips, they sucked up the rest of the cuff, the sleeve, the shoulder, the back, and the tails of the shirt. Once all the way through, the shirt plopped flat as a cardboard into the rinse pail. One by one, Grandma fed another shirt, an apron, and a blue dress into the wooden monster mouth.

Ring-ring! Ring-ring!

Grandma hobbled toward the telephone.

"Oh, look!" I cried, watching the clothes feed through, "Here's my yellow T-shirt, too!" On the hem of the blue dress, dripping, it rode into the rollers. I reached forward to show Grandma across the room.

"Eee!" I shrieked, as the rollers pinched my fingertips.

I tried to pull back my hand. I couldn't. My hand stuck. Through the rumbling crack, my fingernails disappeared.

"Wait!" I tugged.

My knuckles bumped between the rollers.

"Ow!" I felt myself pulled forward. My chair slid back. *Thump,* I heard it hit the table.

"Mary!" Grandma dropped the receiver.

Hung over one side of the washing machine, I couldn't believe what I saw! That monster had ME in its mouth!

The back of my hand squeezed flat. "No!" I yanked, but the rollers sucked it in and in!

"Mary!"

I heard her feet scuffling across the floor.

My wrist crackled under the wood. I tugged as hard as I could. Still the rollers gobbled and gobbled. I felt my whole body yanked closer and closer. Would I get squished into cardboard? "Help! Grandma, help!" I screamed!

Clunk, clunk, the rollers crawled up my forearm. "Ow! Ow!" they flattened the muscles. My elbow twisted. "It hurts!" Tears flooded my face. I shut my eyes.

THUNK! The hard wooden lips let go. I felt Grandma's firm hands slide out my arm.

"Mary, are you alright? Did I pull the switch in time?" Her fingers pressed up and down my tingling skin.

I opened my eyes. The rollers were wide apart. Inside the machine, the wash water drifted murky and still. Grandma hugged me to her soft warmth. Behind her steady breathing, I heard my heart pound.

"Oh, Mary," she chided. "I told you, stay back. I warned you."

"But, Grandma, I didn't know . . . " I started to cry again.

"Hush, hush. It's over." She rocked me side to side. "We got your arm out in time. Once over the elbow, those rollers would have broken the joint."

I held up my bruised fingers.

"The blue marks will fade." She wrapped her hand around them. "But a broken bone . . . Well, that's a serious matter. I remember when . . . "

I covered my ears and burrowed into her apron. I didn't want scary stories. By lunchtime I felt much better and didn't mind hearing how other kids got caught in washing machines. Best I liked Uncle Louis' story about his school friend, Art Brennaman. The rollers pulled him in all the way to his shoulder. For months after, he had to wear a scratchy white cast. Even when he grew six inches in his fourteenth year, that one arm hung shorter than the other.

Uncle Louis patted my unhurt arm. "It's lucky you're such a good scrubber." Grandma told him how I washed his socks. "You won't even need a washing machine when you grow up. These modern contraptions just mean trouble."

Grandma shook her head. "Don't be so old-fashioned, Louis. Besides, you use a milking machine, for the cows."

"Yeah, sure" he replied, "but it sucks out milk. It don't gobble up arms."

They all laughed, but after what the washing machine did to me, I agreed with Uncle Louis. Old-fashioned ideas were best.

*From Susan Ioannou's *A Real Farm Girl.* Edmonton: Hodgepog Books, 1998

IN YOUR LIGHT *

Susan Ioannou
Toronto, Ontario

For Grandmother Wright

Without frame or lens
To freeze this pine-narrowed bay,
You are clear to me still as shallows
Glassing over ridged sand
- the acid clarity of northern rains.

Years have rippled your skin.
Hands like rugged mounts
First through fishless waters,
Thrusting cedar and spruce against
Sky's low, inverted bowl.

Eyes almost transparent
You root along this rock. Through evergreen shade
Twisted feet scramble the slope,
Shore to stairway, step to shore,
Refilling an emptied pail.

When you ease into the boathouse chair,
Pink and mauve pansies
Bob under white eves.
Sunned into morning,
Your chocolate home sways above water
- with love.

A finger begins
Curling, uncurling,
A single strand of white hair.
Memory's mainspring unwinds
Clear as the north's thin light.

It was all forest, then,
Clustered thick to the sand,
Trees chopped down, one by one,
Another rock for the pilings dragged up.
A few feet further each year
The fiddlehead tangle flattened,
While lawn spread up the slope,
A slow tide, 'til it stopped
High enough for four children to run.

Winters back in the city
Curled seven days' work round a week:
All your kids helped with the store.
The Great Depression? Contentment:
Hot food and enough hand-me-downs.

You married for love and it stuck
Fast, on this rock
Above skyless water,
Building three more
Small chocolate houses.
Petunias straightened the lawn.

Cold as the sand
You found him one morning.
Forty-nine years . . .
And now

You still summer here on your own
Water curls, uncurls at your door.
Your granddaughter weeds
Her begonias.
Others come by
And go.

You can't walk far, but your eyes
Absorb the transparent sky.
There are islands
Far down the narrowing bay,
Little fist punching up
Rock, firs reaching
Into the wind.

That's the way things are, and stay,
In your light.

* From Susan Ioannou's *Clarity Between Clouds* (Fredericton: Goose Lanes Editions, 1991)

POEMS FOR MY GRANDCHILDREN

Shirley-Ann Doucette
Burlington, Ontario

Our lives have been enriched and continue to be every day!
Smiles, Hugs, & Snuggles we love to have from you,
Coos, Ahs, and Oos bring along their own treasures too
Cries, Screams may sometimes alarm but they're often golden sounds,
For all are indications, signs that show us all is well with you!

Farther goal! Dare to be all you can be
Attaining to fulfil your dreams and goals in life.

Life isn't always sweet, the road we
Travel has many a rough footage
Making our steps unsteady at times.
But with loving friends, and family
To accompany us, we'll make it
Through each new journey along
The way.

A Grandmother's Prayer

Thank you for . . . Gifts - treasures to behold

These little ones . . . Reflections – of your son (who came to earth as a child)
May I always . . . Appreciate these children, never forgetting from whence they come, (sent to us from above)
Grant to me . . . Discernment – wisdom, in being of assistance (whenever I can)

Let me keep in . . . Mind, their mothers' methods (her ways listening with respect always)

Help me to . . . Offer opinions, suggestions when I'm asked (with consideration, thoughtfulness before I speak!)

Let me . . . Train, teach each child your ways (forever in the direction by which you took each step)

Help me to . . . Have, maintain a good relationship (with their mother as well, giving honour to her roles, given unto her, to raise these little ones for you!)

Give unto me . . . Everyday, in every way the wisdom to know the best things to do and say in all situations or circumstances that may arise!

Enable me to . . . Rise to the challenge facing each new day! (with a prayer in my heart, giving all gratitude honour and praise unto you!)

Grandmothers – Another Generation

Generation – Now the third

Racing, in circles, to and fro
After small children in diapers once more
Nothing much more important than these little ones
Doing whatever a Nanna can - to add a measure of joy
Managing a part of her day – to share in their laughter
Offering assistance as each day passes by
Temperaments, trials a part of daily life - as they grow
Happiness not always, sometimes there's tears, but
Enduring love shines though - with each golden smile!
Reflections, memories we are creating to cherish, to
Surround us during each one of our cares -

"There are the things I prize
And hold of dearest worth -
Found in Nature's beauty
Walking along your way -
Each day, if one would only look."

Parents, children should
Have such a place of honour
And esteem!
Each day a golden moment
You will find, if one would
Really see!

Friends and family of which
I am surely blessed - can find
Their place as well!
Yet above all I should – I must
Reflect upon and Remember
My creator-Thee-O God-Thee!

Welcome to our family
Child from above
You'll be surely loved
A welcome addition
Within our home
Within our hearts
God's gift, a treasure
To each one of us!

A Parent's Prayer
May God always protect you

May He guide your life and turn
Things around so that you live
In the Joy of God's blessedness!
May God's grace shine on us
Providing us with a home
And a meaningful existence
Adding the blessing of His church
To give encouragement and
support!
To be God's child is to be
Permanently held in the
Embrace of His Love
"Nothing can separate s from
The love of God", Oh that
This shall be true of our love
May it always and forever be
shown!

The Gift of Life - New Life

In closing: We'll continue to grow
in Love
To build our lives - including
Each other in many future days,
As we make our way – along
The road of life.
As your sister and you,
Your mother and I,
Travel on the highway
That lies before us!
We may in time separate
When your mother and you
Children move to a home
Of your own - but I will always
Be involved - be nearby - just
A call away - to help as you
Should need, to try to meet you
Wherever you are, emotionally
Or physically, to encourage and
Offer my support, always!

*But my prayer: is for you to know
God*
Needs to be let in
To travel on the journey
Along with you!
He needs to be with you
Through each experience,
In every opportunity
As our guide, as your friend
And Oh what a friend
To always be beside you!

RUTH, THANKS FOR THE MEMORY

Maureen Brown
Hamilton, Ontario

Thanks for the memory.
In my heart I still see you and Alex on your daily walk, arm in arm, often carrying bags of groceries from The Barn.

Always a smile and a "How are you and John?".
Always caring and asking about others.

The joy you got from small gifts such as the embroidered anniversary hanging. The dried flower basket which traveled with you from the hospital to the retirement home, put a smile on your face.

Thanks Ruth for your graciousness, in living, in dying and now a memory, in death.

Thanks for allowing me to visit you at the hospital, and at Elm Villa. Your concern for others was always there. Even at Elm Villa, you would ask, "Can I get you something to drink?"

One afternoon I found you sleeping with your head on the bed and your feet on the floor. When I called your name and woke you, rather than be upset as many of us would be, I got a big smile.

Ruth, your smile is embrasioned in my mind. Your spirit lives on in the smile and caring of your family. You are so proud of them and they of you.

You are now in heaven with God.
When I die, Ruth because I have asked, I know that you will be there to greet me with that same big smile.

Ruth, thanks for the memory.

Life can only be understood backwards:
but it must be lived forwards

Soren Kierkegaard,
Life

CHAPTER 3

CONNECTIONS FROM TWO GENERATIONS

The entries in this chapter are different from the rest of the book. These were submitted jointly. The older persons' submissions, presented in italics, are followed by those from their younger loved ones.

GREAT JOY

Audrey Forster
Orillia, Ontario

A happy one-year-old came swiftly down the dining room pushing his little walker. He made more speed than most of the residents in this Retirement Home. He brings great joy to each one at whom he smiles as he hurries along. Every head turns and smiles illuminate the faces of even the saddest residents.

Older children also bring joy to the hearts of the residents. Some have adopted a grandparent, and child and residents experience the thrill of the relationship.

Once a month we have a Sunday morning church service. Eleven-year-old David comes with his "Nanna" who plays the organ. He helps seat the worshippers and distributes the Hymn books. He is my great-nephew and always likes to stay for lunch with his 85-year-old aunt. Many speak to him for they look forward to his coming as much as he looks forward to his visit. He chooses a game for us to play before he must leave.

I would like to share with you two articles of creative writing, which he did for school. The first he entitled "Grandma Goes to Heaven." The minister requested that he read it at his Grandma's funeral. The second is about a bicycle ride and his 62 year-old Grandpa, who is the husband of "Nanna" with whom he lives.

GRANDMA GOES TO HEAVEN

David Wood
Orillia, Ontario

Have you ever thought about what happens to us when we do not live on this earth anymore? I don't think about it very much but the last few weeks I have had to because my Great-Grandma is very ill in the hospital right now and I think she won't ever be home to our house again. When she was well and my Papa was alive, we had lots of fun together and she was happy. But then a big sadness came over her when he went to Heaven and she had to stay here on earth. Lots of people have lots of ideas about what Heaven is like. Some people say that it is just a place where there is no sadness or sickness or being afraid. Other people say that it is just a state of being nowhere. Other people have a picture in their minds of God being there waiting to give us a big hug and making us feel not afraid of anything ever again. My Nana and Grandpa gave me a book when I was a little younger that talked a lot about Heaven and instead of talking about streets paved in gold it talked about other things. I kind of think that the way my book talks about Heaven is the way it will be. My book says that there are no tears there, no monsters, no mean people, you never have to say, "good-bye," or "good night," or "I'm hungry," you never get sick, cold or afraid and God is so close He can give us big hugs. I kind of think too that we will see the people we have loved lots like my Papa. Right now, my Grandma is getting ready to take her trip to Heaven, only this time she doesn't need to pack any suitcases or worry about spending money, she just needs to let the angels come and take her gently away. We will miss her very much but we will know that she is happy, not sick anymore and in very good hands!!

A RACE WITH GRANDPA

David Wood
Orillia, Ontario

It started out being just a regular Friday morning. I got up, got dressed and had breakfast. After breakfast I got ready for school. So I got on my stuff and went to school on my bike. It took me about five minutes. When I got to school I had a regular day. I had a great day at school in Mr. Clendening's class, doing gym, science and a whole bunch of other stuff. Before I knew it, it was time to go home. So I packed my backpack and went home. On the way home I saw Grandpa in the van. Just as the light was about to change, I peddled a bit faster to make it across the street. As soon as I was across the street and still peddling faster, I noticed that I was off the ground! Then I realized that the faster I peddled, the higher I went! I landed on some old lady's lawn but I kept on going. Then I peddled faster and before I knew it I was over the roofs of houses!! As soon as I got high enough, I was over the van and I came around the corner, landed and skidded into the driveway and beat Grandpa home!! You should have seen the surprised look on Grandpa's face!!

THEODORA KNOWN AS DORA

Elizabeth Averil Thompson
Dundas, Ontario

For Megan and Gillian (known as the Angels)

Your great-grandmother Thompson, from Northern Ireland, was christened Theodora, but was always known as Dora by family and friends. She grew up to be a slim and talented young woman who sang, played the piano and baked the best soda bread and wheaten bread in town. When she was quite young, she had the good fortune to meet and marry your twinkle-eyed great-grandfather. He was a teacher, but in his spare time he sang with a lovely tenor voice and conducted church choirs. So, they became a musical twosome and in due course, were blessed with two musical children, your great-aunt Isobel and your Grandpa Thompson.

When your Grandpa T. grew up, your great-grandmother was happy when he found a wife (me), but a little sad that we lived far away across the Irish Sea in England. She couldn't just drop in for a cup of tea and a chinwag. When your grandfather and I had two little boys (your Daddy and Uncle Simon), your great-grandmother was even more sad about the distance which separated us. In 1968, when your Daddy and Uncle Simon were still young (11 and 10 years old), we decided to move to Canada, where Grandpa T. had been offered a job at McMaster University. Your great-grandmother felt keenly that we would be even further apart but made up her mind to come and visit us in Dundas as quickly as possible. Grandpa T. and I didn't think at that time of warning her that August is usually very hot, hazy and humid in Dundas and that we had no air conditioning. Nor did we mention that Canadian women (even the no-longer slim and definitely plump, like your great-grandmother) favour comfort over glamour and go for shorts and little cotton tops in the heat of summer.

Your great-grandmother visited us in 1969 wearing the same sort of clothes that she wore in cool, rainy Northern Ireland - whalebone corset, petticoat, nylon stockings, dress and lace up walking shoes. The holiday got off to a sticky start in Dundas, and she became quite exhausted with the heat. Fortunately, we had arranged to stay at a cottage near Honey Harbour for two weeks and we thought that this would provide some relief. However, it was not to be, as even in Georgian Bay, a full Northern Ireland outfit is a sure-fire recipe for acute discomfort.

Grandpa T., thinking of blissfully cool breezes on the lake, tried to encourage your great-grandmother to come with him in a rowboat. She finally agreed, with the utmost reluctance, and we set out for the dock with your great-grandmother dressed as for church, complete with large straw hat. Grandpa, with great difficulty, succeeded in persuading your great-grandmother to put her right foot into the rowboat. Unfortunately, as she paused to ponder her next move, the decision was taken out of her hands, as the boat moved gently away from the dock with her right foot in it. What a splash! Poor great-grandmother was floundering in the water with her straw hat floating gently downstream. Your Grandpa T. leapt out of the boat and rescued your soaking wet and "shook up" great-grandmother. He was greatly relieved to find that the water just came up to his chest, as he doesn't swim like a fish the way you do. We made our way dripping back to the cottage, where in short order, your great-grandmother's whalebone corset, petticoat, stockings and dress were soon all flapping merrily on the washing line.

Sadly, your great-grandmother, Theodora, known as Dora, never came to visit us again in Canada.

P.S. This is a true story – just ask your Daddy who was in the boat, or your Uncle Simon, who was on the dock, both wide-eyed at the spectacle.

CHEESE WODGES

Elizabeth Averil Thompson
Dundas, Ontario

My dear Megan and Gillian,

I thought that you might be interested in some memories of my early working life.

In 1949, when I was 22 years old, I was hired as a personnel officer with C & J Clark Ltd. Shoe and Sandal manufacturers in Street, Somerset, England. This huge private business was run by Quakers, good people who worked very hard and provided the village with valuable amenities, such as a school for continuing education and a swimming pool. My hours were from 8 a.m.-6 p.m. (with an hour off for lunch) and I was required to participate in the joint consultative meetings, which were held in the evenings. I was also expected to join the Dramatic Society and contribute in some meaningful way. Learning how to make shoes by hand at evening classes was viewed with favour. My starting salary in 1949 was six pounds per week in paid cash. As you can imagine, there was not much left over after I had paid for my room, food and a few other necessities. Financially, I lived a hand-to-mouth existence but I was very fortunate to work for generous progressive employers and to have such a charming and understanding boss, Miss Kilgour, who was held in high regard, not only at the factory but in the wider world of personnel management.

Each morning, at break-time in this enormous shoe factory, a fleet of trolleys would go out to provide strong tea and heavy-duty sandwiches for the hard-working staff. The well-brewed tea was transported in urns and served in earthenware mugs (no polystyrene in those days). The sandwiches were constructed from doorsteps of bread, each slammed together with a thin slice of processed cheese. Some wit had christened these sandwiches "cheese wodges" and the name stuck. Whenever I think of my first job I think of cheese wodges.

One of my responsibilities was for the canteen, which was run by a dear lady, who was better at balancing the books than the meals. Each day I bought my lunch at the canteen and endured stodgy fare. Finally I resolved to have a heart to heart talk with the manageress regarding meal planning for nutritionally balanced meals. I suggested to her, in a diplomatic fashion, that fried fish with chips, followed by suet pudding with treacle syrup was a rather heavy meal. She was quick to inform me that, on the contrary, suet pudding with treacle syrup was "light." We continued to talk without any meeting of minds, until I suddenly realized that she meant light in terms of cost - fish was expensive, therefore heavy, and suet pudding was cheap, therefore light, and together they made a perfectly balanced meal! I guess this early encounter impressed upon me the need for speaking the same language.

My boss, Miss Kilgour, bless her heart, used to take me to meetings of the Personnel Management Association in Bristol (a long drive from Street). I remember one of the speakers talked about the great importance of "carrying your foremen with you." This is of course very sound advice but it always made me giggle, as I had visions of carrying a couple of our bouncer-sized stalwart foremen, one under each arm.

After a relatively short time at C & J Clark, my boss, charming Miss Kilgour, left and was replaced by Miss Druce, a Christian Scientist. She took a lively interest in her staff, inviting us for meals and outings, and told us that we could call her "Bobby" on the weekends. However, there was some tension, particularly with the factory nurse, regarding Miss Druce's Christian Science beliefs. On one occasion, a young man from the Systems and Methods Department was diagnosed by his family doctor as having diabetes and was offered insulin treatment. As a Christian Scientist, he felt that he could not accept this offer and some time later he died of the disease. Miss Druce thought he had made the right decision and explained to me that the young man was just continuing his journey in the "upstairs" rather than the "downstairs" part of the bus.

Life was very busy with long hours of work and painful plodding progress in making leather slippers by hand. My social life centered on my fellow personnel officers and a boyfriend from Systems and Methods, who was not favoured by Miss Druce. There was little time left for the Dramatic Society, but I acted as secretary and watched curiously from the sidelines as romance blossomed between the flirtatious leading lady and a handsome young married management trainee. One winter, I joined the chorus of the Glastonbury Operatic Society for a production of Good Night Vienna. We practiced diligently. However, in the heat of the first night's performance, when the girls rushed in to bid fond farewells to their handsome soldier boyfriends, I kissed the wrong soldier, much to the amusement of the audience. So much for my operatic career!

In 1954, I accepted a position as a personnel officer with the Kellogg Company of Great Britain in Manchester. My boss at Kellogg's had kindly arranged for me to stay at Alderbank, a Young Women's Christian Association Hostel (YMCA) in Altrincham, which was relatively close to my new place of work. It was an unusual hostel, in the sense that thirteen men were allowed to stay there, but only for one year, while women were allowed to stay for five years. I really enjoyed life at Alderbank - interesting young people, reasonably good meals and a kindly warden all contributed to my happiness.

The work at Kellogg's was rather dull and I didn't have enough to do. One of my jobs was to keep the books for some sort of "Sick Fund." One day, an outside auditor arrived unexpectedly and quizzed me so persistently that I burst into tears. There was nothing wrong with the books and my elderly boss took it upon himself to give the young auditor a little fatherly advice.

At Kellogg's, I used to have lunch with a large lady from customer relations, who regaled me with bizarre stories about strange things found by customers in boxes of cereal - broken glass, a man's tie, etc. Naturally management was pretty hyper about the production line and there were strict rules designed to ensure that only cereals went into cereal boxes.

One night at Alderbank I answered the clanging front door bell and a young man was on the doorstep with his luggage (which included his violin). He had come from London to work in Manchester and he had been booked in temporarily at Alderbank. I thought he looked a little lost in his big army surplus style overcoat, but I quite fell for the innocent look in his blue eyes. His name was Ian Thompson.

Your loving Grandma T.

OUR HOLIDAY IN HONEY HARBOUR

Gillian Thompson
Dresden, Ontario

My Dad's parents, his brother and our family (Megan, Mom, Dad and I) go on a trip almost every year. In 1996 we went to Honey Harbour and stayed at the Delawana Inn.

One day we decided to go canoeing. We had two canoes. Megan, Mom, Dad and I were in one canoe and Grandma and Grandpa in the other. We went along the lake quite happily. Megan and I didn't paddle much. When a wave came, Mom and Dad put down their paddles. However, Grandma and Grandpa didn't put theirs down.

It was partly because of that and partly because Grandma had on a slippery bathing suit, that made her slide from side to side on the seat, that made their canoe tip over.

My Grandpa had his wallet with him! He rescued it before it could get away. He was wearing trousers, a yellow shirt and sandals with socks. I thought he was a little overdressed for the occasion.

A man on a jet ski came by and asked if they wanted to be rescued. Grandpa replied, "No thank you. We are just fine." I wondered if he was used to bobbing in the lake wearing his trousers. Then, my mom asked the man on the Jet Ski to please rescue my Grandma.

While they were being rescued, the Jet Ski tipped over and they all fell into the water. It was very comical for us looking at them. Grandma and Grandpa probably did not find the humour until later.

We went back to the lodge and dried off. Later, at supper, Grandma and Grandpa gave their rescuer the free lunch they had won.

Now when we go canoeing, Grandpa finds a special canoe where Grandma won't slip and Grandpa leaves his wallet behind.

BLITZEN SAVES CHRISTMAS

Megan Thompson
Dresden, Ontario

Dear Grandma,

I just love all the stories that you tell me.
Now I have written a Christmas story for you.
I hope you enjoy it.

Love Megan.

Blitzen Saves Christmas

One Christmas Eve, Santa and his reindeer were entering China. Blitzen who was the closest reindeer to the sleigh noticed that Santa looked a little green.

"Is anything the matter?" inquired Blitzen.

"Oh," laughed Santa, "I am just feeling a little queer from those cookies I had at the Jun's house."

Suddenly Blitzen thought that the cookies might have been peanut butter cookies and Santa was allergic to peanuts! He asked Santa about this though and Santa exclaimed, "I think you are right Blitzen, we had better go down right away."

The first house that they landed on was the Young's house. Fortunately, Mrs. Young was a doctor and knew what medicine to give Santa. Santa told his reindeer that they must save Christmas. Blitzen thought that the reindeer should fly back to the North Pole to get the magic elf to somehow get all the presents to their correct places all around the world. The other reindeer agreed and started to fly back to the North Pole. On the way there they stopped in France for something to eat. The reindeer chose to stop in France because the grass is so sweet there.

Once the reindeer reached the North Pole it was already 10:00 p.m. Blitzen found the magic elf in her workshop. He asked her if she could somehow make all the presents go to their places around the world. The magic elf agreed to this and went to work right away. "Lots of this and a touch of that," she muttered to herself. About two hours later the magic elf was finished. The potion the magic elf had made looked like wine. "How do you work the potion?" Asked Blitzen. "It is simple," replied the magic elf. "You just say, 'Coil and trouble, boil and couble, deliver these presents on the double.'" As soon as Blitzen said those words, all the presents were delivered to their correct places. All the reindeer were so happy that they shouted, "Hurray for Blitzen. Hip hip hooray!"

UNE NOUVELL VIE – CHRISTINE

Jeannine Ringuette
Timmins, Ontario

Quelle joie de vivre une nouvelle naissance ?
Quand l'occasion est la première petite - fille ?
Les émotions débordent dans cette réjouissance,
Car c'est un trésor ajouté à notre famille.

L'attention est centrés sur ce petit être
Qui sait en retour donner tant d'amour ?
Quels heureux moments nous passons à la connaître ?
Nous anticipons toujours ses visites et son retour.

Au fils des années, elle nous accompagne partout.
Intelligente et curieuse, elle veut tout savoir.
Les talents se développent dans presque tout.
Par sa joie de vivre, elle sait nous émouvoir.

Nous la voyons grandir, elle est adolescente.
Les succès abondent en musique, aux sports et aux études.
Son caractère prend force; elle demeure accueillante.
C'est merveilleux de constater ses aptitudes.

Je prévois pour elle un avenir brillant
Si elle met en pratique les sages conseils
Et la formation qu'elle reçoit en grandissant.
De tout temps, je demeure la fière grand-maman.

GRANDMOTHER

Christine Groulx
Timmins, Ontario

Grandmother, you have always been there when I needed you,
But I haven't been there for you.

Grandmother, you have always showered me with lots of gifts,
But I haven't showered you much.

Grandmother, you have always taught me to help others,
But I haven't been helping you much.

Grandmother, you have always told me to forget and forgive,
But I haven't been forgetting and forgiving you.

Grandmother, you have always told me to love others,
But I haven't loved you.

Grandmother, here is my chance to change all of that,

It's my turn to be there for you.
It's my turn to shower you with gifts.
It's my turn to be patient with you.
It's my turn to help you.
It's my turn to forget and forgive.
And, it's my turn to love you.

I LOVE YOU!

BIRTHDAY TRIBUTE

Katie Allen
Lynden, Ontario

As I turned 80 this year my family had a birthday party for me at my daughter's home. Each member of the family read something they remembered about me. It was very touching. This is what Matt Allen, my youngest grandson wrote.

Being the second youngest grandchild in this family unfortunately has meant that I have the second fewest memories of Grandpa. Though I find this extremely disappointing I take a tremendous amount of solace in the fact that I have probably spent the most time with Grandma. Sure she excels at being a grandmother. Mike, Heidi, Kirby and Corky or I could, and do, talk at length about that very topic. The advantage I have is that Grandma employed me for six years.

I used to spend every Saturday in Copetown. It was my first job and I haven't had a better boss, since I learned countless things about gardening and how to use power tools. I guess with Grandma you can't expect anything less. However this sort of thing seems infinitely unimportant.

It is amazing what a woman in her seventies can teach a teenager about the work ethic and energy. There were days I did not want to be there because I was tired, but no matter when I got to the house Grandma was always up and on most occasions already out there working.

The funny thing is, I grew thinking that this was the norm. I thought all Grandparents took fitness courses and were more computer literate than their grandchildren and drove back and forth across the country. I've been asking around and I got to tell ya, this is not the standard.

Whenever I talk to my roommates about my Grandma, they always ask, "What's she up to now?"

DEAR GRANDPA

Helen McGrath
Millgrove, Ontario

This was written by Grandpa McGrath's grandchildren and lovingly read at his funeral

Dear Grandpa,

During the most important years of our lives in which our values and morals were formed, it was an honour and pleasure to experience your humble example. As we continue our journey in life we will always look to you as an excellent teacher, husband, parent and role model. Your kind, generous and selfless ways are an example to us all.

Throughout your life and even in your final days you always thought of others before yourself. Despite the pain you endured throughout your illness, no word of complaint escaped your lips. The love and care you expressed towards Grandma throughout good times and bad will remain in our hearts as we mature in our relationships. The little things you did for her such as vacuuming, threading the needle or doing the dishes never went unnoticed. When Grandma was ill, you stayed after the mass to pray for her recovery. This showed the special bond you shared with her, and the role Christ played in your relationship.

Your immense faith and belief in the power of prayer remains with us today as we reflect upon your Christ-like ways. Every night, as you and Grandma prayed the rosary and said a special prayer for each of us, we felt your presence. We believe your prayers have helped us in our day-to-day lives and we know you will continue to watch over us from your special place in heaven. Even in your final weeks your faith did not waver. Instead of self-pity, you offered prayers for those who had no time to prepare for their own deaths. When your pain was so immense, you warned your daughters not to administer too much morphine, as you had no interest in changing God's plan.

The importance of the Church in your life was reflected in your support of us. At Baptisms, First Communions, and Confirmations, you and Grandma would always be in attendance with words and cards of encouragement. You also taught us to see the beauty of nature, animals and play. What appeared to your unsteady hand while plowing was your attempt to save a young family of birds. The best baseball bat that we ever used was built by you with your lathe. Collecting maple sap on a fresh morning during March break taught us more than any teacher could. More fond memories include summer weekends at North Brant, tractor rides and mechanical explanations that baffled and amazed us, and it always seemed that by the end of the ride you had our names all straightened out. Be sure every time we hear a fiddle play we will feel closer to you, and we will be reminded of the times when our family celebrated with music and dancing led by you. While we will miss your physical presence, the joy of these and other memories and knowing that you are looking over us from a better place will help to warm our hearts.

Do not worry about your bride, for in addition to your sons and daughters, there are 29 grandchildren here to share their love with her.

Love Always,

        Your Grandchildren

Sean O'Reilly	Colleen Haykin (McGrath)	Daniel Ferguson
Maureen O'Reilly	Seamus McGrath	Nadine Ferguson
Kathleen O'Reilly	Sheila McGrath	Mark Ferguson
Patrick O'Reilly	Brendan McGrath	Joe Ferguson
Shannon O'Reilly	Sarah Mercey-Boose	Chrissy Ferguson
Michael O'Reilly	Michael Mercey	Mike Ferguson
Colleen O'Reilly	Christa Mercey	Nicole Ferguson
Siobhan O'Reilly	Laura Mercey	
Pauline Fox	Robert Wallace	
Michael Fox	Mary Wallace	
Margaret Fox		
Helen Fox		

CHAPTER 4

CONNECTIONS FROM CHILDREN

The love and appreciation of a child is never so eloquently expressed as it is through actions that reflect the guidance of their elders.

MY GRANDFATHER

Kendra Benedict (Age 9)
Oakville, Ontario

Ken Dix was my grandfather. He died of cancer at the age of fifty, before I was born. Three wonderful gifts he had were singing, music and people. He interacted with his family by singing with them at weddings and variety concerts and taught my mom and two aunts how to sing and what music was all about. People liked him because he was friendly, outgoing and spoke very well!

Something that made him happy was the foster children. Even though Granny and Granpy had 8 kids they took in at least 14 children and he loved them! That's where my first and middle name came from. Kendra came from Ken and Nicole came from my grandfather's favourite foster child Nicole.

My grandfather would have been proud of his grandchildren and the only one he knew was my cousin Ryan. The rest of us were born after he died. He would be proud of us because of his talents and how we all have a piece of his talents, like singing, acting or musical instruments!

I wanted to write about my grandfather because I didn't know him and I wanted to know a little about him. I learned that even though my cousins and I didn't know him, we all have a piece of him in our own different way and that's better than any gift from a store!

GRANDMA AND GRANDPA

Nina Mirkovic (Age 9)
Oakville, Ontario

Grandma and Grandpa
You're very old,

Grandma and Grandpa
You're worth gold,

Grandma and Grandpa
You're so wise,

Grandma and Grandpa
You make great pies,

Grandma and Grandpa
Your hair is gray,

Grandma and Grandpa
It's time to play,

Grandma and Grandpa
You're so fun,

Grandma and Grandpa
Let's tan in the sun,

Grandma and Grandpa
It's not so dark,

Grandma and Grandpa
Let's go to the park,

Grandma and Grandpa
The day is over,

Grandma and Grandpa
I'll always come over,

They give me treats
They give me candy,

What else will they give?
I get a little spoiled but
That's all right,

Because they are my grandparents
And that's what I like.

MY GRANDMOTHER

Rebecca Schinkel (Age 9)
Oakville, Ontario

I would like to write about my grandmother because she had an interesting life. I admire her because she did something that not many women had done before her.

My grandmother was born in Wiseton, Saskatchewan, where she went to school for two years in a two-room, two-storey school with two teachers. Her family left the prairies when the drought and depression began. They crossed the continent to New York to visit her aunt, and then crossed the Atlantic by ship to Germany, where they boarded a train that took them to Stockholm, Sweden and then on to Finland. A few months later they travelled to Petrozovodsk, Russia, where her father intended to stay; however, they only lived there for six months. They returned to Finland for six months, and my grandmother attended school and taught the teachers English. The family then moved to Toronto, Canada, and lived there for six years. She attended high school for three years, two in Kirkland Lake, and one in Scarborough.

After high school, my grandmother chose optometry as a career. She started the three-year course in 1944 at the School of Optometry. Optometry was not a popular career for women at the time, so only about one percent of the students were women. My grandmother and grandfather met at university, and until 1950, were only the second married couple to practice optometry together in the province of Ontario. They celebrated their 50th wedding anniversary in 1997.

My grandmother was like a trailblazer for women in optometry and after all these years she is still working.

MY GOLIGA AND GRANDPA JACK

Adam J. Clark
Oakville, Ontario

Goliga

My Goliga came to Canada from England in 1953. She sailed to Canada on the ship *The Empress of Scotland*. She said, "it was very, very rough, very cold and I saw 32 icebergs. I was very sea sick." My Goliga wanted to come to Canada because she wanted to see the world. When Goliga was a little girl, she had a Canadian math teacher in her school. Her family lived in Tunbridge Wells in Kent and their neighbours were Canadian. Her family was sad to see her go. "It was a time when all young people in Britain were travelling, we were all heading out to sea to see the world," said Goliga. "It was just after World War II and we wanted to get away." During the war, Goliga lived in an area that was bombed, machine gunned and shelled. She hated the war and was very afraid. She could not get enough to eat and she really missed oranges and bananas. Since Goliga came to Canada, it has changed a lot. "Toronto was not a very big city, now it is huge. I am glad that I came to Canada," she said. "I met Grandpa Jack here and we had three children. Now I have four grandchildren who I love with all my heart. Canada is a good, peaceful country." Goliga got her name from my cousin Kate who could not pronounce "Grandma." Now everyone calls her Goliga.

Grandpa Jack

My Grandpa Jack came to Canada in 1953 too. He sailed to Canada on the Holland America ship the *Ryndam* with his younger brother Victor. "Everyone on the ship got sick because the waves were very, very rough. I didn't, I was one of the few passengers who had a big breakfast everyday," he said. "I had eggs, bacon, ham and toast and lots of tea. I loved sailing on the ship to Canada." My Grandpa Jack was in the army in England. He went to Egypt and worked there. After he finished in the army, he decided to come to Canada. Grandpa Jack wanted to see the world. After Canada, he was going to go to Africa and Australia. Grandpa Jack liked Canada so much that he decided to stay. When Grandpa Jack came to Canada, he lived in Toronto. On weekends, he played rugby on Toronto Island and spent time with his friends there. While my Grandpa was on Toronto Island, he met my Goliga. They got married one year later. Grandpa Jack loves living in Canada. He likes to sail and he loves the opportunity that Canada has given him. "In England, it was very hard to make your own life. In Canada, if you work hard, you can do anything," he said. "Toronto has changed a lot. When I first came to Canada, the subway was just being built. They also had streetcars that were heated by wood stoves. The driver had to stop the streetcar to put wood in."

MY GRANDMA

Nick Pescod (Age 9)
Oakville, Ontario

My Grandma loves tea. She was born in England in 1927. She had twin sisters, who were the world champions in ping-pong. They are in the Guinness Book of World Records. My Grandma was a war bride. My Grandma had three kids, my Dad, my Uncle and my Aunt. My Grandma plays bridge and she loves to move to new places. My Grandma loves clothes and she is a sports fan. Her favourite sport to watch is tennis. My Grandma cares for me.

REMEMBERING

Celine LeFevre (Age 9)
Oakville, Ontario

She walks down the streets of Toronto.

"I'm so old now," she thought, "I wonder how many more years I have to live? Was my life a total waste?"

No, it wasn't.

She can hardly remember yesterday yet she remembers when Islington Avenue was just a dirt road with one lane for each direction. She remembers her husband (my grandfather) telling her about growing up on the prairies and how apples were always a treat. Now she eats apples every day and they're not treats. She remembers growing up in Toronto, living above a store and having her grandmother living above her.

Now with the millennium coming up, her children and her grandchildren (one of which I am) know so much more than her. Would she live to see the new year? I hope she will.

ABOUT MY PAPA

Haleigh DiBattista (Age 9)
Oakville, Ontario

Hi! My name is Haleigh Alexis DiBattista. I am going to introduce you to my papa, Edward Wood. My papa died April 14, 1994, of cancer. He died four days before my gramma and papa's 41st anniversary. My papa died two nights after the doctors found out he had cancer.

My papa had married a fine young lady named Sheila. They met at their cottage when they were 11 years old. They got married April 18, 1953.

My papa's favourite hobby was golf. He was a great golfer. He also liked to swim too. When he came to our house he would always watch some sort of sport, but mostly golf. My papa even got a hole in one!

My papa had been to another place outside of Canada. He has been to the United States of America.

My papa had a few jobs. I remember we always went to visit, so we saw him coming home wearing his uniform. He worked for the TTC, he was a truck driver, a salesman and even a policeman. Now that's a lot of jobs!

When my papa was young he had dogs, cats, rabbits and even birds. That's a lot of pets!

My papa had six kids including my mom. The order of the kids from oldest to youngest is Karen, Nancey, my mom, John, Heather, Paul and Andrew. Now that's a lot of kids!

Before my papa lived in the house before he died, he lived in 5 houses altogether.

My papa made a few things out of wood. He made a lot of things for our cottage because it had barely anything in it.

My papa lived in Whitby, Ontario. The street he lived on was Gadsby Lane. His street was very long and it went on and on.

My papa didn't see my Uncle Paul's wedding because he died before the wedding. My uncle Paul is married to a nice young girl named Suzy.

My papa never got to see my Uncle Andrew's girlfriend Charmange and their baby Rachel. Rachel is adorable!

One of my favourite memories was when we were at my cottage and he threw me into the lake.

I Love My Papa.

MY FRIEND, NANNY!

Willie Brown (Age 10)
Hamilton, Ontario

When my Nanny was living she loved to dress up,
Especially when she was going to dine or to sup.

She loved to wear large, fancy hats,
And she also liked to crochet and make floor mats.

My Nanny loved to ride downtown on the bus,
Over me, her grandchild she made such a fuss.

My Nanny I had was one of a kind,
Until one day when she peacefully died.

She went to heaven to be with the Lord,
There she has found peace so happy and galore.

I have a spot deep down in my heart,
My feelings for her will never depart.

GRANDMA AND GRANDPA

Sarah Labourn (Age 9)
Oakville, Ontario

My grandma and grandpa are great. My grandma bakes the best goods. I have always wished to learn her talented ways.

She taught me how to share, how to cook and many other things.

My grandma loves to knit. If you give her a needle and thread, she'll start making things right away!!

I remember when she knit me a little doll. I still have that doll.

My grandma has no pets. She lives only with my grandpa.

My grandpa is really good with wood. He spends most of his time working in the basement.

Grandpa made two shelves of wood. They are very sturdy.

My grandpa has a good sense of humour. Tell him a joke and he'll laugh his head off!!

Grandpa wears glasses. He looks very handsome. In fact, I would like to have a lad like that myself!

Grandpa loves to read. Newspapers, books, magazines, anything. He'll just keep reading. He's a mean, lean, reading machine!!

Well that is all I have to say except for one thing. I love them very dearly, and when they die they will always be in my heart. Always and forever.

Sarah

MY GRANDPA

Emily Stacey (Age 9)
Oakville, Ontario

Hi! I'm Emily and I'm going to introduce you to my grandpa. My wonderful grandpa is probably the nicest grandpa in the world. (So is my grandma.)

When my grandpa was a kid he had red hair, so all his friends called him Red. My grandpa was born in 1935. He grew up on a farm. My grandpa's favourite subject was math. When my grandpa grew up he worked at a college for a few years. Then my grandpa joined the navy. He did a lot of things in the navy. Here are some things he did. He fired guns, worked on computers and travelled all around the world. The reason he joined the navy was to protect people. While he was working in the navy, he invented something called log cabin potatoes. They are mashed potatoes rolled into a log and then you put breadcrumbs on them.

My grandpa got married in 1956. He married a nice young lady. My grandpa likes to tell stories of when he was a kid and when he was working in the navy.

One of my favourite memories was when my grandpa took all my cousins down to the beach and we had a water fight. Another good memory was when my grandpa and I built a huge Lego castle that I had gotten for Christmas. My grandpa likes to watch football and likes to play hockey.

My grandpa is the best coach in the world. Do you hear me? The best coach in the world! Grandpa makes the best subs.

I will always love you and you will always be in my heart!

JUST A LITTLE TOKEN

Emily Elliot (Age 11)
Oakville, Ontario

For my Grandma and Grandpa Lewington,

It's the little things in life that count. Like when your grandparents take you out for ice cream or give you some money or something. Even if you only get a dime you still feel special. My grandparents give me old books and necklaces and I treat them like they're worth a million treasures. Doesn't it feel good knowing that they are always there? Whether they are next door or miles away, they are always there for you. So tell your grandparents not to go all out for your birthday as long as you have something small as a token of their love.

MY FAVOURITE POEM

Alec Elliot (Age 9)
Oakville, Ontario

To my Granny and Grampa Lewington

I love my grandma very much
and that you can't bend
she also always lends me
at least a buck to spend

I love my grandpa very much
with him I'd never tell a fib,
because he was the one
that taught me the game of crib

GRAMPS AND GRANDPA

Christine Cochrane (Age 9)
Oakville, Ontario

Dear Gramps and Grandpa,

I miss you both. The reason that I miss you is that I never met you. Gramps, you were my mom's dad and you lived from July 2, 1929 to November 17, 1988. Grandpa, you were my dad's dad and lived from November 11, 1922 to May 8, 1982. I really miss you and I wish I got to meet you. Then you could come to my swim meets and see all the ribbons I have and I could have fun with you.

Love,

Christine.

GRANDPARENTS

Melissa Davis (Age 9)
Oakville, Ontario

My grandparents are wonderful. I have two grandmas and one grandpa. So three, but I did have four. I had one more grandpa. His name was Russle. He died when I was five. All I remember is that he used to call me his little Pixy Girl. I know he loved me just like I loved him. I love all my grandparents. My dad's mom Grams helps me very much. She's the one that taught me how to hold a fork and knife. Then there's my dad's dad. He is very nice, old, but wise and loving. You can't forget my mom's mom! She is very smart, old, but young in a way. I do not mind what they look like. I know I will always love them, it's just the way life goes.

THE GREAT-GRANDMA I NEVER KNEW

Sarah Gray (Age 9)
Oakville, Ontario

I wish I knew her.
My Great Grandma Gray

She was a great golfer,
Just like my Grandma and
Grandpa Gray

She lived in a golf store,
When the great World War II was
on

I wish I had known her,
My Great-Grandma Gray.

MY GREAT-GRANDPA

Kaylan McDonald (Age 9)
Oakville, Ontario

My Great-Grandpa was very brave. He died two years ago. My Great-Grandpa lived on a farm. He had all sorts of animals on his farm. My sister and I used to call him Pop. A long time ago he had a plane and it crashed. My Great-Grandpa was my hero, and I loved him very much.

Another adventure is when he had a big log cutter. My mother was standing right by him. He went to push a button and cut off his finger. I loved my Great-Grandpa.

MY GRANDFATHER, THE POLICE OFFICER

Preeti Lal (Age 9)
Oakville, Ontario

A long time ago when my dad was around my age, his father was a police officer. He was called in for many, many crimes and just bad situations. Now, I'll tell you about a time when a man in Africa used to steal luggage and jewellery.

One day there was a train in Africa going somewhere. After the train left the station this man named Alfons Charles jumped on top of the moving train and started to saw open the lock to get in. He and his men threw out the luggage and gathered it in a truck and left. When the train got to the station and people found out that their luggage was gone, they reported it to my grandfather. He sent out with other police officers to catch Alfons. My grandfather instructed one of the officers, "When you hear something sawing through the train you silently go to the back and arrest Alfons Charles." So the officer did as he was told and arrested Charles. But the officer had fallen asleep so Alfons had a good chance of escaping. He quietly slipped his hands out of the handcuffs and left. At the station all the luggage was there. Then my grandpa asked where Alfons Charles was, and the officer had no clue because he fell asleep. The next day my grandpa went on the train himself and caught Alfons Charles. My grandpa sent spies out to look for the hideout where Alfons used to hide the luggage. He found it and he brought it back to the police headquarters.

MY GRANDMA

Colin Stewart (Age 9)
Oakville, Ontario

My Grandma is very kind,
And she also has a really smart mind.
She's really good at cooking food
And she's always in a happy mood.
Her favourite drink is a cup of tea,
And she always says she really loves me.
She's very good at making pie,
And my wish is she'll never die.

THE BIG TRIP

Alex Bouma (Age 9)
Oakville, Ontario

Slow. The plane ride is very slow. Relaxing, I guess. My parents snooze while I watch a Star Trek movie. I bite into a plane ride cookie. Not as good as homemade. Speaking of home, I am 1200 miles from it, up in a plane. We're going to BC to visit my Oma and Opa. I love it there. I'm going skiing on Big White Mountain.

"I think I'll play my GameBoy," I say to my mom. It's a game with a bucket on Mario's head. I get bored of it really fast. Anyway, the batteries ran out.

Our first stop is Calgary. Then we fly to Kelowna, BC. My ears hurt when we land. In Calgary, I get more batteries for my GameBoy. I am eating a turkey and gouda sandwich. I give the rest to my dad. He likes it. He likes anything.

What?! Oh. I must have fallen asleep in the plane to Kelowna.

"Hey, it's Opa!" I yell to my parents. I run over to give him a hug. "Hi Alex," he says. "I'm so excited about your arrival." My Mom and Dad talk to him and I look at the airport. It's very small, but cozy.

The next day we head up to the mountain in Opa's car. My Oma talks to my mom. I hold on for my life. My Opa is a really fast driver. My Aunt and Uncle own a condo at the mountain. My Opa had heart surgery and he still skis. My Oma had hip surgery and she skis too.

I **think** I'll rent a snowboard. I've been wanting to for a long time. I had **better take** some lessons too. Oma and Opa are very kind and generous. They are fun to be around. My Oma is a very good artist. She has sold so many different paintings. My Opa really likes eggs. He likes them poached and I do too.

Opa used to be a very good diver. He would compete in diving competitions. He is a big fan of sports. I wish they could live closer so I could visit them more often. But think of all the fun I would miss on the plane ride!

ME AND MY GRANDPARENTS

Daniel Kneblewski (Age 9)
Oakville, Ontario

To Grandfather and Grandmother,

My grandfather is 80 years old.
My grandmother is 69 years old.
My grandmother and grandfather have a cat. The cat's name is Mindy. My grandfather was in the war. My grandfather always works with tools. I taught my grandfather and my grandmother to play Nintendo and they beat me once. I learned to swim in their pool. My grandmother always buys me ice cream. My grandfather always lets me help him work. When my grandfather and grandmother were in school, if they chewed gum they had to put the gum on their noses for the whole day! My grandfather is 10 years older than my grandmother. My grandmother loves flowers. My grandmother's birthday is April 13. Now my grandmother is 70 years old. My grandfather almost died in the war.

I NEVER GOT TO MEET GRANDPA

Braden Gordon (Age 9)
Oakville, Ontario

I call my Grandpa, Grandpa Gordon. He was born in 1917. Everyone was happy that he was not injured when he was born because his mom had just tipped the Model - T (a car). They named him Clarence Walbern Gordon. He grew up on a farm near Osage, Saskatchewan. He went to war in Europe when he was still a young lad. After the war he worked at a grain elevator for 36 years. He and my grandma had 2 boys and 1 girl. Grandpa had blond curly hair when he was a young kid, black curly hair when he was an adult and then white curly hair when he was old. He loved children but unfortunately I never got to meet him, he died two years before I was born. He died from a pulmonary embolism. My dad was sad but now he is OK. That's how my Grandpa died old.

GRANDMA

Pawan Dosanjh (Age 11)
Oakville, Ontario

G is for grandma who is nice and sweet.

R is for the ring that she always wears.

A is for amazing because you are.

N is for nothing more special than you.

D is for your dazzling jewelry.

M is for the money she always gives me.

A is for always nice all the time.

MY GRAN

Meghan Lawrence (Age 13)
Stroud, Ontario

I met her at the old age home in Alcona. My class goes there every Tuesday to be with our grans. My gran is Ethel Lade. She is a little woman with a big heart! Well, she isn't that small but she is smaller than average. She is so cute!! Ethel, at first was a little quiet, but so was I. Later on, after about a month, we were talking like crazy!

Ethel and I always talked. She didn't play cards or games, she just liked to talk. I remember one of her stories that she told me about when she played the piano and organ. She was a very good musician and loved to play. She was asked to play at the church for a while because the musician had to leave for some reason, holidays maybe? So Ethel would be the great musician, which she was!! She played the organ and played very well!!

One day, at Mass, Ethel went up to play the organ. As she was getting on the bench, she had to put her foot on the foot pedal to get up on it. She didn't know her brother had pumped air into the organ, and as she put her foot down, a loud noise came from the organ. A very loud noise! She quickly sat down and went beet-red from embarrassment. Poor Ethel!

Here is a little history about Ethel. Ethel Ireson was born on December 7, 1906 in Markham Township. She lived with her mother, father, one sister and one brother. She didn't play any sports, but liked to watch hockey and baseball. Sometimes she would go out and skate with her friends. Her favourite colour is turquoise and she is English. Her parents were from England.

In 1941 on August 4, my Mother's birthday, Ethel was married to William Lade! (My mom was born in 1960, not 1941!) Ethel had two boys named Robert and Eric. During this time, Ethel didn't work at all. She did work during the war in a munitions plant. She also worked in Eaton's, but only for a little bit.

Well that's not all, but my essay would take days to write if I were to tell you everything. I have learned that everyone has a story to tell, all you have to do is take time to listen and care. I dedicate this report to Ethel Lade. Thank you for not only being my Gran, but my friend as well. I love you!!

Grade 8
Age 13 years
Adopt-a-Grandparent Program

GRANDPARENTS

Breanna Lewington (Age 15)
Georgetown, Ontario

To my Grandma and Grandpa Lewington,

Grandparents are the heart
Grandparents are the soul
Grandparents are the ones you love
And they're not rock and roll.

They help you sleep
By comforting you at night
They tell stories
While you fall asleep with them hugging you tight

They help you remember
And know the past
From yesterday to tomorrow
And the memories will always last

So I wrote a few verses
To show all my love
To prove I found the best people
Who are as gentle as a dove

The sweetest people I have ever known
Are my grandparents
Being there for me as I have grown.

FOR MY POPPA

Alison Graham (Age 10)
Oakville, Ontario

I will always remember my Poppa
I think of him every day
In his chair beside the pool
I remember him that way.

In the summer he'd watch us splash and play
In the backyard pool you see
He'd clap and cheer at all our dives
And wished he could jump in after me.

He'd come home for dinner on Sunday night
To visit with his family, he would say.
Without you Poppa, it won't seem right
And I will miss the card games we used to play.

He loved to spend time with us
And listen to all our stories
Especially about our soccer
And of all its glories.

For my Poppa isn't really gone
I will remember him like this
He will always be in my heart
Goodnight Poppa; with a kiss.

Dedicated to my Poppa, January 13, 1923 to October 24, 1999.

ALL ABOUT MY GRANDMA

Alison Wiseman (Age 9)
Oakville, Ontario

Hello! My name is Alison Wiseman. I will be telling you about my Grandma, my dad's mom. She died of cancer. When my dad and his two brothers were born she was always there, but when she started to smoke and work she was never there. Just a minute, I call my grandma Nanu because when my Nanu was teaching my big sister how to say Grandma she said Nanu so all my cousins call her Nanu. My Nanu always took us to fairs and bought us things because she loved us. When she was in the hospital my family was very disappointed. When I came home one day my parents said she had died. She had black hair and brown eyes, she was born on a farm, she had 7 or 8 brothers or sisters. Her name was Evelyn and she played with us and read to us. Nanu I miss you. Well, I hoped you liked the story. Bye.

She was born on November 12, 1932 and died April 10, 1996

MY GRANDMA

Anita Jaitly (Age 11)
Hamilton, Ontario

Dedicated to My Grandma

My Grandma is nice
and she always gives big hugs.
She likes to use spice
and she loves drinking tea from mugs.
She's always there to make me smile
and even when I'm sad
she makes me feel very glad.

My Grandma is very special.
She helps me clean
even though I may be a little mean.
She's always there for me
she walks with me.
She even squawks to her friends about me.

She's one terrific person.
She's loving and caring.
She's kind and she's sharing.
I couldn't have asked for a better Grandma than you,
I love you Grandma.

A SPECIAL MEANING

Emily Elliot (Age 12)
Oakville, Ontario

To: My Grandma Elliot and Vic Sparrow
75 and 82 years old

Across the world there are many different languages, Chinese, Mexican, Latin, English and many more. I'm sure of all of these different ways of saying grandparents all have the same meaning - sweet, gentle, caring, supportive, smell good, always smiling and give great big hugs.
But I think my Grandparents are more than that. If I had to write a definition about them in the dictionary, there would be many a page full of all of the wonderful things about them. I mean not many grandparents would be so caring to volunteer at the hospital, give generous amounts to charity, and are so hard working that they build their own garage.

Also, while we're on the topic of dictionaries, I don't think there's a word in the biggest dictionary in the world that expresses how much I love my Grandparents.

LETTER TO OMAMA

Rachel Muller (Age 8)
Hamilton, Ontario

Dear Omama:

I hope you come to Hamilton soon. I want to see you because I want to give you hugs and kisses and have a picnic with you on Bubba's hill. Do you want to come to Hamilton and have a picnic with me? I love when you read stories to me. I think you are very cheerful, sweet, funny and nice. You cheer me up when I am sad. I hope you write back soon. Hugs and kisses.

Good Luck.

Love,

Rachel

MY GRANDMA AND GRANDPA'S GREATEST GIFTS

Payton Levy (Age 8)
London, Ontario

My grandma is giving,
My grandpa is thoughtful,
My grandma bakes cookies,
My grandpa eats meat.

My grandma is giving,
My grandpa is jolly,
My grandma plays bingo,
My grandpa is funny.

My grandpa colours,
While my grandma sweeps,
My grandma cleans,
While my grandpa eats.

Grandmas are sweet,
Grandpas have big sizes of feet.

Punch line: If you have a grandma or grandpa love them like crazy!

MY GRANDPA

Sarah Elliot (Age 12)
Dundas, Ontario

On the occasion of her Grandfather's 75th birthday

My Grandpa, Bob Shimmell, is now 75
He has lived a long life, and somehow survived!
He's a Grandfather to eight and a father to three
He is special to everyone – but most of all me!
One day my dear Grandpa had a magnificent thought
He gathered the Grandchildren to hatch a fine plot!
He dressed them in costumes and hustled them in
To sell Kiwanis peanuts to family within!
That man with the peanuts also makes wine
And everyone says that it tastes just divine!
On special occasions we all raise our glass
I wish I could have just a sip – I'll pay cash!!
Another great thing that my Grandpa can do
Is whip up some burgers for him and for you!
He thought up the recipe when my mum was a kid
No one knows the ingredients – he keeps them well hid!
My Grandpa is brave and was in World War II
He fixed up the airplanes that other pilots flew!
To this day he loves airplanes, especially the Dakota
When it flies overhead there's no time for a soda!
My Grandpa continues to golf and to curl
He's busy and active and life is a whirl!
Happy Birthday dear Grandpa, may your wishes come true
And you must remember that I will always love you!
Happy 75th Grandpa!!!
Love Sarah
XOXOXOXOXOX

WHAT I REMEMBER ABOUT MY GRANDPA

Ryan Elliot (Age 14)
Dundas, Ontario

On the occasion of his Grandfather's 75th birthday

It's not every day my Grandpa turns 75, so I thought I'd write and tell him what it's like being with him.

I remember a few summers ago when he took me to see the air show in Hamilton. We left early in the morning and got a great parking spot. We had a lot of fun looking at the old planes, especially the Dakota. After the air show was over, we left to go find the car. However, we had forgotten where we parked. We spent almost an hour searching for his car – we even got parking attendants to help us! Finally, we found his car. We had been looking in the wrong half of the lot!

That's one thing we have in common – we both like old planes. A lot of what I know comes from Grandpa telling me facts and stories about World War II planes. Grandpa got me interested in planes and I've chosen aircraft books from our library.

I also remember going over to his house to help him put up a fence so that deer couldn't eat one of his trees. When I came over that morning, he was wearing a hat that said "Boss" in capital letters. There was no arguing with the Head Honcho. After all our hard work, the deer could hop the fence. We were both angered and amazed by this!

My grandpa was in a parade last May. I was proud when he walked by. He asked my Uncle Bob to see if he could get the picture negatives so that he could have a picture to remember this special day.

Grandpa is an author too. He wrote a book about West Hamilton. He wanted to preserve its history for other generations. I may want to become an author too.

My Grandpa works hard – some say he's even a perfectionist. Maybe that's why my Grandpa and I get along so well – we're perfect. Grandpa taught me how to do things right.

Grandpa is daring too. What other 70 year old would climb an apple tree and cut it down himself?

I think that Grandpa did a good job of raising three "great" kids. If not for him, I couldn't baby-sit for Auntie Ben, play catch and almost break our neighbour's window with Uncle John, or have my mom look after me and Sarah. Grandpa used to call me "Tigerman" – now I'm taller than my Grandpa, but will I ever be wiser?!

Love,

Ryan

MY GRANDPA

Emily Hutton (Age 8)
Ancaster, Ontario

On the occasion of her Grandfather's 75th birthday

My Grandpa I love
As true as can be.
As much as a bear,
Loves a honey tree.

My Grandpa is really nice
Because he listens to me
When ever I'm sad or happy.

My Grandpa helps me
So it's always fun
So that makes him
The best #1.

My grandpa is special,
Special to me
I love him a lot.

I LOVE YOU

Wyatt Baldwin (Age 11)
Nepean, Ontario

When I need courage,
I think of you.
When I need respect,
I think of you.

You wrote poems,
And I'm writing a poem for you.
You lost your husband,
And I lost you.

You are my light.
You are my friend.
You are my angel.
You are my grandmother.

I LOVE MY GRANDPARENTS

Laura Elliot (Age 5)
Oakville, Ontario

I have very nice Grandparents,
they are very nice to me.
So I picked up some nice daisies,
put them in my hand,
then gave them to my dear grandparents,
who had my Mommy who had me.

MY GRANDMOTHER

Nicole Settimi (Age 13)
Little Britain, Ontario

Awesome, sweet, nice and cool,
That's my grandma. She has a pool.
She goes shopping almost every day.
She hardly has any time to play.

She never argues.
I hope that's true,
But grandpa, was that a rumour that she threw
her shoe at you?

She tells me stories every night.
Then I go to bed without a fright.
She hugs and kisses and holds me tight,
And then she says, "Good night! Don't let the
Beddy - bugs bite."

A devoted grandma, mother and wife,
Having a good grandma sweetens up my life.
I love my grandma; she's quite a treat.
As I said in the beginning,
She's really sweet.

Grandma, I love you

Nicole
XOXOXO

MY GRANDMOTHER

Cathleen Settimi (Age 11)
Little Britain, Ontario

My Grandparents are the coolest dudes.
In their red rag-top,
They like to cruise.
My Grandpa likes to country drive.
And about the children,
They have five!
My Grandma likes to SHOP, SHOP, SHOP!
She loves it so much,
She'll never stop.
For wonton soup, she's off to Chan's,
With Grandpa, Aunt Nelly or Aunt Joanne.
Grandma writes the greatest books.
Oh! I didn't mention the way she cooks.
Her meatball soup, her homemade bread.
With this great cook,
We'll always get fed!
Almost single-handedly
Grandpa ran the railroad.
Using honesty and fairness as his code.
No "lolly-gagging."
No "frittering time away."
He makes the most of every day.
Forty-five years together
On this Happy Day.
Grandma and Grandpa,
I love you so much,
In every way.

Love Cat

CHAPTER 5

CONNECTIONS FROM YOUNG ADULTS

I WANT YOU TO KNOW

Colleen Lowe
Kleinburg, Ontario

Dear Grampa,

I want you to know a few thoughts that have been on my mind.
I know that life is finite and there is no time like the present to share these with you.

I want you to know that I remember the train rides you used to take me on when I was little.
I know that I was sometimes a handful, but you were always patient.

I want you to know what a thrill it was for me to visit your condominium as a little girl and peer over your seventeenth-storey balcony.
I know times like these gave me my sense of adventure.

I want you to know how glad I was to have you at my high school graduation.
I know that your faith and pride in my accomplishments have encouraged me to persevere when the going gets tough.

I want you to know that I admire you for working long past when you could have retired, if for no other reason than personal satisfaction.
I know that you have inspired me to always work hard and dedicate myself to all tasks, no matter how small.

I want you to know how grateful I am to you for bringing our whole family together for the holidays.
I know that these times are very special and they are memories I will always treasure.

I want you to know how much I appreciated the way you took care of Gramma when she was ill.
I know that you made her final hours peaceful.
I want you to know how proud I am of you for having the courage to go on with life after Gramma passed away.
I know that living as a widower after 58 years has not been an easy adjustment for you.

I want you to know that you have shaped my dreams for the future.
I know that my desire to help others lead healthy lives has stemmed from watching you live your own life so gracefully.

I want you to know how much you have influenced my life.
I know that you will always be my hero.

Love,

Colleen

REMEMBERING MY GRANDPARENTS:
SITTEE AND GIDDEE

Janic Gorayeb
London, Ontario

When I was a little girl, my family spent many weekends at my grandparents' apartment. All the grandchildren in the family called our grandparents Sittee and Giddee. Sittee is "grandma" in Lebanese and Giddee is "grandpa" in Lebanese. My sister Elise and I always felt happy and excited as our parents drove us to Sittee's and Giddee's place. I have so many wonderful memories from our visits with them.

When we finally arrived at Sittee's and Giddee's small apartment, it would be full of relatives and great smells of simmering Lebanese food coming from the kitchen. Sittee would make grape leaves with rice, Akibbi, a meat dish, homemade cheese, fresh Syrian bread and of course, her famous chocolate cake. Sittee's food was so delicious! Even a regular bowl of cereal or a peanut butter sandwich prepared by Sittee tasted so good.

After dinner, the entire family sat in the small living room telling jokes and funny stories. We would laugh, and laugh, and laugh. Sometimes hearing Sittee's laugh made me laugh even more. Sittee had a silly laugh. It was infectious!

I remember being able to do whatever we wanted to do, and never being told "No"! It was a kid's paradise. We would run up and down the halls of the apartment building, or chase each other playing a game of tag. Other times, I would do cartwheels all the way down the hall, make myself dizzy and then flop down on my back for a rest.

Sometimes Sittee and Giddee would treat us and give us money to go to the store. My sister, all of my cousins and I would run down to Johnny's

269

variety store to buy candy. Since I was the smallest and the youngest of all my cousins, my sister would always hold my hand. I always felt safe with my sister and my cousins.

We would all race back from the store singing and laughing. We ran into the spare bedroom, my cousins jumped onto the bed and started gobbling up their candy. I would sit quietly and practise writing my name in all of the colouring books. I often wondered if we would keep on doing these fun things for the rest of our lives.

I remember when I was a young girl, Sittee became very ill and I realized that my life would change. Mom and Dad reassured me that everything would be okay and if I felt comfortable, I should say good-bye to Sittee. I knew that I was not responsible for Sittee's illness and although she was dying, I had my family to talk to and to cry with. I said good-bye to Sittee; I told her that I loved her and thanked her for being the BEST Sittee in the world. That night Sittee died. Although I was very sad, I imagined the most beautiful and magnificent place in the universe to keep my spirits up. Then I knew that Sittee was safe and happy there.

After Sittee's funeral, everyone came back and filled the tiny apartment. We sat around with plates of food and drinks. We hugged each other. We talked and laughed at wonderful stories about Sittee's life. It's funny, even though the apartment was small and often bursting with people, I never felt cramped or uncomfortable. I always felt safe and secure.

Giddee lived with us for a few years after Sittee's death. During those years, Giddee and I would take long walks and play cards. Sometimes Giddee would play his clarinet and Dad would play the drums. Mom and I would get up and dance. I can still hear them playing my favourite song: "You've Got The Cutest Little Baby Face."

I remember when I was a young adult, Giddee became very ill and I realized that once again my life would change. Mom and Dad reassured me that everything would be okay and if I felt comfortable, I should say good-bye to Giddee. I knew that I was not responsible for Giddee's illness and I knew that I had my family to talk to and cry with. I said good-bye to Giddee; I told him that I loved him and thanked him for being the best Giddee in the world. That day, Giddee died. Although I was very sad, I imagined the most beautiful and magnificent place in the universe to keep my spirits up. Then I knew that Giddee was safe, happy, and with Sittee once again.

I remember after the funeral everyone had lunch together in the apartment. We sat around with plates of food and drinks. We hugged each other, we talked and laughed at wonderful stories about Giddee's life.

Now that I'm older, I sometimes experience feelings of sadness from the loss of my Sittee and Giddee. My sister and I are always talking with our cousins about the things we did at Sittee's and Giddee's apartment. Constantly reminiscing has helped my family and I to cope with the loss of our grandparents. I will never forget what a wonderful and loving childhood I had. I will never forget my Sittee and Giddee. I am truly blessed.

IN MY DREAMS

Mignon Lau
Toronto, Ontario

It has been six years since my grandmother passed away and there have been many times when certain things will trigger memories of her. Of all my grandparents, I was the closest to this one (my mother's mother) and I have many wonderful memories of her that I now call upon to comfort me when I miss her. I would like to share my extraordinary experience of having a grandmother that was, not only a loving grandmother, mother and wife, but also a wise individual.

I remember when I was younger my grandmother used to take my cousins and I to the corner store and buy us treats. We would all ride our bicycles and tricycles while my grandmother walked along behind us making sure all her *ducklings* were safe. It was a trip that we all looked forward to and even though at the time we all appreciated it for its face value, I now also appreciate it as a special memory.

My grandmother was the type of person who kept in touch with all her children and made sure that everyone was all right. She was a selfless person that gave of her time, love and patience whole-heartedly, regardless of who the individual was. The most vivid memory I have of my grandmother's unending love is from my childhood.

As a child, I was inflicted with whooping cough. One night I had a severe case of whooping cough that lasted through most of the night. My grandfather had gone to another room to sleep so that my grandmother could care for me through the night. Although I had kept my grandmother up all night, never once did she complain or leave my side. Instead, in the middle of the night, my grandmother went down to the kitchen to fry some minced ginger (a traditional Chinese remedy) to rub on to my back to ease my coughing. It was only after my grandmother had persistently rubbed my back with the ginger that my coughing ceased. I will never forget the love, patience and selflessness that she blessed me with that night - and every moment I shared with her.

In March of 1994, my grandmother was diagnosed with lung cancer. It was a devastating realization for my family, but not unexpected, for she had smoked her entire life. Although we never told my grandmother of her condition, she knew deep down what was happening to her body. As she gradually declined in health, our family finally admitted her to the hospital in September. The several months that she was in the hospital remain very clear in my mind.

While my grandmother was in the hospital, my aunts, mother and I took turns staying with her because she did not speak or understand English very well. So every Friday night I would stay with my grandmother. By this point, the cancer had spread to her brain and her memory sort of came and went depending on whether she was having a "good" or "bad" day.

One night, I was awoken by child-like cries. I realized that my grandmother had gotten her leg caught in the bed rail. I helped her out and asked her where she wanted to go. She told me that she wanted to go to the washroom. So I helped her to the washroom and then assisted her back to her bed. When she was back in bed she thanked me for helping her, she said, "Thank you nurse for helping me, you are so kind."

I will never forget the heartache I felt when I realized that my grandmother no longer recognized me. Though I spent all those nights with her, there were very few times that she actually recognized me. She would either confuse me with my mom, aunts or nurses. At first, I was hurt that she did not know that it was me, but I realize that by that point the cancer had taken over and it was not her fault.

When my grandmother passed away in December, we buried her in a traditional Buddhist ceremony. The traditional method of burial consists of a wake, a cremation and then a mourning period of forty-nine days. It is believed that the spirit remains on earth for seven days after the individual has passed away and it is believed that the spirit takes this opportunity to say good-bye to its loved ones and finish anything they have left undone. On the seventh night after my grandmother passed away, I woke up in the middle of the night to go to the washroom and I saw my grandmother. My washroom is next to the guest bedroom that we reserved for my grandparents when they stayed over. When I was walking to the washroom, I saw my grandmother's figure in the doorway. She was wearing the dress that she was buried in and had her head thrown back laughing. Although, at the time, I did not really absorb the experience or understand it, I was not afraid. The following morning I told my mother what had happened and she felt that my grandmother had visited me to say good-bye and to let me know that she was happy and no longer suffering.

None of my other relatives saw her after she had passed away and it makes me feel special and honoured that she said good-bye to me before she left. It also comforted me to know that when I saw her, she was laughing and happy - I know she has gone to a better place where she will no longer have to suffer. I miss her terribly and sometimes when I come across something that reminds me of her - like certain foods or smells - I smile and remember what a wonderful person she was. I have not seen her since that seventh night, except for in my dreams, and often times when I really miss her, I hope that I will dream of her so that I can see her once again.

IN REPLY

Sherri Batenburg
Beamsville, Ontario

I said to him in reply:

Today Sir I will not make the tea.
For today, Sir, you have offended
me.
All my life I have been gentle,
But today is the day I stand
strong.

When you look at me Sir,
What is it that you see?
No Sir please . . . allow me.
You see a small, grayed matron,
With wrinkled hands and faded
eyes,
A woman who even in her age
has to wait on others for a poor
wage,
You probably even pity me,
Poor old woman, nice old lady,
Shouldn't have to . . .

But Sir, if I may,
When I look at me, I see me.
I see a strong young woman who
in the days that woman didn't,

went to - despite it all,
I see an accomplished mother,
I see a dedicated wife who loved
with all her heart,
I see hands that show
workmanship,
I see eyes in the mirror that are
warm,
thoughtful and wise.

Sir, what you don't see is me.
You see only that which I let you
see.
So today, Sir, I will not serve you
your tea.
But I will freely give you this
lesson,
That whoever you are or think
you may be,
Someone else will think of you
differently.
Therefore, judge not what you
see,
or think you see,
For those who are not judged Sir,
Love to brew tea.

MRS. AUGUSTINE

Dorothy Nytko
Niagara Falls, Ontario

If there was one person in the world who absolutely loved music, it was Mrs. Augustine. Her name and memory will stay with me forever as she played a significant role in my life as I was growing up. I was an eight-year-old girl with no siblings and she was a recently widowed eighty-year-old woman. Sometimes, I believed that our friendship was meant to be one that would last for a long time. Her passion for classical music not only encouraged me to nurture my own talents, but it also gave me a sense of ambition and drive which I apply to everything I do.

My piano lessons were always on Friday at four o'clock in the afternoon, and I had to be on time because Mrs. Augustine did not like her students to be late.

"Hello, who's there?" said the old but sweet voice as I entered through the door.

"Hello Mrs. Augustine, may I come in?"

"Of course, dear. Come in." Her plump, rosy face lit up when I entered the tiny living room where, in the center, stood the most beautiful baby grand piano I have ever seen. At first our relationship was strictly student-and-teacher, but over the course of that year, we had become the best of friends. Mrs. Augustine would tell me about her arthritis or stories about her husband, and I would tell her about my friends and school and how hard grade three math was. It had gotten to the point where my half-an-hour piano lesson turned into an hour-and-a-half and my parents would have to call her house to get me to come home for supper!

One day, after I finished playing Beethoven's "Turkish March," Mrs. Augustine turned to me with a slight smile and said that I played very well. At the same time, she took my hand and looked at me very seriously. Throughout my lessons we had not really spoken on a personal level and I was wondering why this was. I knew that our conversations were vital because it was the only way in which Mrs. Augustine would socialize with anyone, as she rarely left the comfort of her own home.

"Dorothy, if I die, will you come to my funeral?"

"Mrs. Augustine, what are you talking about? Please don't think that way!"

"Promise me you will come to my funeral."

"I promise, but I wish that you wouldn't talk that way." Her question really bothered me. Why was she thinking of her death and why would she ask me to come when she knew that I would go? We were good friends, how could I not go to her funeral?

"The reason why I ask you that question is because I will be going to get surgery done on my knee. My arthritis is really acting up and the doctor told me that it would be better for me to get this surgery. I will be in the hospital for a couple of weeks but I am scared that I will not make it through the surgery. You will have to go to another piano teacher during that time."

I did not know what to say. Hearing that my good friend was going for surgery made me really sad. I did not want to go to another piano teacher, and I definitely did not want to see Mrs. Augustine in pain. But if the surgery was going to help her walk better, then I knew that she had to go.

Mrs. Augustine had her surgery a few months after she had talked to me about it, and it went very well. My mother and I would visit her in the hospital every week after my piano lesson, since it was located near the hospital. Seeing Mrs. Augustine get through her surgery with such determination has influenced me to be the same way with everything in my life. She also exemplified this in her teaching. We would not finish up a lesson without mastering one part of a song with perfection.

A couple of weeks after her surgery, Mrs. Augustine's physical health began to deteriorate. My mother and I would go and visit her but she would either be sleeping or, when she was awake, she could not speak to us. Then, in the last week of her life, my mother and I went for a visit and we took a bag of Doritos and some pop for her to drink. When we entered her room, she was awake and so lively. I have never seen her like that before. She especially enjoyed the snacks we had brought her because they were her favourite things to eat. We sat and talked for hours.

The next day, she passed away. My mother did not tell me this until a couple of weeks after her death. I had just broken my promise to Mrs. Augustine. How could she forgive me? I told my mother that I had promised her that I would go to her funeral and now it was too late. My mother did not want me to know about her death because she thought that I was too young. But it was the one and only thing that I had promised her, and I did not fulfill it. To this day, I have always wanted Mrs. Augustine to forgive me. Maybe she knew that I could not go, but I have always felt guilty about it and I have carried that feeling around with me for my entire life.

Every time the anniversary of her death comes, I acknowledge it in my own special way. I always play her favourite piano piece, "Waltz in A Flat" by Brahms, and I talk to her, even if she is not able to answer me. In my conversation with her, I always ask her to forgive me. I really hope that she does.

REMINISCENT THOUGHTS OF ME AND MY GRANDPA

Heather Findlay
Burlington, Ontario

I find it interesting to look back at the evolution of the bond that I shared with my gran and grandpa. It probably would have been easier to achieve these bonds if we had lived closer to each other, but, instead, we were an ocean apart, as they lived in Scotland. I remember when I was much younger that I just adored my grandpa. It seemed to me that he would do just about anything for me, and, well, he did that. He was great, and so much fun. He did not care what others thought of him as he would get "down and dirty" with the grandchildren. He was merely just a big kid himself and that's what I loved. I will never forget the time that he chased an ice cream truck for blocks just to get me an ice cream cone. The visits with the both of them were wonderful. The unfortunate thing about it all is that I was so young and a lot of the things that I remember about my grandpa are stories that I hear and not vivid memories.

I remember him well, and the things that we did when I was older, but it was different then. He had started to change. He would have little 'black outs' and not remember things and I was still young enough to not understand it all. All I could remember was being scared. The last time that he came over to Canada to visit us, well, now that I look back on it, it was as though we had switched roles and I was the adult and he the child. One day he went for a walk like he used to do. He was such a great walker. I remember this because he used to walk me to the store every day to buy me the treat of my choice. But suddenly his memory was not as sharp as it used to be and he took a wrong turn. I just happened to be on a bike ride with a friend and noticed him so I walked him home. I was so confused as to why he was lost. I never really understood, until now, exactly what was going on with my grandpa. I knew he was getting sick, I could almost see it in my gran's face; however, I did not want to believe it.

The last visit that I had with my grandpa was over in Scotland just before he began to get really sick. I remember that visit being one of the hardest times I had ever had leaving the airport; maybe deep down I knew that I was not going to see my grandpa again.

When I found out that my grandpa had passed away I was crushed, and so upset that I did not know what to do. In a way, I felt empty, after all I was grandpa's little girl and now that was gone. Now that I am older and look back on things, I think about how Alzheimer's was such a heartless disease for such a smart and witty man to experience.

The first shared memory/moment of my gran and me was after my grandpa had passed away and she gave me the locket that he gave to her. Oh, how I still cherish it. For it is these small mementos that keep the spirit and memory of the dead alive.

Even though my grandpa has been gone for a number of years, he still lives on in my memories and actions. Every once in awhile my mom will say to me, "That is something grandpa would have said/done." I feel proud, that to this day, he lives on with me. The only good thing that came from my grandpa's death was the wonderful bond that I now have with my gran.

Maybe I do put him on a pedestal, but he was my only grandpa. I learned so much from both my gran and grandpa, so many valuable little things that I will always cherish, for they are both so special to me.

THE VISITOR

Laura Chambers
Clinton, Ontario

Mrs. Lobb had lived down the street from me for as long as I could remember. She was your typical old lady who lived in the average little house with the rickety little picket fence around it. As a little girl, I remember how the magnolias in the front yard used to blossom every spring as the last of the snow melted away. They were the first brightness after a long, dreary, cold winter. The vibrant pink of the magnolias was soon joined by the clear yellows, reds and purples of the tulips that next pushed their way through the freshly-thawed earth.

Mrs. Lobb's busy gardens seemed to encourage the other plants and flowers in the neighbourhood to struggle into bloom and thrive. Mrs. Lobb demonstrated that same encouraging force when it came to the neighbours. Every Canada Day she organized fireworks, and at Christmas time she organized the swapping of baked goods. Through all her work and enthusiasm, Mrs. Lobb's husband stood just a step behind, silent, yet always there, smiling his approval. Mr. Lobb was a small, fragile man. Years of work in a welding shop had left him bent over, and he hobbled about slowly through his daily tasks, stopping to catch his breath while leaning heavily on a gnarled old cane, seemingly growing smaller in his every task. He was not a weak man. He was simply old and tired, beaten down by his years of hardship. I don't think that I ever heard Mr. Lobb utter a word for the seven years that he lived just four doors down. The wheezing, snuffling old man seemed afraid to sap his energy by speaking. When suddenly one day my mother announced that Mr. Lobb had 'passed away' during the night, I thought of the silent smiling man. As a seven-year-old, I only knew that he was gone, and I noticed only that Mrs. Lobb began to come and go alone, and the reserved space that stubbornly remained two steps behind her was strangely empty.

As I passed through childhood and into adolescence, I took little notice of anyone other than my friends, pulling away from my family and their acquaintances. I was a selfish young person, struggling to break out of childhood and gain the independence of an adult. I was a typical teenager. Mrs. Lobb and her long-dead husband were far from my mind. I hadn't noticed that Mrs. Lobb no longer brought us her homemade jam every summer, or how there hadn't been a fireworks show on the street in nearly ten years. I hadn't even noticed how the neglected magnolia trees had become wild and overgrown, their flowers obscured by the thick foliage, and tulip bulbs had not been planted in years. It was not until a Family Studies course in my last year of high school that I gave Mrs. Lobb a second thought. My course required me to perform fifteen hours of community service. Annoyed at being forced to give away any free time, but resigned to the fact that I wanted to graduate from high school, I approached a home visit agency, and in their attempts to match me with someone in the community who lived nearby, I found myself assigned to visit Mrs. Lobb twice a week.

My first visit to Mrs. Lobb unfolded in late September. The air was still hot, as summer's grip still held tightly against the impending autumn. I climbed the steps up onto the porch, tripping over the rumbling branches of untamed bushes, and I kicked through a pile of untouched daily newspapers, headlines screaming out the newest crises. I rang the doorbell, and then knocked sharply just for good measure. Before I could withdraw my hand, the door swung open, and I found myself face to face with a stranger. The stranger smiled, greeting me like an old friend. Had it been so long ago that I had come to play around this woman's house, all the children shouting out instructions as they attempted to restore order to their games? Could it possibly be the same woman who used to put lemonade and cookies on her porch for us when we were too tired to run anymore? A faint glimmer of that woman peered out from the stranger's tired, moist eyes. Her wild white hair stood out on end, and her long terrycloth robe was so bulky that it appeared to have swallowed the rest of her body. Her red lips, smeared clumsily with bright colour, trembled as she sized me up. Without a word, she turned and walked into the depths of the house, leaving me at the open door, peering in uncertainly. I timidly stepped inside, and was greeted by darkness, and a thick musty smell that threatened to overwhelm me. The floor, the furniture, every corner was incredibly dusty, and cobwebs shimmered in the sunlight that spilled through the cracks in the blinds. I tiptoed forward, in search of the stranger. The only sounds were the uneven creaks of the old house, and the faint ticking of a clock, somewhere out of sight. Down the hall, the only place to go was up the stairs, and so I climbed the flight, groping in the semi-darkness. One of the doors in the hall was open, and I approached the lighted doorway, eager to escape the darkness of the rest of the house. Mrs. Lobb sat on a window seat in the bedroom, and she distractedly gestured for me to take a seat on the bed. Of all the times that I had played in her house (which once was full of bright sunlight, every inch spotless), I'd never been in this room. I settled awkwardly on the bed, and nervously attempted to start a conversation, drawing on the techniques that the home-visiting agency had suggested. Mrs. Lobb's enthusiasm was overwhelming. After a few minutes of small talk, we were both revealing the general details of our lives. I listened to Mrs. Lobb's stories about when she was my age. I think that I was surprised to think that she was ever my age. I was thrilled to hear of her past loves. She was the first adult in a long time that I had willingly listened to. And it seemed that I was the first person of any age that had listened to her in a long time. In fact, when I asked whom she usually talked to, she absentmindedly replied, "Well dear, I prefer talking to my husband, but he doesn't talk much to me." At first I wasn't sure if she was serious or if she was trying to trick me into thinking she was a crazy old lady who talked to her dead husband. I later learned that her humour often took this puzzling form. I never really did figure out when she was serious. She liked it that way.

Throughout the autumn and into the winter I continued to visit Mrs. Lobb, each time venturing up to the bedroom in the hallway upstairs. We talked about everything and she insisted on being kept updated on my life. I don't believe that she left the house once throughout those months (you can find delivery services for practically everything these days), and she hungered to know about the other people who still went about their daily lives, just as she once had, in the days before her self-inflicted isolation. She cried when I told her about school dances and when I described such simple events as going for coffee with a group of friends. But she was reminded of herself in younger years, and she then delighted in regaling me with stories of her wild times. As she spun her stories, she would laugh and smile, lose herself in the past. My specified fifteen hours were well behind us. I became her listener and her friend.

When spring came, our visits moved outside of the stuffy old house, and we began to work around the yard. Soon the magnolia trees once again blossomed, now that they had been pruned, and tulips grew up and out of the ground, their bulbs freshly planted. I also helped Mrs. Lobb (or Edna as she now insisted that I call her) do some simple repairs and painting. Work that I would have cringed at, had my parents asked me, was suddenly something to be proud of. It was our project. I tried many times to help Edna with her inside housework and cleaning, but each time she refused politely. The atmosphere inside was for no one but herself. Everyone could enjoy the outside improvements, but the inside was for her alone, her sanctuary. She firmly denied that anything in the house should change. To this day, I still believe that Edna was afraid that if she changed anything in the house, she would chase away any remaining pieces of her husband. In this way, time stood still inside the old house. Perhaps that was why she never left. Edna was stopping time.

But time never stops, never slows down. It rages on, knocking down those who oppose it. It was a stifling mid-summer, and I was getting ready to leave school to go straight to Edna's house. Today we were going to look through some of her old photo albums. The secretary came over the loudspeaker and requested me to come to the office to pick up a message. I retrieved the square yellow paper, with the school name and crest neatly printed in the top left corner. Printed neatly, the note simply read:

Your visit to Mrs. Lobb will not be required today
Sadly, she passed away this morning.
Thank you for your time.
If you would be interested in taking on another client,
it would be greatly appreciated.

The note was from the home-visiting agency, and I felt the cold, flat paper in my hand become heavy. I trudged home silently, pausing absently at Edna's front gate to pluck a stray weed from the flowerbed. But I continued home. That night, and for the next week, I wept, I screamed, I sat in silence. I was unbearably sad, but more than that I was angry. Angry at losing a friend. Angry at Edna for leaving, angry at the agency for being so cold, angry at myself for becoming so attached to an old woman.

I went to Edna's funeral that week. Only a handful of neighbours attended and her only son flew in from Winnipeg. He had not been home since his father's death. I tuned out the service, bombarded by my own thoughts of Edna. The woman who loved her husband so dearly that she essentially tried to stop time in order to preserve his memory. The woman, who had a rich past, a love of children, a love of gardens, an interest in me. A woman, that was forgotten inside her old dark house. I felt guilty that we as neighbours had so easily allowed her retreat.

A week later, Edna's son knocked on my door. He handed me a small shoebox and an envelope, explaining that his mother had left it in full view with instructions for it to be delivered to me when she was gone. Alone in my room, I opened the envelope and withdrew a letter, flowery writing relaying a message. It read:

Now that you are reading this, I am gone. I wish only to thank you for your companionship these last few months and wish you well in the future. Although you have made me happier than I've been in years, I am relieved to finally join my husband. It has been a long time, and I am ready. Enjoy your life. Commit it to memory. Life will move on, even when you're dragging your feet.

I stared at the letter for a long time, grateful for this piece of evidence that our friendship had really existed. Then I opened the shoebox, carefully untying the twine that bound it. Inside were three items. A magnolia blossom, carefully dried to preserve the vibrant colour. Underneath the blossom, was a small packet of seeds and some tulip bulbs.

The next spring, I planted the seeds and the bulbs in the flowerbeds around my house. I cared for them like I would a child, watering, weeding, and obsessively protective. As the flowers grew to show off their magnificent colours, their effect seemed to spread to the yards of the other neighbours, as everywhere flowers bloomed and trees blossomed. Once again, Edna Lobb had spread joy. And this time, I had helped her.

NOSTALGIA

Aja Larche
Hamilton, Ontario

In the eyes of a child
Grandad was his leather chair -
Rigid and black,
Permeated with the pungent stench of tobacco.
I wept when forced upon his knee;
I hope he forgives me.
He fought in World War Two;
I don't remember if he spoke of it.
He died when I was seven;
I don't remember if I was sad.

Today I study his life
Through the eyes of history,
Just one of many ordinary men
Who suffered - a result of the war.
I have tattered photographs and
Soiled soldier's medallions,
Yet the essence of his life
Has escaped my memory.

He died thirteen years ago;
Today I mourn his death.

THE VIOLIN

Kara Happy
Hamilton, Ontario

I was about to purchase my first violin. I had been searching for one for many years and yesterday I received the call. I had lain awake all night, and finally it was morning. The violin was reported to be over a hundred years old, and I was plagued by visions of the secrets it must hold. Perhaps it had been played for peace or love. The possibilities exceeded imagination. I swear I ran all the way to the owner's home.

As the door opened, a frail gentleman in his eighties appeared. He spoke very little before beckoning me to follow him. He led me down a dark staircase to a small room richly coloured in green and blue. There, in a dusty corner, lay the violin, gleaming under the soft light from a lone window. I asked the man if he knew the history of the instrument. At this he simply looked at me and smiled. Then he picked up the violin in his wrinkled hands, drew a sharp breath, and suddenly the most heart-wrenching melody echoed from the strings. As he played, his lips moved with his own tale, dusty and ancient in its own right.

He told me of being a small child in Austria with no food and no home. He lived in a convent where music was his only escape. At the age of eight, a music teacher from Vienna came to hear him play; his talent had been proclaimed as a gift from God. The man accepted him as a pupil and removed him from the convent. He studied for many years and played for many people in high society. He even gave a private concert for the King of Vienna. Then he met his love.

She had been a schoolteacher, a painter, and his soul mate. She was the essence of youth and beauty, with rich brown hair and dark brown eyes. They became consumed by each other in a matter of days. He used to play for her in the moonlight. They married soon after they first met, but they were separated abruptly at the start of the war. He spent years he cannot begin to forget in a concentration camp. The horrors he survived were unimaginable. But his greatest loss had been his violin.

Once released, he spent a decade roaming the country searching for his wife. His hope finally died in a small garden bordering the walls of an Italian Villa. There, behind the gates of a tiny chapel, he found a handmade gravestone with her name carved into the charred wood. He cried for days. It was here that an old man found him and gave him the violin. With the instrument came the elder's own tale of life; a life of love and grief which filled the strings. He was told of the memories that were held within. Like his own, they needed to be heard and to be remembered. He played in memory of her all day.

At that time he was nearing his fifties, but his only pain was in his heart. Armed only with the violin, he boarded a boat to America to escape the misery of his homeland. Many of the passengers died of a plague that struck the ship that voyage. Despite his prayers, God had spared his life again. His health remained strong when the vessel docked in New York. Facing poverty and homelessness once more, he sought refuge in a shelter and taught music to the families in the neighbourhood. Eventually, he was able to rent a small home - his current residence.

His sixty-first birthday came and brought decline with it. His vision started to fade. His body began to feel heavy and weak. The students stopped coming. The violin attracted dust. Like the man himself, it had been forgotten and cast away. Unlike himself, the instrument had become more valuable with age. It was desired and yearned for. Its care was fought over. It was to be cherished, and he knew it was time to pass it on. It was the only piece of himself that he had left to give; the legacy that had kept him alive and its release would finally end his suffering.

The wrinkled hands then stopped playing and placed the violin in mine. He told me, "A life can take many paths, and you can never tell the value of age unless you look at what it has surpassed and left behind. You are young; this instrument is in need of a new melody. It has become tired of the old. Make it a happy one."

Later that morning I left with the violin under my arm, cherishing the history and the mystery it held. And I wondered, how can we value that which has not earned its worth through age and experience. For the violin, age is the richest melody.

AN ODE TO GRANDPARENTS

Carla Coruzzi
Hamilton, Ontario

Grandparents were made to love and to hold,
Grandparents are seen as the ones who've grown old.
However age doesn't matter - it's who they are,
And mine stand out like a big, bright star.

Their gentle hands would wipe my tears,
Or their loving hugs to calm my fears.
When I was ill, they would show their care,
By staying at my side and always being there.

When I was young they would tuck me in bed,
And gently bend down to kiss my forehead.
I remember our outings to the park
And the bedtime stories read after dark.

I will never forget my childhood days,
How their love showed in so many ways.
Although precious moments can't always last,
They're recalled in our memories of the past.

These memories make me feel glad,
Of the fun times that we once had.
Always there with a helping hand,
To fill my needs as they each demand.

I will always remember everything you've done,
Your presence makes me shine like the bright sun.
You are two special people who always help out,
You show our family what love's all about.

Their love is shown in a gentle way,
It's in their actions or something they will say.
They're there to help you make it through,
Grandchildren appreciate everything you do.

I can take out many pictures to look and see,
The everlasting memories of you and me.
Two unique people so loving and true,
Thanks for everything and 'I love you!'

Always in my mind, forever in my heart,
No one could ever fill a grandparent's part.
Those with grandparents have really lucked out,
They know what a family is all about.

FOREVER

Debra Kuipers
Palmerston, Ontario

When I accepted the position as a Nurse's Aide at the Nursing/Retirement Home, I never could have imagined how an elderly woman of 88 years could have impacted my life so drastically. At first she appeared to be just another one of those 'old ladies' that needed some help with her daily activities, but who also loved the company of the 'young girls' that worked with her. The more I sat and talked with her, the more I realized that she wasn't old at all, but rather she was a young woman in an aging body.

Jean (that is her name) has become a huge part of my life. I love her not as a grandmother, but instead as a close and dear friend. She has brought extreme amounts of joy and satisfaction to my life and there are not enough words to give her the thanks she deserves. I see it as only fair that I share with you, the readers, the story behind my friendship with Jean.

In 1997, I took the job as a Nurse's Aide, but it wasn't until late in the fall that I met her. In the beginning she was, just as I said, another person, another face with a name. But I remember one day that she asked me to sit and talk with her. I sat there only for a few minutes, because honestly I really didn't know what to say to her, seeing as I really knew nothing about her. But over the next few weeks, I went out of my way to go and talk with her because she had so many interesting stories to tell me about her childhood. I learned about all her trips she took as a young lady to places as fascinating as Trinidad and Tobago, and her few trips to Europe. She spent her first years around Listowel, a small town an hour north of Kitchener-Waterloo, but moved around a lot from place to place where she could find work. She finally settled down in Peterborough where she worked until her retirement. In 1996 or 1997, she moved to a retirement home, and that is still her home to this day. Through reading her diaries, I learned what it was like being a teenager in the '20's and doing the things teenagers did back then.

During the time I was learning about her, she was also learning about me, and what it is like being a teenager in the '90's. She was curious about my goals and aspirations for the future. She knows my family and has met a few of my friends and she thinks it is such a treat when I bring them by to visit. Jean has also introduced me to some of her nieces and nephews and that means a lot to me. She has been there for me through my hard times and heartaches and always lends an ear and a kind word. She recently told me that she can't keep all the names of my 'boys' straight, but I know she likes to hear about them anyway, because she always asks.

I worked in the Retirement Home until August 1999, when I resigned my position to go to school here in Hamilton. It seems to me that after the first few initial weeks of getting to know her, I found myself going to see her everyday that I worked and even some days that I didn't because I wanted to spend time with her. Now, being two hours away from her, I cannot see her as much and when I surprise her with a visit or a phone call, the look on her face or the expression in her voice I receive is priceless. I can tell then that she misses me as much as I miss her. I have a close friend that still works there and she tells me that Jean is always asking about me and just hearing that puts a smile on my face and a warm feeling in my heart. When I leave to say good-bye I get a big hug and a kiss, and it makes me wish I could spend more time with her.

On August 21, 1999, Jean celebrated her 90th birthday, and I was so delighted to be able to share that wonderful and special occasion with her. While there I was able to meet some more of her family, but some of them already knew who I was. I felt somewhat embarrassed, yet flattered, to know that she shares with her family the bond that we have. A few days before her birthday, a friend and I took Jean out for a picnic so that we could celebrate her birthday on our own. My friend and I made her a cake and a small lunch and we took her to the park she knew well. We all enjoyed ourselves immensely and to this day she reminds me of the seagulls and the swans that were there that day. Before I left to go to school, Jean went through some of her little treasures that she had and she gave me a small spoon with a seagull on it; she said she never wanted me to forget the picnic. I hope to return there this summer, so I can spend lots of time with her, and we are planning to go on another picnic this year to celebrate our birthdays together.

Being with Jean, and also working with the elderly, helped me decide that I would like to spend the greater part of my life working with the elderly and helping to make their lives better and easier.

Jean, I thank you for all the love and support you have given me; you will forever live in my heart.

THE NEWSPAPER ARTICLE

Maryjane McLaren
Winnipeg, Manitoba

"This morning," George joked, "we have with us a celebrity." An excited whisper ran through the congregation.

"If any of you read the Winnipeg Free Press you probably stumbled across her picture in the 'Most Wanted' section. Maryjane is wanted for being too perky early in the morning at a near-by grocery store last Monday. Penny, her immediate supervisor, vows to give her that shift for the rest of the summer as it helps to wake up the customers." The small congregation laughed at the joke. George, the minister, dying of heat in his angelic white robe, swayed back and forth at the podium of the one-room church trying to get air-flow between him and his robe. "Just kidding Maryjane. Actually, Maryjane's picture, name and a very well-written article appeared in yesterday morning's editorial section of the Free Press. It was a thank you to a good Samaritan for helping Maryjane and her family when the motorhome broke down as they headed out to camp for the weekend. They have started a new tradition called the Girls' Weekend Away. So this is the tale of the adventure that the McLaren women had. Gary wants us to note that it is Wanda and Gary's motorhome, as opposed to OUR motorhome, like it's referred to in the article."

"Mr. Sinclair told me to write *our*. He's the journalist. He writes for a living, what was I supposed to do - tell the man he's wrong?" I protested aloud in fun.

"Wouldn't be the first time you put someone in their place," Andrew, my younger brother, joined in. People chuckled.

"I encourage you to read the article as it will be posted on the bulletin board at the back of the church. Congratulations Maryjane . . . " George continued. The open windows allowed chirping birds and buzzing bees to be heard between the hymns. Those lucky enough to sit near a window felt the gentle, cool breeze, which blew teasingly every now and then. The sunlight danced on the windowsills reflecting the sunshine throughout the small church. "Also, I'd like to extend a warm welcome to any visitors we have with us today and welcome you all back for another year of worship and work. Now let us pray," George said. I could still remember standing in the wet wind in a sweatshirt and jeans at the Brunkild gas station parking lot.

*   *   *   *

"Stephenfield or Grand Beach?" Aunty Wanda asked as she hopped into the motorhome, buckled up and started the engine.

"Stephenfield!" The girls replied.

Mom and I looked at each other in shock. Not their favourite spot in the whole wide world, Grand Beach? The stress of the summer must have affected their brains too.

"Is that all right with you guys?" Aunty Wanda asked Grandma, Mom and I.

"Yeah fine," I spoke for the three of us with what I hoped looked like a casual shrug. I loved Stephenfield Provincial Park. We'd camped there for years and though probably the most part of why I loved to return was for the memories, there were some childhood friends who'd grown into really cute teenage boys.

"Then Stephenfield here we come. And nothing better get in our damn way!" Aunty Wanda said and laughed. Pulling out of the gas station with the sun shining in our faces, no one other than ourselves knew how true that was. Downsizing and computers had finally affected our family. Men with temperaments like time bombs were only adding to the stress of life.

So we were starting our own little tradition. This was the first annual Girls' Weekend Away. We were looking for the fun in life, born to be wild, spreading our wings, exploring our independence and looking for a place with no technology or stress.

Passing wheat fields and canola and flax and mustard fields, our roots were coming back to us and relaxation was beginning to take hold.

The highway passed by without effort and finally the setting sun peeked through the clouds to dry up the puddles on the highway.

Crack! Pop!

"What was that Lorna?!, Mom did you hear that?" Aunty Wanda asked, eyes wide, looking carefully around, her foot easing of the gas pedal. She sat straight up and clutched the wheel so tightly that her knuckles turned white.

"I don't know, let's try to make it to the garage over there," Mom said. "The shoulder of the highway is wet and we'll only get stuck."

'Welcome to Brunkild' the brand new sign read as we crept past. My cousins and I looked at each other frowning and turning down the *Sister Act* soundtrack we were listening to in the back of the motorhome. Heather, April and Allison put down their *Archie* comic books and peeked out of the curtained windows as the motorhome rolled to a stop. I pulled on a sweatshirt, tied my hair back and jumped into the wind of the small muddy parking lot of the Brunkild garage.

"Just my luck, I can't get the hood up," Aunty Wanda said, "Gary said he didn't want us going out of town and did I listen? No, I said if he didn't want to come, then he should shut up. And now . . . ?"

"Here let me try," Mom said, trading positions in front of the motorhome to fiddle with the hood.

"I wonder if there's anyone who'll know about this sort of thing inside," Grandma said looking toward the large square window of the gas station. "Lorna, didn't this used to be a garage?"

"Yes, isn't-- ", Mom stopped. The gas station had once been a full service garage. We'd driven by it millions of times on our way out to camp for the weekend or family vacations.

"Let's go inside and talk to the girls," Aunty Wanda suggested.

The bell rang over top of the door as we walked into the small gas station. Beside the counter where you pay for the gas there were a couple of chest-tall shelves with convenience store food and a wide variety of videos for renting. Behind the counter were two teenage girls, the night's gas attendants.

"Hi, is something wrong?" asked the brunette gas station attendant. Neither of them were wearing name tags.

"Our motorhome broke down. Is there a garage in town?" Aunty Wanda asked.

"No. This used to be the only garage but that changed about three years ago - new management," the girl explained.

"What's up?" the blond asked holding her hand over the receiver.

"They need help, Mel. Their motorhome broke down," the brunette repeated.

"Is there a phone I can use to call my husband? We're from Winnipeg, it'll take him about twenty minutes to get here but at least we'll have a ride back to the city," Aunty Wanda asked. "So much for Girls' Weekend Away," she said to us.

"Just out there." The girl pointed to the pay phone outside the gas station.

"Thanks," Aunty Wanda said as she walked outside.

"You don't know anything about cars by chance do you?" I asked, hoping maybe they were aspiring mechanics.

"No, Melanie and I are just gas attendants. Sorry," the brunette said.

"Huh? Yeah, sorry Dad. I am listening. These women just came in. Their motorhome just broke down and they were asking if there's a mechanic in town," the blond, Melanie, repeated into the phone. "Uh, do you know what's broken?" Melanie asked us holding the phone away from her mouth.

"No clue. It just made this funny sound, then the heat gauge went up and we thought we'd better stop," Mom said.

Melanie repeated the story into the phone. "Okay, bye Dad," Melanie said and then hung up the phone. "Dad's coming," Melanie informed us.

Aunty Wanda came back inside and with her came a gust of cold wind. We told her "Dad" was on the way. "Oh that's really nice of you. Uh, so is Gary," she said.

He never introduced himself, we just knew him as Dad. Dad drove up in a big old gray car and hopped out. He'd barely had it turned off before he got out, took off his clean coat and started rolling up his sleeves. We found cardboard for him to lie on, from inside the motorhome, and Dad crawled underneath the front part of the motorhome with his son as his assistant.

"You blew a fan belt." Dad said, getting up from the cardboard. "I don't suppose you have a spare, do you?"

"A fan belt?! We just got that thing fixed this week! Oh Gary's going to be so mad. No I don't think we do have a fan belt," Aunty Wanda said.

"I wonder if they'll have one inside?" Mom asked.

"I doubt it. It's not a garage anymore," Dad replied.

Grandma silently slipped away into the gas station and a few minutes later came out with the girls holding an assortment of different parts.

"Dad, will any of these things work? We don't know what they are but we found them in the back room," Melanie announced to her father.

"Well I'll be . . . these are fan belts. At a guess we'll try this one," he said trying to match the broken belt with one of the belts in his daughter's hand. He disappeared under the motorhome again and we crossed our fingers.

When he came back out he announced, "Done."

"It's fixed?! That's terrific. What do we owe you?" my Aunt asked in relief.

Taking the package from Melanie's hand, he read, "$6.59, uh, plus tax."

"And what about you?" my Grandmother asked. "You didn't have to come down and rescue us."

"Nothing. You don't owe me anything. But you must excuse me because I have somewhere I have to be so I'll leave this for the girls to clean up and finish. Excuse me," Dad apologized. "Have fun at camp."

"Thank you," we all said in unison.

And the gray car drove away.

*   *   *   *

The organ snapped me back to reality, ending the hymn and cueing George to begin the benediction. The congregation responded with an

299

"Amen." The service had ended. Everyone sat down, to gather purses or talk with people beside them, except my grandfather. The quiet and shy man who all my life waited for me to come to him because of my extreme shyness as an infant, came over to the pew where I was sitting, like a little child with a secret at Christmas time. Grandpa stood before me smiling and asked, "Guess what?"

"What?" I replied.

Grandpa answered, "Yesterday, Lloyd and Ruby phoned." My grandfather's cousin and her husband live in the country and travel as often as they change their socks. Grandpa continued, "Lloyd was in Brunkild the other day getting gas and he got to talking with a few of the locals – you know Lloyd, could talk forever that man – and the people in Brunkild have a copy of your article framed on the wall of the gas station office. They saw it in the Free Press the other week and they cut it out and damn neared framed it and hung it on the wall. Now everyone who visits Brunkild will see your article." Grandpa chuckled. Something he didn't do very often due to his pessimistic view of life. He stood there in his Sunday suit – the gray pants and jacket, white shirt and blue tie – the one he'd worn for years, with his hands in the pockets. The Sunday suit that came off immediately after church as though he still had animals to feed and fields to work, the prairie farmer routine still embedded deep within him. His almost bald head with its summer tan, and his slim five foot eight figure were before me, smiling and awaiting my response.

My eyes got wide with surprise and a smile spread across my face. I turned to Robert, my friend seated beside me in the wooden pew, "Did you hear that?" I asked him.

"That's pretty cool," he commented, nodding.

It could have been the way the sunlight was reflecting off the windowsill but I thought I saw a tear glistening in Grandpa's eye when I looked back at him. When he swallowed it was apparent there was a lump in his throat.

My grandfather was proud of me. I'd never realized that before. I supposed I always knew that deep down, but he was from the old school that never showed emotion, especially the men. And here he was standing before me, a step away from me, a step away from hugging me, gushing with pride.

Ironically this display of pride was uncomfortable. Pushing past Robert and Grandpa, I went over to my Mom across the carpeted church aisle. "Mom, guess what?" I interrupted the conversation in which she was engaged. Excusing myself for being rude, I repeated the news to her. Mom made some positive comment but I didn't hear it. Grandpa was still standing in the same spot of the church, mesmerized in his own pride. He stood there chuckling to himself. His very own Granddaughter on the wall of the Brunkild gas station because she wanted to say thank you to a kind stranger. Grandpa was still muttering quietly to himself, "Hah, what do you know? They framed it," I did a double take when I saw him wipe a tear from his cheek . . .

IN MEMORY OF A CLOSE FRIEND

James Gregory McHarg
Ancaster, Ontario

The salty waters broke on the incandescent sands.
A small schooner without a cargo of gold or ivory
But with riches far greater came steadily past my bay.
It frolicked lively over the waves of life, and in its
Weathered but full sails blew the winds of vigour,
Strength, and guidance.

To view this ship for but the few seconds it passed
Into sight was to know peace and happiness and to
Have greater insight into the gales one must face.

The moon waned and the vessel came silently to rest
On a jagged rock.
The salty waters broke on the incandescent sands.

I shall remember this ship - and just as it taught me
To set sail so too shall its memory teach me to brave
The depths of the vast oceans of the world.

FEELS LIKE HOME

Amy Johnson
St. Catharines, Ontario

One of the greatest influences in my life has been my grandmother. I remember some of my classmates in elementary school who loved visiting their grandparents because they always got gifts of money or a really expensive present for their birthday. Some of the children hated visiting their grandparents because either they were mean or gave them lousy presents. I always loved visiting my grandma and always will. She is the only grandparent I have known in my lifetime, as my other grandparents died before I was born. A lot of my friends have two sets of grandparents. I only have one grandma – and I believe that God only gives us what we can handle or need.

When I was young my teachers always got the class to write about who our role model was and why. I would always write about my grandma – and the reason back then was because she was the nicest and kindest person I knew. Today my answer would be the same only it would include a deeper understanding of my grandmother's life. It was what she went through growing up and in her marriage, that has made her my ultimate role model. It seems impossible to convey my respect for my grandmother without letting you know about her past and present.

She was born Mildred Otilia Strader, in 1917, on her parents' farm in the small town of Walkerton, Ontario. She was the oldest of sixteen children. After Grandma was born her mother had seven boys, and she was not very close to her sisters because of the large age gap. There were not very many rooms in the farmhouse, so she shared a room with her brothers (the warmest room). Grandma loved school and learning; she was not very athletic. During the summer while other children were learning to ride bikes, she was longing to go back to school. In those days it was not proper for girls to be educated, especially beyond the elementary grades. She was very clever in school and was only eleven years old when she entered high school. She finished high school at sixteen and, because she was too young to become a teacher (which was her desire), she went back to school to take a business course and became a secretary. She married my grandfather, August Richard Voisin, when she was 20. She said that she was first attracted to my grandfather because he had a car and offered her a lot more freedom than she had ever experienced. She had the first of fifteen children a year after she was married. At this time Grandma and Grandpa moved into the house that Grandma is currently living in. The house is a three-bedroom stone house in the middle of town. Grandpa was a factory worker, so there was never enough money; however, grandma always made do, with a large portion of their food being grown in her garden – a garden that is still in existence today, yet a lot smaller. Grandpa died before I was born, when Grandma was 52 years old, so the only things I know about Grandpa are the stories his children tell about him.

Of the children, eight were girls and seven were boys. Her oldest was a girl, and I remember overhearing one story where Grandpa did not think it proper for her to be always studying and focusing on education. Instead, he thought that she should be helping Grandma with the young children. Grandma, on the other hand, always regarded education very highly and she set up a desk and lamp in the girls' room to allow her oldest daughter to secretly study without letting Grandpa know. This eldest daughter eventually achieved Grandma's dream of becoming a teacher. Of the eight girls, the majority are nurses and teachers. Grandma still encourages her children, grandchildren and great-grandchildren to attain a good education and to be in a profession that they love.

Today, at 82 years of age, she fills her time by reading, quilting, writing in her journal, gardening in the summer, and going to church every day. She is the nicest person I know and should be very proud of how her family has turned out, all thanks to her encouragement and positive attitude. I believe that Grandma's Christian faith has gotten her through some of the roughest times of their lives. Often when we go to visit Grandma, her sons and daughters stand around the kitchen telling stories about the old days. We visit Grandma on every holiday or weekend that we can, and I never plan on changing this habit. Even though she has forty grandchildren, she is always so glad to see us and lets us know what it has meant to her to have us there. She is the center of our family, the glue that keeps us all together and our moral leader; when visiting her, it is the time that I feel most like I am home. I do not know what would happen to our family if we ever lost her.

God bless you Grandma!